GLOBAL ANTITRUST

T0299926

Global Antitrust

Trade and Competition Linkages

YUSAF H. AKBAR

Associate Professor of International Business,
Southern New Hampshire University, USA

LONDON AND NEW YORK

Contents

List of Figures

List of Tables

List of Interviews

Anonymous Official, Chemical Industries Association, UK. January 24, 1996.

Malcolm Harbour, Director, International Car Distribution Programme, UK. May 24, 1996.

Mr S. Iijma, Industrial Policy Division, Ministry of International Trade and Industry (MITI), July 4, 1994.

Professor K. Ishiguro, Professor of Law, Tokyo University. July 22, 1995.

Professor M. Ito, Professor of Economics, Tokyo University. July 14, 1994.

Ms U. Pachl, Chief Legal Advisor, BEUC, May 20, 1999.

Mr Y. Sadamitsu, International Trade Policy Division, MITI. July 4, 1994.

Mr Y. Sasaki, Director, Toyota Kaikan and General Manager, Public Communications, Toyota Motor Corporation. August 15, 1994.

Mr K. Smith, Manager – Purchasing, Toyota Motor Manufacturing, US. July 14, 1995.

Mr E. Tabor, Assistant General Manager – Purchasing, Toyota Motor Manufacturing, US. July 14, 1995.

Mr H. Tadokoro, Machinery and Information Industry Division, MITI. July 18, 1994.

Mr Y. Takahashi, Manager, Government and Industry Relations Group, International Public Affairs Division, Toyota. July 5, 1994.

Mr T. Ueda, Project General Manager, International Purchasing Division, Toyota Motor Corporation. August 17, 1994.

Mr A. Uesugi, International Trade Counsellor, Japanese Fair Trade Commission (JFTC). July 11, 1994.

Mr H. Welge, Head of Unit, DGI, Commission of the European Communities. January 25, 1996.

Mr Y. Yano, Manager, International Trade Division, Japanese Automobile Manufacturers Association. July 21, 1994.

List of Abbreviations

ABA	American Bar Association
ACEA	Association des Constructeurs d'Automobile Européene
AML	Japanese Anti-Monopoly Law
ANSAC	American National Soda Ash Council
BE	Block Exemption
BEUC	Bureau Européen des Unions des Consommateurs
CECRA	European Committee for Motor Trades and Repairs
CEFIC	European Chemical Industry Council
CFI	Court of First Instance
CKD	Complete Knock Down Kits
DG I*	Directorate-General for External Affairs (now DG Trade)
DG IV	Directorate-General for Competition (now DG Competition)

(* the use of roman numerals for DGs changed following the Kinnock reforms of the EU Commission. However, the time period covered by this research predates the reform and therefore the 'old' system is referred to throughout the book).

DOC	US Department of Commerce
DOJ	US Department of Justice
DSM	Dispute Settlement Mechanism
ECE	East and Central European States
ECJ	European Court of Justice
ECSC	European Coal and Steel Community
EEA	European Economic Area
EFTA	European Free Trade Association
EU	European Union
FDI	Foreign Direct Investment
FTC	US Fair Trade Commission
GATS	General Agreement on Trade in Services
GATT	General Agreement on Tariffs and Trade
G7	Group of Top Seven Industrialized Countries
IB	International Business
ICDP	International Car Distribution Programme
IO	Industrial Organization
IPE	International Political Economy
ITO	International Trade Organization
JAMA	Japan Automobile Manufacturers Association
JFTC	Japanese Fair Trade Commission
JMPIA	Japanese Marine Products Importers Association
JSAIA	Japanese Soda Ash Importers Association

LdPE	Low Density Polyethylene
LR	Long Run
MAI	Multilateral Agreement on Investment
MES	Minimum Efficient Scale
MITI	Japanese Ministry of International Trade and Industry
MMC	Mergers and Monopolies Commission
MNE	Multinational Enterprise
MOF	Japanese Ministry of Finance
NCC	National Consumer Council
OECD	Organization for Economic Co-operation and Development
OJ	Official Journal of the European Communities
OMA	Orderly Marketing Arrangements
PVC	Polyvinyl Chloride
SEA	Single European Act
SED	Selective and Exclusive Distribution
SEM	Single European Market
SMMT	Society of Motor Vehicle Manufacturers and Traders
TRIM	Trade Related Investment Measure
TRIP	Trade Related Intellectual Property Right
VER	Voluntary Export Restraint
WTO	World Trade Organization

Preface

Understanding the relationship between trade policy and competition policy took on considerable importance in the 1990s. Strengthened by the development of theories of imperfect competition in economics and globalization in international political economy, scholars turned their minds to understanding the conflicts and complementarities between these two policy domains.

Moreover, the strength of empirical evidence against our static and models of policy interactions was growing. The decision of the Reagan and Thatcher governments in the US and UK to de-regulate their economies encouraged a more general process of trade and capital market liberalization. The success of the GATT Uruguay Round negotiations resulted in the biggest ever trade liberalization package and pushed international liberalization into new policy domains such as intellectual property and trade related investment measures. By the mid-1990s, the OECD had proposed a wide-ranging treaty to liberalize rules on foreign direct investment among member states.

Indeed Sylvia Ostry's 'System Friction' suggested that the process of trade liberalization began in the 1980s had led to significant conflict between differing systems of national regulation in the domains of social, environmental and antitrust policy. This is the focus of our book. More specifically, the relationship between trade policy and antitrust policy is examined by analysing their relationship under different industrial structures.

As the complexity of industrial structures increases, we should realistically expect that a simple relationship between trade policy and antitrust policy would break down. On the surface we should expect trade policy and antitrust to be mutually reinforcing tools of liberalization. However, as we demonstrate in our book, as industrial structures become more complex, this relationship breaks down. We examine two specific kinds of industrial structure: natural resources and complex manufacturing. Using case studies, we demonstrate how in the case of natural resources, there appears to be a simple relationship between trade and antitrust policies i.e. they should be mutually reinforcing tools. However, in the case of complex manufacturing, e.g. the car industry, there may be instances in which a liberal trade policy can undermine legitimate antitrust policy objectives to promote quality of service provision in pre- and after-sales of cars.

Given these complex relationships, we argue that there is a need to develop mechanisms for agreement on common rules for antitrust policy in order to reduce 'System Friction'. It is clear that different policy approaches to trade and antitrust exist among the 'Triad' of the US, EU and Japan. We examine the threat posed by a resort to extraterritoriality as a means of 'solving' these differences. In the light of the extraterritorial threat, we argue for the internalization of competition policy and for the development of both multilateral and mini-lateral mechanisms for promoting the internationalization of antitrust policy. We argue for the potential elimination of anti-dumping measures. However, while the theoretical policymaking arguments for such a move may be compelling, we recognize that the political economy of trade and antitrust suggests that this is unlikely to occur quickly.

I would like to thank many people and organizations for their help in the research for this book. First of all, I would not have completed this task without the invaluable advice, support and encouragement of my supervisor, Professor Alasdair Smith, Vice-Chancellor of the University of Sussex. I would also like to thank the School of European Studies, University of Sussex for financial support for my DPhil upon which this book is based. Professor Helen Wallace, then Director of the Sussex European Institute helped me greatly in developing contacts and providing advice on the completion of my thesis. Dr. Peter Holmes and Dr. Michael Gasiorek also offered useful advice for the case studies.

My research on the car industry would not have been possible without the support of a Research Fellowship from Toyota's Institute for International Economic Studies (IIES) in Tokyo. I also received invaluable support from the Department for International Studies at the University of South Carolina and from the suggestions of Dr. Robert Angel there.

I would also like to thank the European Business School and Mike Potton and Eric de la Croix in particular who gave me teaching and administrative relief while I was completing the dissertation. I would also like to thank my students over the years who have had to put up with my lapses in meeting deadlines for grading and other administration. I also thank Dr. Nigel Grimwade for comments on my manuscript for Ashgate.

Last, but not least, I am indebted to the emotional support and love of many people. In particular, the love, pride and support of my father and sisters have been crucial to me. Thanks to my friends, Matt, Jon, Lisa and Prem for putting up with my inane talk about academe. And, I can say without doubt that I would not have completed this task without the love of Els who during the period 1993-1998 had to deal with tremendous demands from me at a time when she had many a problem herself to deal with.

Chapter 1

Introduction

Introduction

This book is an analysis of the linkages between trade policy and antitrust. In a world in which traditionally separate international and domestic policy domains have become increasingly related, our study aims to examine the extent to which trade policy and antitrust complement and conflict with each other. Based on a series of case studies, our book explores the conflicts and complementarities between these policy domains given different industry conditions and market structures.

Our essential argument is that different market and industry structures lead to different policy requirements in the domain of trade and antitrust. In the extreme, there may be grounds for the creation of international, transnational antitrust mechanisms. The book attempts to classify these different industry conditions into four categories: natural resource, complex manufacturing, R&D (Research and Development) intensive and internationally traded service industries.

The key theoretical starting point is to contrast traditional explanations for trade and investment with models that attempt to introduce market imperfections into their explanatory variables. Thus traditional models of international trade rely upon country-cost or factor endowments as the explanation for international trade. By assuming the immobility of firms internationally, these models cannot explain the existence of a faster growth rate in FDI over trade flows. By contrast, a number of new approaches in the international business literature (e.g. Porter, 1986, Yoffie, 1993) and the IPE literature (e.g. Milner, 1988) have attempted to introduce the role of multinational enterprises (MNEs) and the existence of market externalities and failures as explanations for international trade and investment. For its part, the international economics literature has also developed models of trade and imperfect competition still somewhat under strong assumptions.[1] The crucial aspect of all these literatures is the realization that trade and investment cannot be explained in the traditional way. The policy implications for governments have been that while a traditional approach would unambiguously support trade and competition liberalization *per se*, once an imperfectly competitive world is accepted the aims of trade policy and antitrust may need to change. By implication, the role of an interventionist approach to trade and antitrust could be admitted including the selective targeting of 'strategic industries'.

While a significant amount of work has been done in R&D intensive and internationally-traded service sectors on the relationship between trade, industrial and antitrust (e.g. Tyson, 1992, Woolcock, 1993, Bar and Borrus, 1997, Bar and Murase, 1997, Vogel, 1996, Baldwin, 1990, Borrus, Millstein and Zysman, 1983, Martin, 1997, Freeman et al.,. 1990, Hobday, 1995, Sako, 1992, Suzumura and Goto, 1997 and Yoffie, 1997), there has been relatively little detailed case study work on natural resource and complex manufacturing sectors in the context of trade and antitrust.

The choice of complex manufacturing and natural resource industries is thus an instructive one in that it allows us to contrast sectors where market imperfections lead to an increased role for non-country cost factors in explaining international trade (complex manufacturing) with a more traditional country-cost sector (natural resources). It therefore provides an important comparison for the analysis of the links between trade and antitrust. The case study method which is based around a detailed 'unpicking' of the nature of the industry and the policy formation process provides a positive analysis of the linkages and informs a more general debate on the policy implications. The primary research for our study has been based on in-depth interviews and analysis of primary documents from industry and government used in the policy formulation process. This has been complemented by the extensive use of secondary official documentation, media sources and related research work done by other scholars.

Increasing Economic Interdependence

Milner (1988) argues that increasing economic interdependence has altered the way in which international economic exchange occurs. The implications for her analysis are that firms' preferences for protection have changed too. While this latter aspect is not of direct relevance to this book, the realization that changes in the international economy in the last few decades has altered the nature of international trade, investment and competition is an important aspect of this book.

This process is often referred to as economic globalization.[2] For some, economic globalization is an indisputable truth – it has become a dictum for international business (Turner and Hodges, 1992, Dicken, 1998, Ohmae, 1993) and a 'buzzword' for journalists and politicians. It has become part of a justification for a renewed debate on the governance of the international economy. It is argued that changes brought about by the process of increasing economic interdependence have rendered traditional notions of state boundaries and policy dichotomies between 'domestic' and 'foreign' increasingly questionable. This process has created a sufficiently high level of interdependence and spillover between national economies that domestic policy regimes are now being scrutinised for their impact on international trade and investment. Increasing economic interdependence has been characterised by an increasing interdependence of the domestic economy with external economic events. This has been encouraged by policies of de-regulation and liberalization undertaken by the G7 governments and the WTO and by changes in the technological space in which economic activity takes place. How far this process has gone is a matter for debate (e.g. Hirst and Thompson, (1996), Strange, (1996)). The impact of increasing economic interdependence has varied across sectors. In the financial sector, it is hard to argue against views that within the industrialized world (and beyond) that markets are truly embedded in a highly interdependent structure. On the other hand, goods markets such as agriculture and textiles may remain substantially segmented along national lines due to the continuing presence of trade policy used to shelter domestic producers. Pauly and Reich (1998) provide evidence that MNEs may not be as 'global' as is often suggested. They show that MNEs tend to have strong home country and regional bases. This is in terms of revenue and profitability generated for the MNE as well as corporate control.

Frequently noted characteristics of increasing economic interdependence have been an faster growth rate of FDI over trade; rapid falling transportation and telecommunication costs and increasing level of intra-firm trade as the dispersed activities of MNEs require the co-ordination of complex value chains (Porter, 1986).

Economic deregulation and liberalization has played an important role in the process of economic globalization. Recent decades have witnessed an emphasis on the promotion of competition and the prioritizing of the private sector over allegedly outmoded statist and interventionist policies. Thus, the view that competition is the life-blood of the economy and distortions of competition should be proscribed has become dominant in recent years not just among neo-classical economists but more generally in the disciplines of economics and politics. Neo-classical economics places at the core of its analysis the market and the competitive motive. The general presumption is that more competition is preferred to less competition. Economic theorists have for many decades suggested that increasing economic interdependence is a positive phenomenon for the domestic economy as far as it promotes competition. By opening the national economy to global competition, policymakers can ensure that domestic sub-state actors (e.g. firms and labour unions) cannot engage in anti-competitive conduct with the negative impact that this conduct implies for consumer welfare. In the extreme, governments should pursue completely free trade policies in order to provide external discipline on domestic firms and to ensure the ensuing gains in aggregate consumer welfare.

Indeed, Hoekman and Mavroidis (1994) have claimed that the best *antitrust* policy for nations to pursue is a *free trade policy* because of its pro-competitive impact. Similarly, Bhagwati (1983) showed that in a rather stylized situation of domestic monopoly and perfectly competitive world markets, a move from autarky to free trade would transform the domestic market, lowering prices, raising output and enhancing consumer welfare. Again, the key to these effects was the introduction of competition in the form of imports. By contrast, Fingleton et al. (1996) points to shortcomings in this argument. In particular, if foreign markets are imperfectly competitive, there is no guarantee that trade liberalization will ensure that domestic market contestability can be achieved. Indeed, conventional economic analysis has been faced with the criticism that many of its models are unrealistic i.e. the world economy is not perfectly competitive. This is not just due to the existence of government induced barriers to trade. It is because in reality, many markets are imperfectly competitive, e.g. structures that exhibit economies of scale can only sustain a limited number of firms. This means that it is necessary to relax the assumptions of perfect competition. Most importantly, the range of potential market structures that emerge in imperfectly competitive market conditions can be considerable.

The Implications of Imperfectly Competitive Markets for Trade and Investment

With the increasing influence of economic theories embodying the notion of imperfect competition and strategic interdependence of firms in international as well as domestic markets, theorists have recognized that there are situations in which competition can have a detrimental impact on social welfare.[3] One of the central outcomes of the recognition of the complexity of imperfectly competitive conditions is that there are no universal theories that can explain the multiplicity of potential outcomes – an issue which is central to the policy implications that are present in this book.

Imperfect Competition and Economic Efficiency

The starting conceptualization of economic efficiency is based on the concept of the allocation of economic resources, whereby efficiency is maximized when a given set of resources cannot be reallocated leading to an increase in the benefits to consumers and producers without making others worse off. This is termed Pareto Optimality. Through a process of perfect competition, the most efficient firms emerge thereby supplying consumers with improved consumption possibilities. This scenario is static in its approach in that it examines changes in efficiency on a comparative static basis. Thus one of the more common changes analysed in this framework is when prices of a good fall. The standard approach is to compare the gains to consumers from that price fall in terms of the increased consumption of the good. Lower priced supplies are available by virtue of the fact that lower cost producers have entered the market hence the gains to efficient producers and consumers alike. The 'losers' in this approach are the higher-cost ('inefficient') producers. A similar approach has been traditionally applied to the analysis of the welfare implications of a move towards free trade (Leamer, 1984). Both Ricardian and Hecksher-Ohlin (hereafter termed static trade theories) approaches assume markets that replicate the model of perfect competition as analysed above. They thus use the same static concept of efficiency – based predominantly on static cost considerations. In the Ricardian model, it is the productivity of labour (cost-output ratio) which determines the international division of labour and hence the most efficient trade patterns in a world of free trade. In a Hecksher-Ohlin framework, relative factor abundance determines the most cost-efficient pattern of production and international exchange in a world of free trade.

There are two essential welfare implications of the static trade theory models. First, a move away from a situation in which domestic producers are protected from international competition (and by implication more cost-efficient producers) towards a situation of free trade will be globally welfare enhancing. Traditionally, protection has been conceptualized as taking place at the borders between nations e.g. tariffs, quotas. The static welfare implications of these different types of protection differ. At this stage, it is not necessary to follow through the arguments here.

This is due to a more (statically) efficient allocation of resources internationally. High cost domestic producers are required to reduce output and the factors of production used in the high-cost sectors will be freed up to be reallocated more efficiently in another sector. This is a consequence of trade liberalization as foreign producers enter the domestic market. Thus, increased competition is welfare enhancing (in the comparative static framework).

Second, there will be a redistribution of income domestically between sectors and factors of production because of trade liberalization. Thus, trade liberalization will negatively impact on owners of factors of production in high-cost industries that have hitherto been protected from international competition. Thus, workers and owners of capital in highly protected sectors may seek to resist trade liberalization in this sector if increased competition (in the form of imports) causes domestic firms to lose market share. Similarly, trade liberalization will promote the interests of export sectors over import-competing industries. This is due to the fact that import-competing sectors will be forced to adjust to the newly competitive situation by releasing factors of production out of the sector. These factors of production are likely to be reallocated in the export sector more efficiently. Export industries can thus expand their output – to the benefit of both the international and domestic economy. International trade is unambiguously a positive-sum game.

The central implication of this is that trade liberalization is an efficiency-enhancing process and should be encouraged. In this traditional (static) framework, where governments intervene to frustrate international competition, there can only be welfare losses globally. There may well be gains to specific sectors in specific nations but there will be a net global welfare loss. Thus if a nation decides to offer trade protection to a specific sector, owners of firms and factors of production in this industry will gain. However, losses occurring to other sectors that may face retaliatory protection from other nations may further undermine this gain to these specific sectors.[4] Moreover the rents gained from protection in this sector will attract other factors of production which may be more efficiently allocated in other sectors had there been free trade. In this framework, antitrust has focused on assuring competitive conditions in domestic markets. To quote OECD (1998a), 'competition policies tended to focus on promoting consumer welfare by protecting competition between and domestic firms' OECD (1998a: 5). In this sense, antitrust is concerned with how the competitive process can maximize allocative efficiency. Its focus is on how private actors can restrain competition and trade and in situations in which these restraints of trade are predatory, antitrust seeks to act against these restraints of trade. In this sense, trade policy's central aim should be complete trade liberalization. *Domestic antitrust and international trade policies are complimentary or mutually reinforcing tools of liberalization.*

There are two important differences between trade policy and antitrust in this context. First, trade policy focuses on the role of state activity and how it attempts to control the international flow of goods and services from. Antitrust focuses primarily on the activities of private agents. Second, trade policy and liberalization have historically been based on varieties of multilateral negotiations. In some cases, these negotiations have been on a regional basis (e.g. EU, NAFTA). By comparison, antitrust normally has a microeconomic, fact-specific, case-by-case approach. Importantly, antitrust has remained the preserve of national governments – with the notable exception of the EU. Trade liberalization is normally applied *ex-ante*. With the exception of merger notification, antitrust is applied on an *ex-post* basis.

There are arguably problems with the conceptualization of efficiency in a static sense both in general and in application to trade and antitrust. In particular there are shortcomings facing static trade theory models of international trade and the assumptions upon which these models rest. To reiterate, the clear conclusion of the above approach is that competition is an unambiguously welfare-enhancing process. However, the assumptions behind the model of perfect competition that are used to characterise international trade can be criticized. Thus when considerations such as R&D, learning-by-doing or other market externalities, the link between competition and static efficiency can be challenged. First, under perfect competition, there is an absence of increasing returns to scale both internal and external to the firm. A model of perfect competition cannot explain the importance of scale production (where average costs decline with increasing output). Firms in perfect competition are assumed to be small and thus produce a small part of total industry output. Nor can it account for the importance of learning-economies of scale where firms require a certain amount of time and productive effort to reach their most cost-effective production. This latter aspect implies an important role for research and development (R&D) in the commercial success of firms.

Competition can also have an adverse impact on the economy and the public interest if it discourages R&D. This is not to suggest that R&D is unambiguously beneficial to the economy and society. There may be situations in which firms carry out too much R&D. Nevertheless knowledge-intensive industries require significant investment in R&D which may not be guaranteed in a situation in which firms were forced to compete in a 'perfectly competitive' manner. In economic theory, this is often explained by the need for firms to focus on short term cost considerations rather than medium or long term investments to survive. Domestic government policies designed to encourage co-operation between firms can also significantly impact on international trade in favour of these states. There may be situations in which judicious use of subsidy and other export promotion policies may offer advantages to domestic firms over their foreign competitors. In addition, export subsidy may also offer broader advantages to society. These include the creation of employment and the diffusion of technology across society.

Static trade models are also unable to explain the existence of FDI and the role of the MNE. This is due to the emphasis on the location of economic activity that causes trade rather than the ownership and internalization aspects of an MNE's activities. Of greatest importance to the discussion here is that the MNE is a result of the need to internalize transactions or specific assets within the firm. To quote Dunning,

> [A]s societies become more sophisticated, not only are markets likely to be less perfect (i.e. in a Pareto-optimality sense), but any imperfection is reflected in increasing co-ordination costs of using this organizational mechanism. Such endemic failures [...] reduce to the presence of uncertainties, economies of scale and externalities, and the increasing public good characteristics of intermediate and final products, which contain a high ingredient of created (as opposed to natural) assets (Dunning, 1998, p.128).

Thus, there are several arguments to suggest that explaining international trade may be not be complete if static trade models are used exclusively. It is necessary to use a range of models or approaches to understanding the nature of international production, trade and investment. Porter (1986) was a groundbreaking study into how the MNE is an important explanation for trade and investment. The starting point was the realization that competition and competitive advantage were multi-faceted concepts that were not reducible to 'universal' axioms or laws (as suggested by both Ricardo and Hecksher-Ohlin). While some kinds of international trade and investment could be explained by the relationship between factor cost/abundance or productivity and efficiency of firms, it was not possible to explain numerous other kinds of international exchange. This is especially where *who produced* rather than *where production occurred* mattered.

> The global competitor can locate activities wherever comparative advantage lies, decoupling comparative advantage from the firm's home base or country of ownership. Indeed, [this] suggests that the comparative advantage story is richer than typically told, because it involves not only production activities [...] but also applies to other activities in the value chain, such as R&D, processing orders, or designing advertisements. Comparative advantage is specific to the activity and not the location of the value chain as a whole (Porter, 1986, p.2).

Porter notes that during the 1970s, nation states imposed increasing levels of 'behind the border' measures thus frustrating trade. When combined with falling labour content in production, this suggests that 'more foreign direct investment [flowed] to developed countries (to secure market access) instead of low-wage countries', Porter (1986, p. 55). Above all, Porter argues that competitive advantage in global industries is determined by 'a game of coordination – getting dispersed production facilities, R&D laboratories, and marketing activities to truly work together. Successful international competitors in the future will be those who can seek out competitive advantages from global configuration/co-ordination anywhere in the value chain, and overcoming the organizational barriers to exploit them'. Porter (1986, p. 56).

Although not directly related to this study, Milner (1988) attempted to analyse the link between increasing economic interdependence and the preferences of firms for protection. The approach taken by Milner was to draw a link between two 'variables': the degree of export dependence of firms and the degree of 'multinationality'. She defined multinationality in terms of the extent to which firms undertake FDI and the change of FDI over time; the profitability of foreign operations and the extent and direction of intra-firm trade. She hypothesized that as firms become more export dependent and multinational, they will resist attempts to erect trade barriers. She developed a series of hypotheses which is reproduced in figure 1.1 below.

Thus firms of type III are highly multinational and export dependent and would favour open markets both domestic and international. By contrast type I is where firms rely heavily on domestic markets and there is relatively low MNE activity. Type II and type IV firms are intermediate cases. While type IV firms are heavily multinational in their structure, they tend to produce in and for national markets (possibly because this is the only means of overcoming trade protection). Thus while they may favour liberalization abroad, they may seek protection for domestic markets in order to reduce the degree of competition in their sheltered market positions domestically. Type II firms will be keen for international market liberalization and this is their primary objective as they are heavily export dependent. They may not be so keen on domestic market liberalization.

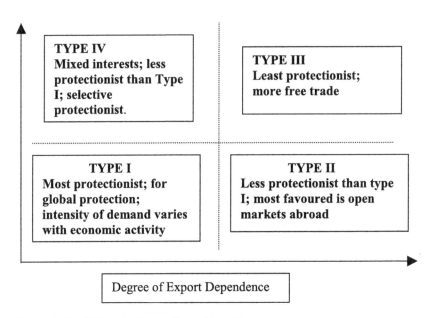

Figure 1.1   **Milner's (1988) Four Hypotheses**

Source: Milner (1988), p. 25

She compared the situation in the 1920s where economic slowdown should have led to calls for increased protectionism. She also looked at the 1970s when a similar economic situation was taking place. She compared French and US firms in the two time periods. Her central argument was that as the 1970s world economy was significantly more interdependent than its 1920s predecessor, protectionist pressure from firms both in France and the US should be lower. This is despite (a) the relative decline of the US as an economic power and (b) France's different domestic political institutions which have historically followed a less liberal stance in trade policy than in the US. She found that her arguments held and that therefore the essential difference between the 1920s and the 1970s was increased economic interdependence.

Thus for this book, the interesting implication of Milner's work is that she demonstrates the role of oligopolistic and multinational structures in the explanation for trade and investment and hence in the attempts of firms to influence the policy mix of states. Static trade models tend to ignore the importance of MNE activity, Milner emphasizes the latter while still showing that there are industries which are relatively domestic in their outcomes. It implies therefore that when an attempt is made to explore the linkages between trade and antitrust, it is necessary to consider the role of MNEs and their strategies depending on the nature of industry conditions.

Building on the work of Porter, Yoffie (1993) is a study that sought to re-conceptualize systematically the nature of international trade and investment. Its focus was on how the nature of competition between firms in the industry can condition and explain the nature of international trade and investment. Yoffie (1993) developed five propositions that attempted to classify why trade arises which in turn allows him to classify industries. The study argued that country-costs, MNE strategy and government intervention matter in determining trade and investment. The implications for trade policy and antitrust are important in this context.

Yoffie's Five Propositions

A When industries are relatively fragmented (and competitive), national environments (i.e. relative abundance of factors of production, domestic demand) will largely determine the shape of international competitive advantage and hence the pattern of trade. A corollary of this is that 'nascent' industries tend to be dominated by these country-cost advantages. An important implication of this kind of industry is that cost-factors determine trade. In other words, firms will seek to produce in the lowest cost location. As long as barriers to entry are low, firms will produce in the lowest cost location and export to the rest of the world. Factor abundance determines the cost competitiveness of the firms in the industry. MNEs will seek to produce in this sector by seeking out the lowest cost production site.

B If an industry becomes internationally concentrated with high entry barriers, then MNE strategy becomes an important aspect of global oligopolistic rivalry. In internationally competitive markets (A) where cost advantages are crucial in determining the patterns of trade, it would not be possible for an MNE to produce in an inappropriate i.e. high cost location as new entry would drive down costs and force the exit of the cost-inefficient firm. Thus in global oligopolies, (i) the success of one firm depends on the actions of others i.e. strategic interdependence and (ii) there are barriers to entry in the industry e.g. economies of scale and scope, R&D, capital intensity, advertising costs, government regulation. These barriers are determined by MNE strategy e.g. predatory pricing, standard setting, government lobbying. Thus, the fundamental difference with (A) is that firm strategies determine the pattern of trade and investment in (B). The competitive advantage of firms rather than comparative advantage of nations determines trade and investment.

C In global oligopolies, firm-specific characteristics e.g. the structure of ownership and organizational form have an identifiable influence on trade and investment. The implication for nations is that these factors can determine success for a nation in global competition. If profit maximisation is not the key measure of performance in these industries, managers will make use of risk reduction strategies or similar strategies that will reduce the risk of loss of competitive advantage to other firms.

D Extensive government intervention in oligopolistic industries can alter the relative balance between firms of different nations – even in fragmented industries. In industries which in absence of government intervention would be similar to category (A), it is likely that the forms of government intervention would be to support the cost-inefficient firms e.g. raising rivals' costs by tariffs, quotas, anti-dumping. In industries that display characteristics of (B), government support can be crucial in maintaining the fortunes of the industry through support for structural adjustment, technical progress etc. A related concept is strategic trade policy. The founders of this idea were Brander and Spencer (1983, 1985). They showed that in a two-country (A, B), two-firm (1, 2), one-product world, firms were assumed to compete by choosing the level of one strategic variable e.g. output, productive capacity, or R&D. The objective implied by choosing a particular level of the strategic variable would be to demonstrate aggressive intent in competing for market share. The problem faced by both firms is that they must make their decisions credible in order to succeed.

Brander and Spencer argued that trade policy can enhance a firm's credibility in setting strategic variables. This point is best illustrated through an example. Assume that R&D costs are the particular strategic variable. If the government of country A provides subsidies for R&D costs, firm 1, in receipt of these subsidies, can then threaten large outlays in R&D credibly and rationally (the subsidy has lowered firm 1's total costs) because the other firm is aware that its rival has government support. It should be clear that this basic and *limited* result could be easily used to provide support for government intervention in industry through 'strategic' selection of 'winners'. Thus, there is a case for the exercise of industrial policy in combination with trade policy. Antitrust, in its purest sense, would argue that government subsidies only distort incentives in the market and in the end, the taxpayer has to find the resources to pay for the subsidy. However, the strategic trade policy literature offered an alternative view. If a government can promote industries in international trade, the resulting positive national gains from increased market share in export markets will outweigh the initial national costs of the subsidy.

In a similar way, Doz (1986) also outlines a model of MNE 'development' directly related to the intervention of government policies. In figure 1.2 below, he demonstrates that how over time, MNEs emerge and how they internationalize.

His two key variables are national firms' capabilities and country factor competitiveness. The former relates to the ability of firms to compete based on their internal strategy and capabilities (e.g. the production system, co-ordination of the value chain or management structure). The latter is related to the availability of and competitiveness of resources or factors in the firms' home country relative to those in other countries. Thus at the start of the industry's development, it is likely that neither domestic factors nor the organization of the firms would allow for global competitiveness of the industry (T0 and T1). However, with national protection and import substitution, the domestic factors will develop aided by strong domestic market growth. An example is where an increasingly educated workforce (encouraged by sectoral and macro education policies) improves labour productivity. This enhances the productive capacity of the firms which leads to higher real returns to labour thus increasing their consumption demand as they become wealthier (T2). Through appropriate antitrust, the government allows the most competitive (or nationally capable) firms to emerge (T3). When a series of national champions have emerged (T4), the government pursues trade and investment liberalization as it is clear to governments that their domestic producers are true global competitors based on internal capabilities and national factor competitiveness. Finally, as the domestic opportunity cost of production of the national firm's increase, these firms will move 'offshore' for production purposes. Doz (1986) argues that this analysis can be used to explain the emergence of Japanese MNEs in cars and electronics sectors and the role played by the Japanese government in this process.

E   In industries where firms make long-term commitments, corporate adjustments and patterns of trade tend to be 'sticky'. In other words, past decisions of governments and firms have long-lasting effects on trade and investment. For example, investments in productive capacity may outlive the conditions that drove the decision in the first instance. In industry-type (a), such inertia will lead to firm failure, in global oligopolies; slack (created/enhanced by barriers to entry) may allow less-than-optimal structures to persist for some time. In figure 1.3 below, Yoffie uses two variables: the degree of market concentration and the degree of government intervention. He thus determines four 'kinds' of trade and investment flows.

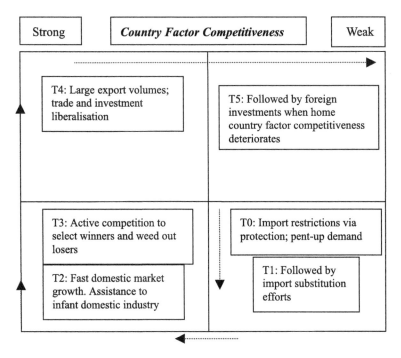

Figure 1.2   Accelerating the Development of a Competitive National Position in a Global Industry

Source: Doz, 1986, p. 240

(a) *Country comparative advantage* trade (bottom left): where global markets are fragmented and in the absence of government intervention, trade will be determined largely by national comparative advantage.

(b) *'Political Competition'* (bottom right): Where markets remain fragmented and where there is a high degree of government intervention (in the form of at the border barriers e.g. Anti-dumping), the extent of the 'success' of government intervention will determine the flows of trade and investment.

(c) *Global 'Oligopolistic competition'* (top left): where market concentration is high (e.g. caused by economies of scale) and government intervention is low, trade and investment will be determined by the strategies of firms (MNEs) and by the existing technology in the industry.

(d) *Strategic Trade Policy or 'Regulated Competition'* (top right): where the interaction of firm strategy and government intervention determines the pattern of trade and investment.

Yoffie introduces an element of dynamic competition into the 'model' by arguing that specific sectors can shift between these 'types' of competition over time. Thus as barriers to entry change over time, we should expect to see changing levels of market concentration over time. As government intervention changes over time, we should see specific sectors changing their position in the schema below. Yoffie and others (including Laura Tyson) develop case studies in the three forms of competition that Yoffie tries to conceptualize: regulated competition (cases: semiconductors, computers, telecomm, automobiles); oligopolistic competition (bearings, construction equipment, minerals) and political competition (insurance). Country-cost advantages shift over time – thus in automobiles, a major shift occurred in 1960s towards Japan (away from US). Subsequent shifts occurred (East Asia 1970s to South East Asia 1980s). This is the concept of dynamic comparative advantage. The logic of dynamic comparative advantage dictates that the most successful firms should make long-term commitments to countries that will act as the best platforms over time for a broad array of activities, beyond pure cost minimisation. Yoffie finds that in fragmented industries, government intervention is rarely successful. If barriers to entry are low, capital is highly mobile and comparative costs were driving forces behind trade, then in the LR government protectionism at the border was relatively unsuccessful. This implies therefore that trade policy measures such as anti-dumping are only likely to shelter the firms from competition. At best these measures may facilitate an adjustment process by slowing the pace of structural adjustment which otherwise would be politically difficult to sustain. The 'breathing space' granted by the protection might focus minds in the industry on the necessary changes in the sector. In oligopolistic markets, cost-considerations are not the only factors driving corporate strategy. For example, MNEs sometimes pursued FDI in order to prevent their competitors from gaining an advantage, preventing their rivals from having safe havens. This also may take the form of 'follow the leader' investment strategies, if one firm is entering a new market, should my firm follow suit? This was also replicated in the formulation of global alliances e.g. if one group of MNEs formed an alliance, then it was likely that another group would follow suit. The strategic reasons behind this policy were to ensure that each firm had a 'foothold' in their rival's markets and to ensure access to the relevant technologies in each of the markets.[5]

Yoffie's Framework and Static and Dynamic Efficiency

Yoffie's framework has implications for conceptualizations of efficiency, competition and trade.

A   Efficiency is a *dynamic* concept. As competition between firms is not 'perfect', neither is competition the unambiguously best approach to maximising welfare. Thus for example, where there are significant learning economies of scale that can only be appropriated through sunk investments, there is no guarantee that firms will gain from these potential economies if they are required to compete with each other. Thus, co-operation between firms may enhance dynamic efficiency and welfare. Another example is the case where there are significant transaction costs in the acquisition of intermediate products upstream or in the provision of services related to sales of final goods. Transaction costs are caused primarily by imperfect information caused in turn by bounded rationality.[6] In this case, if firms are required to purchase intermediate goods in 'arms-length' markets (examples of 'arms-length' markets include commodity markets or competitive tendering),[7] they may not have sufficiently high level of information in order to select the best supplier for the purposes of their production. It may therefore be preferable for firms to build close, long-term relationships between the firms concerned.

A third case, as illustrated in chapter 4, is related to the provision of services required after the sale of a product. This form of after-sales service may require significant investment in capital and personnel. Unless the firm providing the service can be guaranteed that once consumers have bought the good, they will return to it for after-sales service, they will not provide the service. Thus if firms are forced to compete for the provision of after-sales service, it will be undersupplied. Efficiency can thus be 'engineered' beyond the static cost approach. From the perspective of domestic governments, this may increase the range of policies available. This further suggests that government subsidy can help the development of industries that may be of the 'regulated competition' kind. Similar studies (Zysman and Tyson (1983), Tyson (1992)) have also pointed to the feasibility of industrial policy and the 'engineering' of comparative advantage. The fundamental aspect of this approach is that trade is not a positive-sum game – nations compete with each other for finite gains from international trade. Thus, it is imperative for nations to capture these gains before other countries do.

By contrast, Krugman (1996) argues that the main problem with industrial policy designed to encourage certain sectors is that first the 'value-added' in these sectors is little higher than in 'traditional' sectors. Even if certain sectors were special, there is the problem of how can governments 'pick winners'? It is unlikely that governments will know more about an industry that is seeking support than the firms producing in that industry and thus, governments will be prone to regulatory capture and invest resources into an industry that does not merit support.

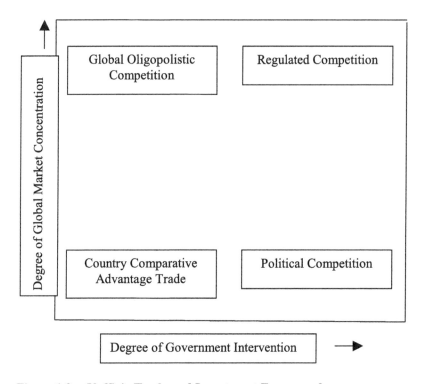

Figure 1.3   Yoffie's Trade and Investment Framework

Source: Yoffie (1993), p. 19

B   As Yoffie (1993) and Porter (1986) suggest, MNE strategy becomes an important aspect in determining trade and investment flows. *Thus, competitive advantage of MNEs becomes more important as discussed above.*

C   Given market imperfections, internationally mobile factors of production and a *dynamic* concept of efficiency, national comparative advantage may not be able to explain completely international trade and investment. *Thus, international trade policy making based on the traditional view of international trade may not be optimal.* Thus Tyson (1992) argues that a US trade policy based on multilateral trade liberalization would mean that nations which make use of government intervention to direct resources into key industries, would gain at the expense of the US firms. If firms are increasingly important in determining the economic success of nations, Reich (1991), Tyson (1992), Zysman and Tyson

(1983) and others argue that it is vital for the US government to play a key role in supporting US MNEs.

'System Friction', 'Deep Integration' and the Consequences for Trade and Antitrust

A consequence of the re-conceptualization of the causes of international trade and investment has been the realization that MNEs are increasingly important in determining international trade. Importantly, the gains from international trade and the depiction of the international economy, as essentially a potentially competitive space governed by nation states, requires reconsideration. In particular, the increasing interpenetration of national economies by the activities of MNEs has blurred boundaries between traditionally separable policy domains. This process of increasing interdependence is regarded as qualitatively different from previous eras because of the pre-eminence of FDI flows over trade flows – this is evidence itself of the crucial importance of the MNE in facilitating this process. This is in turn related to the changing nature of production technologies in that rapid technological change in communications and transport has reduced costs of international business significantly. This change has facilitated the development of MNE strategies that aim to exploit the increasing ease with which international business transactions can be carried out. While the claim of some MNEs to being 'global' companies may remain an unachieved objective, there has been nevertheless a fundamental change in which MNEs operate. The most important consequence of this qualitative transformation in the world economy has been the extent to which *different* national policies or systems of governance have been brought into conflict with each other.

Ostry (1990, 1991) coined the term 'System Friction' to describe how different models of economic organization (more specifically differing market models) between countries was a source of international conflict over and above traditional trade protection disputes. According to Ostry, these differences stemmed from both historical and cultural legacies in the different countries. This led to the development of differing national policies designed to govern the domestic economy. These differences affected a firm's international competitiveness which as Yoffie (1993), Tyson (1992), Zysman and Tyson (1983) suggest is determined by the interaction of firm cost-efficiency characteristics and a broader national institutional framework in which these firms were embedded. In Yoffie's framework, there would be some sectors in which competitiveness would be determined by the nature of domestic regulation (e.g. telecommunications) which would over time lead to the development of 'global players'. Thus when these nationally regulated sectors became more liberalized, these new MNEs, strengthened by government support both explicit and implicit, would be well-placed in competing in a global oligopolistic setting (Doz 1986). 'System Friction' leads to the notion that as national economic boundaries are blurred, not only do different national policies conflict internationally, but also the interaction and effects of different national policies can be highly complex. Jacquemin and Sapir put this succinctly:

[T]he distinction between 'internal' and 'external' competition is more and more blurred given the transcontinental nature of direct investments and the importance of intrafirm trade, the increasing mixing up of the local and international content of final products, the continual delocation of activities all over the world. In such a setting, a strong [...] antitrust, coupled with a relatively protective external trade policy, will not only limit the benefits of competition, it will be unable to control effectively the multiplication of restrictive and monopoly practices in world markets (Jacquemin and Sapir, 1991, p. 168).

Ostry (1994) argues that certain sectors require policymakers to reconsider the ways in which firms enter markets. In particular, in service industries where a local presence is required by the firms concerned, the term effective market access is crucial in understanding competition between MNEs. Effective market access begins from the premise that barriers to entry for imports are no longer confined at the border. They can also be determined by the nature of domestic regulation. For example, rules on domestic retailing can affect international trade and investment.[8]

Ostry (1997) argues therefore that in a world economy depicted by increasing international competition for market share, MNEs require market access in most of the major markets i.e. North America, West Europe and Japan. This is in order to achieve the necessary economies-of-scale and scope; to respond to rapidly changing consumer tastes and the provision of after-sales service; and to access technology from both inter-MNE co-operation and MNE-government R&D (Stopford and Strange 1991).

A truly level playing field for multinational firms would not only require reasonable symmetry of access for trade and investment but also [...] prevention of collusive behaviour and other abuses of dominant market position, thereby necessitating harmonization of competition policies (Ostry, 1997, p. 32).

As Ostry suggests, the source of 'System Friction' is the different models of governance employed by different nations. It should not be surprising therefore that as national economic boundaries become blurred, differences in the model of antitrust employed by different nations and regional authorities can become a source of conflict. Indeed, it cannot be precluded that nation states may 'impose' their domestic antitrust rules extraterritorially on the increasingly transnational nature of economic activity (see chapter 5 for an in-depth analysis of extraterritoriality). Current examples of differences in national competition rules are numerous. An example of asymmetries in competition rules is that of the respective competition laws of the EU-US-Japan 'Triad'. The US and the EU have relatively rigorously enforced anti-cartel policies (the Sherman Act in the US and articles 85 and 86 in the EU Treaty of Rome and the EU merger regulations). By contrast, Japan's AML has a number of exemptions from cartels such as depression cartels, rationalization cartels, and regulated industry cartels. It is also worth noting that the EU has exempted car distribution from the full pro-competitive effects of articles 85 and 86 by allowing exclusive distribution networks. In addition, the European Coal and Steel Community (ECSC) has provisions for the creation of 'crisis cartels' in the steel industry. Even while substantive differences may exist between the EU, Japan and the US, a more important issue relates to *asymmetric enforcement* of antitrust.

It is alleged that although the Japanese AML in theory is substantively as stringent in most circumstances as EU and US policies, Japan has a relatively weak enforcement record of its competition law. This has afforded Japanese firms protection in their domestic markets through forms of horizontal and vertical integration (*keiretsu*) that would not be permitted in the US and the EU. The Japanese Fair Trade Commission (JFTC), the body with responsibility for enforcement of the AML is argued to be weak and under-researched compared to Japan's Ministry of International Trade and Industry (MITI) and is thus unable to carry out its job effectively. Thus, it is claimed that Japanese producers in 'sensitive' industries such as cars, consumer electronics, telecommunications equipment and semiconductors have been able to exploit the enforcement asymmetry. They have thus gained market shares in the US and the EU 'unfairly' at the expense of their US and EU rivals (Tyson 1992).

A further elaboration of this view is that the JFTC has been deliberately weakened by Japanese government in order for MITI to exercise its industrial policy objectives similar to the strategic trade policy issues discussed above. Thus Robert Lawrence suggests that Japanese inter-corporate linkages (*keiretsu*) are a case in point where 'the existence of collusive private agreements are not simply the result of private decisions; they reflect permissive government policies.' (Lawrence 1993, p. 16). A related case could occur where trade and investment takes place between countries where one of them has no readily enforceable antitrust laws. In this case, there would be no means of *domestic* control in the country without antitrust should a firm decide to engage in activity deemed anti-competitive by this county's trading and investment partners. An example of this is where the countries of East and Central Europe as well as the Newly Industrializing Countries (NICs) of East Asia who are only now beginning to formulate competition policies. This is despite the fact that the latter group in particular has been trading extensively with other industrialized nations in Europe and North America for many decades.

These differences imply that if the international system wishes to reduce the incidence of 'System Friction', then states would need to agree on where there could be agreement and convergence. Of course, this is a huge question as convergence would have considerable implications for state sovereignty and the problems of harmonisation go beyond the scope of this book. The consensus of those who have explored these issues is that it is unlikely that a grand multilateral agreement would emerge in the years ahead (Akbar and Mueller, 1997, Hope and Maeleng, 1998, Scherer, 1995, Waverman, et al. 1997). In the absence of agreement on international antitrust, there is the possibility that states will decide to tackle the international spillovers that are at the heart of 'System Friction' by applying their laws in an extraterritorial manner. Three issues emerge from this. First, to what extent is the extraterritorial application of competition law is an optimal policy for tackling instances of MNE activity? By imposing domestic laws upon the activities of MNEs nation states are arguably frustrating the competitive advantage of firms who have chosen to produce in certain countries for strategic reasons. It may be that MNE X is producing in country A because in this country's preferential institutional conditions e.g. government support for their activity exists. If those conditions did not exist, *ceteris paribus*, the MNE would seek to produce elsewhere. One solution would be to harmonize or encourage convergence on those laws and practices that cause 'System Friction'. In that way the potential for conflict could be reduced, as nation states would have less to argue over if their rules were similar.[9] Ostry (1990, 1997) suggests that the optimal 'benchmark' for harmonized rules on competition should be based on the principle of maximising the innovative capacity of firms. This suggestion has much to commend it in that it is likely that future sources of economic growth will be in those sectors where innovation is key to competitive advantage.

Second to what degree are existing politico-legal notions of nationality appropriate in the context of increasing economic interdependence and MNE activity? As Reich (1991) suggests, the concept of ownership and nationality is complex when economies are so interrelated that US workers are employed by Japanese MNEs in the US and US MNEs decide to produce in Malaysia for sale in the US. Whose interests should US legislators serve? Japanese firms employing US workers or US firms who have moved production offshore (from the US) in order to employ lower cost labour in East Asia? Third, if the analysis of international trade and investment is based on an imperfectly competitive framework, then a strict conceptualization of antitrust based on the notion of 'free and unfettered' markets may not be economically optimal. Therefore, there may be justifications for policies that diverge from a strict interpretation. Thus, the EU exemption from competition rules can be justified because in the presence of market externalities, EU economic welfare may be harmed if pure liberalization was pursued. This may not be acceptable to US lawmakers who refuse to exempt the same kinds of activities but is extraterritoriality the best policy for the multilateral system in this case? These events and actions are all a symptom of what Lawrence et al. (1996) term 'deep integration'. This concept is similar to Ostry's 'System Friction' in that it explicitly accounts for the role of 'behind-the-border' integration as opposed to 'shallow' integration by which Lawrence refers to trade liberalization. The main consequence of 'deep integration' is that political sovereignty is inevitably eroded as traditionally domestic policies are modified to take into account the demands for deeper integration on the part of firms e.g. the need for stable multilateral investment regimes. As Ostry suggests, it is the meeting of different national regulatory systems caused by deep integration that leads to 'System Friction'.

Trade and Antitrust: Conflict and Complementarities

In this section, the implications of economic interdependence and imperfect competition for trade will be explored. Given the changes in the world economy, it is necessary to reconsider the relationship between trade and antitrust. As Tyson (1992) suggests, if a source of Japan's MNEs has been derived by judicious support by the Japanese government (e.g. through the relaxation of antitrust disciplines), then the imposition of trade barriers against Japanese imports may be justified. Importantly, Tyson argues that they come from sources other than traditional arguments related to regulatory capture and interest group politics. If the increasing success of Airbus in its competitive struggles with Boeing in the market for wide-bodied aircraft can be partially attributed to the role played by investment subsidy by European governments, is it not acceptable for other governments to pursue similar policies to foster similar commercial success? These are normative issues in that they inevitably lead to a discussion of 'fairness' – especially in an historical context. Thus, US governments have argued that Japan's economic success has been achieved 'unfairly'. In the post World War II period in which the US has been slavishly respecting and promoting the multilateral trading system, successive Japanese governments, while publicly agreeing to GATT/WTO agreements, have systematically sought to protect their key sectors against foreign competition. Thus even if complete trade liberalization had been achieved Japan's market would remain closed (Ostry 1997).

If the nature of industry conditions (e.g. necessity for R&D) implies that competitiveness can be manufactured by government support then the interface of trade and competition policies is more complex than in a perfectly competitive framework. If the source of MNE competitive advantage does not arise from traditional concepts of cost minimisation (i.e. a perfectly competitive or contestable world)[10] but is derived from the exploitation of economies of scope or learning economies, then complex patterns of international investment, ownership and trade will emerge. As chapter 2 will seek to explain, the interface of trade and antitrust is determined by the nature of industry conditions, e.g. MNE strategy and the degree of government support offered to firms prevailing in the specific sector that is analysed.

Structure of the Book

It has been argued above that to understand and explore the contemporary nature of trade and competition governance, it is necessary to develop methods of understanding trade and investment through a range of models and approaches. Above all, *it has been argued that in order to understand the linkages between trade and antitrust, it is crucial that the analysis considers the impact of different industry conditions and structure.*

The objective of chapter 2 therefore is to develop a framework in which it is possible to analyse the linkages between trade and antitrust given a range of industry conditions. An important realization is that there is a range of explanations for international trade. Thus, some industries remain explainable based on comparative advantage. There is however no universal model to explain trade under imperfect or oligopolistic competition. This has two implications. First, the presumption that government intervention is unambiguously harmful (demonstrated using comparative static analysis) does not always hold in situations of imperfect competition. As will be explained in more detail in chapter 2, where market externalities are present, there may be situations in which national policy intervention may be beneficial to the nation undertaking the policy. Second, debates over how trade and antitrust conflicts may be resolved have to be considered given the imperfectly competitive world economy.

In chapter 2, there is a discussion of the case study methodology and the motivations for using such a methodology. The chapter then examines how industry conditions can be classified which then links to a discussion of the relationships between different trade and competition policies that are relevant to the case studies. Having developed industry classifications and examined the links between trade and antitrust, the chapter forwards propositions on the relationships between trade and antitrust given the different industry classifications.

Chapter 3 is one of case studies which explores the linkages between trade and antitrust in natural resource industries. In natural resource sectors, it is argued that trade can be explained largely using traditional models of trade as the role of MNEs and the existence of market externalities are not important. There is a detailed analysis of the soda ash sector and how anti-dumping policy relates to antitrust. It analyses how the introduction of anti-dumping measures against US exports to the EU facilitated an intra-EU cartel between the principle suppliers in the EU. In particular, the central finding is that anti-dumping policy can facilitate domestic collusion (thus undermining antitrust objectives). The main conclusion is that in these types of sectors, trade and antitrust should be mutually reinforcing.

Chapter 4 is the second case study that explores complex manufacturing sectors. Here, the linkages between trade and antitrust are considerably more complicated due to the enhanced role for MNEs and market failures in explaining international trade and investment. Related to this is the fact that government intervention in these sectors can be considerably greater with industrial policy or strategic trade policy being prevalent in these sectors. The industry covered by this case is the car industry. There is a detailed analysis of the relationship between the EU-Japan 'Elements of Consensus' trade agreement which restricts Japanese imports into the EU and the introduction of a Block Exemption (BE) on competition rules for car distribution which permits selective and exclusive distribution systems (SED). In a global oligopolistic market such as the car industry, there is evidence of the anti-competitive impact of Voluntary export restraints (VERs) not just in the traditional sense of a trade barrier but in two additional, but important ways. First, the EU Commission recognizes that the EU-Japan agreement could not work without the need to weaken antitrust within the EU hence partial justification for the BE. Second, the need to allocate the 'forecasts' under the EU-Japan accord has definitely fostered government-industry co-ordination and may have also required firm-firm co-ordination in order to hand out shares of the total EU market 'forecast'. Past experience of the UK-Japan bilateral accord demonstrates the need for firm-firm co-ordination. Where there are important externalities in global production and where the existence of MNE activity and strategy are central to understanding trade and investment outcomes i.e. in complex manufacturing, liberalization *per se* in competition and trade policy may not be the optimal policy. Policymakers need a much richer understanding of the relationships between trade and antitrust.

In particular, where there are genuine arguments for a relaxation of competition rules, antitrust policymakers must also be aware of the 'spillover' effects of such policies on trade policy. Similarly, where a trade policy such as a VER is introduced, policymakers must be aware of the competition effects of these policies in sectors where firm strategy is an important determinant in international trade and investment

Chapter 5 examines the case of a global merger between two US companies General Electric and Honeywell. If it had gone through, it would been the world's largest industrial merger. The case is useful for our study in that it examines both how the complex bundling of services and products can produce dilemmas for trade and antitrust policymakers. Second, it also highlights the dangers of extraterritorial use of antitrust laws as this case involved the EU vetoing a merger between two US companies. It interesting in that the case itself could be interpreted as the sign of things to come in global antitrust.

Chapter 6 is a concluding chapter that draws together the findings of the case studies and offers some more general implications of the research in this book. The implication of the two case studies is that there is a need for reform of existing institutional frameworks for trade and antitrust governance. In particular, both the car and soda ash cases point to intra-EU institutional conflicts both within the Commission and between the Commission and the ECJ/CFI. In a world in which 'System Friction' intensifies with the activities of MNEs, attempts by one nation to capture the benefits of MNE activity may lead to conflict with other nations. This may lead to an increase in extraterritorial application of domestic laws if the conduct of states or firms abroad have spillovers into domestic jurisdictions. Thus chapter 5 examines the trends in extraterritoriality in antitrust in the US and EU. This analysis points to an increasing incidence of extraterritoriality – especially in those sectors that are imperfectly competitive. Lastly, the chapter details some attempts at co-operation in trade and antitrust and examines the GATS and TRIPs agreements as potential 'models' for co-operation on trade and antitrust governance. While a discussion of a move towards the internationalization of antitrust is important, this is beyond the scope of this book.

Notes

1   For a detailed survey of this literature, see Krugman and Smith (1996).
2   While recognising the importance of the globalization debate, this book does not attempt to provide a detailed analysis of this phenomenon. Instead, the term increasing economic interdependence is used. This is because the debate on globalization has become tangled in normative debates. Should certain aspects of the globalization literature be omitted, it is likely that this author would not do justice to this important normative debate.
3   See Krugman (1996) for a discussion of both theoretical and empirical implications.
4   An excellent illustration of this is the decision of the Bush Administration to impose 30 percent tariffs on imported steel. While this may have provided temporary relief to the relatively high cost US steel industry and help the Republican administration win key mid-term congressional contests, it has led to retaliation and an escalation of a potential trade conflict between the US and its trading partners.
5   This is sometimes reflected in merger battles. Recent cases include the battle for Rolls Royce by BMW and VW or the Mannesmann/Vodafone debacle. Firms want to ensure that their rivals do not gain a disproportionate control of specific markets. It also forces rivals to pay a higher price for the company that they wish to take control of which can have important implications for the predators balance sheet. Shareholders may be concerned that the company has paid too much for the firm concerned – did VW pay too much for Rolls Royce because of BMW's entry into the takeover battle?
6   See Williamson (1983) for a seminal analysis of transaction cost economics.
7   See Sako (1992) for a detailed analysis of transaction costs (in particular trust) in the determination of quality production in printed circuit boards.
8   The *Daiten-Ho* (Large-Scale Retail Law) in Japan restricts the size of retail outlets. This reduces the ability large scale retailers to enter the Japan.
9   This approach has been adopted in the development of an OECD treaty on investment – Multilateral Treaty on Investment (MAI).
10 Even if the assumptions of perfect competition are regarded as unacceptable, models such as perfect contestability founder on the assumption of zero sunk costs.

Chapter 2

Developing a Conceptual Framework

Introduction

The objective of this chapter is twofold. First, to develop a framework in which to analyse trade and antitrust linkages in a systematic way and second to introduce the case study based research that is the empirical heart of this book.

Methodological Issues

While it is unlikely that there is an optimal methodology, the approach of this book is to combine broad and tractable conceptual propositions with a case study approach. This approach recognizes the theoretical difficulty in attempting to model different industry conditions in a universal way. A case study is 'an umbrella term for a family of research methods having in common the decision to focus on inquiry around an instance' (Adelman et al. 1977; p. 142) It is much more than mere description of an event. The strength of the case study method is that allows the researcher to concentrate on a specific instance or situation and to identify, or attempt to identify, the various interactive processes at work. These processes may be ignored or hidden in a broader or large-scale survey and most importantly better explain the causes of phenomena being explored. The main criticism is that the case-study method is strongly sensitive to two problems. First, the ability of the research project to select the appropriate cases and second, an insufficient number of cases to be able to generalize around the specific outcomes in each case.

Classifying Industry Conditions and Structure

The industrial organization (IO) literature is rich in case study work. Recent collections of case study work include Scherer (1995). The strength of the IO work is that through descriptive analysis, it is possible to build a picture of the historical development of the industry by 'tracking' the evolution of key variables. IO studies have included the role of technical change, internationalization, the nature of production, market structure and changes in consumer preferences as key variables. These key variables are compared across case studies. Thus, for example, questions related to the importance and impact of technical change on the nature of production and market concentration can be analysed. In turn, these insights can be used to inform both corporate strategy and public policy.

Classifying Industry Conditions

The main objective of this section is to define industry conditions by prevailing cost structures, sources of competitive advantage, the nature of competition, the role of MNEs and the nature of government intervention. Each of these criteria enables the analysis to build a picture of the kinds of industries where trade and antitrust linkages are important.

Where international trade is determined by *natural resources*, the degree of MNE strategic involvement is low, the pressure for trade protection is likely to be of a classic 'at-the-border' type. If economies of scale are present, then there will also be strong domestic pressures for collusion faced with falling demand. Thus this industry type can cover a range of industries from agricultural trade, commodity (raw material) trade and industries that involve the basic elaboration or processing of a natural resource whose production technology is common and widely used.

Where oligopolistic strategic interdependence matters, the type of competition that emerges is quite different from a natural resource industry. Thus in *complex manufacturing* sectors in which the presence of large MNEs is common e.g. consumer electronics and automobiles the decisions of MNEs have a crucial impact on the nature, location and distribution of production.

Two factors are important. First, is the degree of MNE interdependence and second is the success with which firms can minimize transaction costs within the firm that determines competitive advantage. There is also clearly a link between the size and distribution of firms in the market and the nature of transaction costs. If a merger between an assembler and retail distributor takes place in a complex manufacturing sector for reasons of transaction cost minimisation, then this has an impact on the nature of oligopolistic interdependence. For trade and antitrust, it is likely that there will be a range of complex interrelationships and linkages. Antitrust authorities may come under pressure from firms in complex manufacturing sectors to 'help' in the efficient co-ordination of such a sector e.g. selective and exclusive distribution rights in consumer electronics and autos. At the same time, as the role of the MNE increases, issues of the treatment of FDI production become important – thus what is the link between trade protection and the arrival of FDI? In what ways do 'at-the-border' measures such as voluntary export restraints (VERs) create further trade flows as the MNE seeks to transfer intermediate products between affiliates internationally? This industry classification is thus able to encompass sectors that range from TVs and VCRs, 'white goods' sectors, automotive products to the production of semiconductors and telecommunications equipment. The following sections outline the system of classification adopted in this book. There are four 'types' of industry classifications used: natural resource-based sectors, complex manufacturing systems, internationally traded services and R&D intensive sectors.

Natural Resource-Based Industries

This type of industry is where the efficient production of goods is based on access to natural resources. Competitive advantage of firms is thus derived from access to lowest-cost sources of these natural resources. In other words, scarcity of natural resources determines competitive advantage – a firm's success will depend significantly upon the country location to the extent that natural resources specific to certain countries determine costs.

In industries of this kind, there is the possibility for production structures to display both constant and increasing returns to scale (i.e. economies of scale). Thus for example, the production of wood pulp may well entail economies of scale whereas small scale farming may not.

As natural resource industries can involve the extraction of raw bulky materials, there may be high transport costs. Given economies of scale, there are problems of excess capacity when demand for these products decline. If the goods are prone to cyclical demand (e.g. if they are intermediate products), then the problems of excess capacity can be substantial. Price competition can be a strong feature of these industries. Where homogenous goods are produced, the incentives and factors facilitating collusion can be considerable. If sunk costs are significant, the propensity for collusion may rise too (Sutton, 1991). In terms of public policy, these sectors can be subject to 'traditional' regulatory capture. Where MNE ownership of capacity is important, then MNE strategy is often based on risk-reduction (Yoffie, 1993). Examples of such sectors include basic chemicals, iron and steel and other metallurgy sectors.

Complex Manufacturing Systems

As the name of this industry type suggests these sectors are depicted by a multi-tiered or layered production system with discrete but interdependent stages such as components, assembly and distribution.

These sectors benefit from both economies of scale both internal and external to the firm. The external economies of scale are related to access to key inputs e.g. skilled labour, R&D and other learning economies. If these industries sell to final customers (especially consumer goods sectors), marketing costs are high. This is because marketing and advertising serve as means of product differentiation and are therefore an essential competitive weapon used by complex manufacturing firms. Transaction costs in these sectors can be considerable (Williamson, 1983). This is due to the multi-layered nature of production.

One of the sources of competitive advantage for complex manufacturing firms is the ability to develop and use efficient parts supply processes. In the car and microelectronics sectors, the relationships (and hence transactions costs) between parts suppliers and assemblers are crucial in determining the success of these firms. The development of parts inventory minimisation and 'just-in-time' delivery systems are in part an attempt to minimize transactions costs. There are therefore incentives to develop forms of vertical integration. The public policy implications are that policymakers may need to consider the need for exemptions for vertical restraints.

In these industries, there are complex issues of ownership and foreign direct investment involved. Competition in these industries can be of both price and non-price competition. Compared with natural resource industries, the propensity for cut-throat price competition is lower. Nevertheless, where the need for market share to reduce costs is important, there can be claims of international 'dumping'. These sectors can be exposed to the business cycle and economic shocks and as with natural resource industries that have significant economies of scale, periods of excess capacity can occur.[1] In terms of public policy, both 'traditional' pressures for protection and demands for consideration of industrial policy measures are prevalent (Holmes and Smith, 1995).

Internationally Traded Services

The most important aspect of internationally traded services is the need for effective market access (Ostry, 1990, 1997). This can be achieved through local presence and FDI. The relative cost of acquiring real estate, local and national rules on business activities can all have an impact on effective market access. An example is the Japanese small-scale retail law (*daiten-ho*) which restricts the maximum size of a retail outlet. This has allegedly frustrated the attempts of large US retailers gaining access to the Japanese market as the exploitation of retail economies of scale is significantly reduced by this law.

Another aspect of these sectors relates to concerns over the protection of intellectual property rights and branding. In some cases, some of these sectors are emerging from privatisation and state regulation. Therefore, they remain heavily influenced by the nature of current and previous regulations i.e. 'regulated competition' (Yoffie, 1993). Gaining market access offers first mover advantages to the firm as it is able to set the level of switching costs that the consumer faces. A number of factors including access to service provision networks (Tyson, 1992), ability to innovate, and the effectiveness of marketing strategy determine competitive advantage. The regulatory framework is also an important aspect in determining market outcomes in these sectors (Vogel, 1996). Both price and non-price rivalry is present in such sectors. A frequently adopted strategy is the need for 'loss leaders' through price cutting in order to capture market share. As far as public policy is concerned, the key issue of market access and the degree to which market access is restricted due to the need to protect 'national champions'. Another issue is how to treat FDI and the demands for 'local content' e.g. European TV and film media. Examples of such sectors include banking, telecommunications, audio-visual and retailing.

R&D Intensive Industries

R&D intensive industries are industries in which competitive advantage is determined by the ability of firms to gain a return from investment in product and process development. In particular, it is the ability of firms to gain economic rents from innovation that determines the degree of R&D undertaken.

Production in R&D sectors is influenced by the need to undertake large, risky investment in product development and innovation. Given these sunk costs, three strong incentives emerge. First is the need for protection for the innovation. Second, there is a desire for market share in order to recoup the investment through turnover. Third, there are strong incentives towards co-operation with other firms in the form of research consortia. In some sectors, the importance of government support is strong e.g. Airbus as well as more general support through public procurement (e.g. pharmaceuticals). In other cases, legal protection in the form of patents offers protection for innovation. Competition in these industries is commonly of a non-price variety as the source of competitive advantage in these sectors is the ability to innovate and protect that innovation so that the innovating firm or firms can reap the full benefit of innovation.

There are a number of complex public policy issues specific to R&D sectors both in trade and antitrust. In antitrust, there are questions that arise including the role of government subsidy, the permission for research consortia, mergers and acquisitions and public procurement. Whether certain kinds of co-operation between firms should be exempted from standard competition rules is an important challenge facing competition authorities.[2] From a trade policy perspective, should governments protect domestic industries in order for them to develop? Examples of protection and support would be the use of export subsidy. Examples of such sectors include aerospace and pharmaceuticals. Table 2.1 below summarizes these industry classifications. Given these classifications, it is now possible to focus on how trade and competition policies interact in each of these kinds of sectors.

Relevant Trade Policies and their Relationship with Antitrust

As a prelude to an analysis of the case studies in this book, it is necessary to present the main types of trade and competition polices and their interaction which are analysed in this book.

Voluntary Export Restraints

International trade policy and competition policies come into conflict where one government requests another government to persuade its producers to restrict voluntarily their exports. Reasons for such requests may be that the former nation may believe that the latter nation's producers are dumping their products or that the exports are subsidised (Scherer, 1995, p.49)). These policies are commonly called Voluntary Export Restraints (VERs) but are also called Orderly Marketing Arrangements (OMAs) or Voluntary Restraint Agreements (VRAs). The US and EU member states have used these types of agreements frequently and especially in so-called 'sensitive' sectors such as automobiles and consumer electronics.

In a simple trade model based on perfect competition, by voluntarily restricting output, these VERs act as quotas. The price effects of the VER are similar to those of any quantitative restriction. However, they have effects on the distribution of rents between countries; and more subtle effects on the nature of domestic competition in the importing country and on the structure of world production. With a 'traditional' quota, the quotas are distributed to the importing companies. The importing government could capture any revenues from the quotas if it auctions the quotas. As VERs are export country specific, the most common means of allocating the quotas is for the industry to engage in market share policies that fix market share through the handing out of the specified quotas by the exporting industry or the government of the exporting industry. In any sector, regardless of the nature of market structure, economic theory suggests that the restricted supply that emerges from an import quota or VER, will lead to higher prices in the industry both of imported goods but also domestic produced import competition.

Table 2.1   Classifying Industry Conditions

Industry Type	Natural-Resource Industries	Complex Manufacturing	International Traded Services	R&D Intensive
Features of Production	Sometimes E-o-S, high fixed costs	E-o-S, E-o-Scope; vertical integration; marketing and distribution externalities	FDI; intellectual property; importance of service networks; switching costs	E-o-S; scope; learning E-o-S; sunk costs, IPRs
Nature of Comp.	Price comp.	Price/non-price rivalry	Price/non-price rivalry	Non-price rivalry
Competitive Advantage	Key access to raw materials MES is important	MES, product innovation; production-distribution chain co-ordination	Effective market access; market share, protection/ exploitation of intellectual property; strategic alliances	Innovative capacity; market share; strategic alliances and consortia
Degree of MNE role	Mixed	High	High	High
Degree of gov't influence	Anti-dumping; Antitrust exemptions on export cartels	VERs, anti-dumping; Antitrust include exclusive distribution; subsidy, merger control	Domestic regulation government ownership; Industrial policy; control of service network; merger control	Export subsidy; Antitrust: exemptions of R&D consortia; merger control
Examples	Basic Chemicals, Steel	Automobiles, consumer electronics	Financial services; Telecoms; Audio-visual	Pharmaceutica ls micro-electronic

Source: Author's own table

Given the imperfectly competitive nature of many industries in which VERs and import quotas are present, the resulting contraction of supply from the restrained import levels allows the domestic producers to raise prices for domestic production. Thus, consumers have to face reduced choice for products and have to pay higher prices for the same product. Since a certain amount of inter-firm co-ordination is required, such arrangements effected for trade policy reasons may fall foul of importing nation laws that seek to discourage restrictive practices. This has consequences for antitrust: what should competition authorities do to protect consumer interests? Are they able to do anything given that the VER is a consequence of governmental policy? Government compulsion would allow the firms involved to claim sovereign immunity from prosecution should they be involved in market share agreements.

An additional side effect of VERs is that the exporting nation's producers will be able to raise prices on each unit of their quota due to the restricted supply. This is of course because they cannot sell as many units as they would like. One method of raising unit revenue would be to 'upgrade' export products – the VER effectively forces the exporting firms to enter higher-income market segments. An illustration of this is in the car industry where Japanese manufacturers who have been subject to VERs have tended to upgrade the quality of their export cars into higher priced luxury models.

Anti-Dumping Policy

Price discrimination is the selling of identical products at different prices to different consumers or different groups of consumers. In international trade, the export of goods at prices lower than the prices of similar goods in domestic markets is a form of price discrimination and is called dumping. Where this is alleged to occur and there is injury caused to the domestic import competing firms, nations resort to the use of anti-dumping policy. Antitrust also has measures to deal with inter-market price discrimination. For price discrimination to be prosecuted, it must be proven that it is being used in a predatory fashion.

Thus, despite their apparently similar objectives, these two tools of economic policy can come into conflict. The main difference between anti-dumping law and antitrust law aimed at stamping out inter-market price discrimination is that the former is arguably oriented towards protecting domestic producers rather than promoting competition. Price discrimination in domestic markets is only prosecuted if the domestic authorities deem it to be predatory. The proof required to prosecute alleged injurious dumping normally requires showing that exporters were selling abroad at below average cost even though there may be a sound economic rationale behind below average cost pricing. For example, an exporter may wish to price below average cost if launching a new product. This is especially the case where it is at the start of its product life cycle. Due to the nature of 'learning curves' at the start of a product life cycle, total average costs tend to exceed marginal costs. As a firm moves down its 'learning curve' i.e. experience in production increases, total average costs fall. However, in order to gain market share, a necessary pre-requisite for learning in production, it may be necessary to price aggressively the product, at a short run loss. Also, a similar pricing rationale may occur where during an economic downturn, output is below full employment levels, overhead or fixed costs per unit are higher.

Thus, the use of average cost calculations in anti-dumping measures may discourage this behaviour at the expense of lower-priced products and to the consumers detriment. This is a corollary of Yoffie's 'global oligopolistic competition' industry classification i.e. MNE strategy is crucial in explaining trade and investment outcomes.

A particular variant of alleged dumping is predatory dumping where it is claimed that exporting firms systematically sell products in export markets below cost in order to eliminate competition. Predatory dumping however is gauged not by average cost. In fact, there has been a vigorous debate among legal and economic scholars as to what the appropriate measurement ought to be. The consensus seems to be that pricing below marginal cost (which fails to maximize short run profits) is an adequate measure. There is a practical problem however in using below marginal cost pricing as a measure of predation. This is because it is virtually impossible to observe and measure marginal cost and thus some proxy for marginal cost must be used. Consequently, trying to prove predatory dumping in courts has been very difficult. In this book, the term predation does not imply below marginal cost pricing. Rather, it implies intent on behalf of the firms concerned to eliminate competition in order to gain long run monopoly profits. The EU has only upheld one case of predatory dumping, the *Wood Pulp* judgement and perhaps one of the most famous cases in the US of alleged of predatory dumping, the *Zenith-Matsushita* case, failed. For detailed analysis of the case in question, it is worth exploring Scherer (1995) and Belderbos (1996) in particular.[3]

Another reason why the objectives of anti-dumping and antitrust may come into conflict is where anti-dumping actually assists collusion in domestic markets. Thus, Messerlin (1990) has shown that EU chemical producers used anti-dumping measures imposed against East European competitors as tool for cartelization in order to maintain higher prices in the EU market. In this particular case, the EU Commission authorities upheld the first action, the anti-dumping case, launched by the EU producers, and anti-dumping duties as well as price undertakings were imposed on East European producers. A second case, brought by the EU Commission Directorate General for Competition (DG IV) against the EU producers some years after the successful anti-dumping suit, alleged cartelization and price fixing for chemical products in the EU market. The EU upheld this second case noting that the anti-dumping case aided the collusion. Messerlin has shown however that the benefits from anti-dumping: higher prices and profits for EU producers far outweighed the later fines imposed on the EU producers by the EU authorities as punishment for illegal cartelization of the EU market. More generally,

> anti-dumping actions have a pro-cartel and pro-merger propensity. Such actions increase the capacity to cartelize for firms unable to collude without some kind of public support: they also induce [...] firms to merge with foreign firms operating in [domestic] markets to the extent that [domestically] owned foreign exporters are more immune to anti-dumping measures (Messerlin, 1990, p. 10).

Export Cartels

Where the promotion of exports through the exemption of export cartels in domestic antitrust is allowed, trade and antitrust may come into conflict – especially export cartels may have adverse consequences on competition in third markets. In fact, chapter 2 on the chemical industry focuses on the potential impact of an export cartel on soda ash trade. An export cartel is formed in order to enable a group of exporters to co-ordinate their export activities. In this sense, export cartels, like any cartel seek to enhance market power of the group of firms. In the US, export cartels are exempted from antitrust law under the Webb-Pomerene Act of 1918. Although the stated objective of the act was to facilitate exports by allowing firms to reduce joint costs of export administration, export cartels have been allegedly used to fix prices and control export supply. An obvious conflict here arises between trade policy and antitrust. If allowing an export cartel to fix export prices results in anti-competitive behaviour in import markets abroad, should the export cartel participants be prosecuted in the country that receives imports? A good illustration of this kind of activity was the Wood Pulp case in which a group of non-EU wood pulp exporters organized a cartel to export products to EU paper manufacturers. The EU Commission prosecuted this group of producers under EU competition laws even though the alleged concerted practices took place outside the EU.

Import Cartels

Where a group of domestic producers wish to restrict import supply but are unable to do so through tariffs and quotas, then the firms may decide to collude to prevent imports. Setting up an association that would be an exclusive import agency for the imported good can do this. They frequently negotiate with the export firms on raising the price in order to restrict supply. In this way, both groups of firms (exporters and import competing firms) would benefit. It is likely that the exporting firms would prefer to sell an unrestricted quantity if they could. However, if these firms are competing in an oligopolistic market, then it is possible that the domestic producers might have created incentives for the exporters to collude. An example would be ownership of capacity in the competitors' home markets as a threat to the exporters should they attempt to undercut the import cartel. Another method of facilitating the functioning of the import cartel would be to purchase the imported good and distribute the good domestically. The key for the import cartel would be to drive down the price that they purchase the good and then sell it on at a higher price to consumers. This policy could only work if the import cartel firms were able to prevent the exporting firms from selling directly to their final customers. This could be done by placing restrictions on distribution channels such that the only way exporting firms could sell was through the cartel's own distribution channels. Clearly one of the most expensive and risky export strategies for a firm is to set up 'greenfield' distribution networks. There are many measures that domestic firms could employ to facilitate an import cartel through regulations such as phytosanitary measures in the case of food products. Other examples would be technical safety standards related to the 'handling' and distribution of the product.

Theoretical Propositions

This chapter has so far attempted to classify industries by the nature of production, competition, competitive advantage, degree of MNE activity and the extent of government intervention in these sectors. It has identified four 'types' of industry: natural resource industries, complex manufacturing industries, internationally traded services and R&D intensive industries. To some degree, creating categories and taxonomies is sensitive to a number of criticisms: the actual selection made and justifications for leaving other types out. It is thus necessary to put a theoretical framework in place to justify these categories. As discussed in chapter 1, Yoffie's framework is a useful one in that it focuses on how the degree of market concentration and government intervention affect sectors. Figure 2.1 below reproduces Yoffie's framework with the industry categorisations superimposed on it. As can be determined from the graph, *natural resource industries* can normally be located in those sectors which are relatively fragmented because of the nature of production e.g. high transport costs, access to raw materials. An important aspect though is to realize that in Yoffie's framework, global market concentration implies strategic interdependence, something which relative to other industry classifications is relatively unimportant in these sectors. Government intervention, where it occurs, tends to be of the 'at-the-border' variety and is lower and less complex than in other industry classifications.

Complex manufacturing systems are frequently dominated by MNE activity, they have become increasingly concentrated globally (through a process of merger and acquisition). Government intervention has played a role in the both the development of these industries and today, governments respond to demands for protectionism (in trade policy) and can offer exemptions and special derogations in antitrust. *Internationally traded services* remain heavily influenced by the degree of government regulation. However, by definition, internationally traded services are predominantly supplied by MNEs who have market presence in several countries.

Trade and investment in *R&D intensive sectors* is determined by firm's undertaking the risk of investing in the development of new products or processes for the most part. Government intervention, where it occurs is generally designed to promote the interests of firm strategy (e.g. patents, where firms need to recoup the investment by being granted temporary 'monopoly' in the particular product or process). Clearly, natural resource industries can as well display characteristics of oligopolistic behaviour. At the same time, R&D intensive industries could also display characteristics of relative market fragmentation – this may be caused by reasons of national protection e.g. non-tariff barriers such as technical standards.[4]

An important aspect of this approach is that the objective of this framework is not to gauge absolute levels but to appreciate relative levels. Thus *relative to* natural resource based industries, it is more likely that MNE strategy will be important in complex manufacturing systems sectors. Relative to complex manufacturing systems, R&D industries and internationally traded services will have a higher degree of government intervention. In the case of R&D sectors, this will be related to subsidy, exemption of research consortia etc. In the case of internationally traded services, it will be intimately related to the regulatory framework set by national or regional governments/authorities. Having placed the industry classifications in

Yoffie's framework, it is now possible to derive a set of theoretical assertions on the relationship between trade and antitrust that could form the basis of empirical appraisal. It is important to note that implicit in this analysis is an awareness that the incidence of trade policy and antitrust measures is a function of the political motives for protection. In the four sections below, a relationship between the nature of industry conditions, the pressures for protection and the implied links between trade and antitrust are drawn.

1   In industries where competitive advantage of firms is related to *country-cost factors* e.g. natural resource industries, producers who face new entry from lower cost suppliers may attempt to seek protection in the form of 'at-the-border' measures e.g. tariffs, quotas. Where the number of producers *domestically* is low (for example caused by the presence of MES), the trade protection can also serve to facilitate domestic collusion. This is the 'classic collusion' case.

2   Where competitive advantage requires the *co-ordination of complex stages of production* e.g. complex vertically related manufacturing chains, trade and investment will be determined, to a large degree, by corporate strategy that seeks to minimize the costs of co-ordination. As complex manufacturing sectors are depicted by global oligopolistic interaction, the resultant trade and investment flows will mean that attempts to shelter domestic/regional markets from this oligopolistic market (e.g. trade policy) will require support from other policies e.g. antitrust. There have been several cases of this in the past. For example, in the EU automobile sector, attempts by the EU and member state authorities to protect West European auto manufacturers has arguably encouraged FDI flows from Japanese assemblers who now produce in the EU. A similar argument is forwarded by Belderbos (1996) in other electronics sectors and Tyson (1992) more generally:

> Both U.S. and other multinationals invest abroad primarily to improve their shares of foreign markets. When protectionist trade barriers block access to markets, or even when barriers are only being discussed, foreign firms often respond by making direct investments in local production facilities. Protectionism is not a sufficient condition to explain foreign direct investment; foreign firms must be able to compete with domestic firms after incurring the higher costs of establishing local production to serve the domestic market. But protectionism may be a necessary condition to explain such investment, since when they have no reason to fear import barriers, foreign firms typically prefer to supply markets through trade rather than local production. Trade friction between the U.S. and its trading partners is a major reason for the substantial foreign investment in America's consumer electronics and automobile industries. Honda's extensive operations in the U.S., for example, were largely stimulated by U.S. trade policy. Among Japan's automakers Honda stood the most to lose from the restrictions on Japanese auto exports to the U.S. that were in force between 1981 and 1985 (the so-called 'voluntary export restraints') (Tyson, 1992, p. 41).

Thus as Tyson suggests as important as trade barriers is the realization that FDI was central to Japanese MNE strategy as means of achieving competitive advantage independent of trade barriers.[5] As the West European car market has historically been segmented along national lines, the arrival of Japanese firms required controls on the flow of intra-EU trade in order to maintain the segmented markets. As intra-EU trade barriers were not permissible, the use of exclusive distribution systems (through an EU-wide BE on automobile distribution) was required. Another example would be the case of consumer electronics which have been the subject not only of trade restrictions (in the form of VERs) but calls by domestic producers in the EU for 'local content' rules on 'foreign' producers located in the EU. Thus where the pressure for protection has succeeded in imposing barriers to trade and investment, it has been necessary for trade and antitrust to be used at the same time to control trade and investment in this type of industry. This is a direct result of the nature of complex manufacturing.

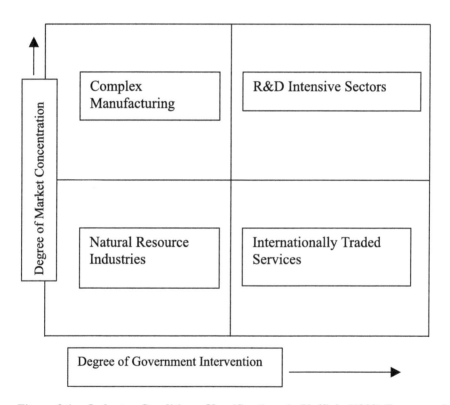

Figure 2.1   Industry Conditions Classifications in Yoffie's (1993) Framework

Source: Author's, adapted from Yoffie (1993)

3   In sectors where competitive advantage is determined by *effective market access*, a lax antitrust can effectively serve to restrict imports. Thus it is likely that governments may in support of their 'national champions' who face difficulties

in accessing their targeted markets may use 'countervailing' trade measures to prevent market entry into their 'national champions' home market. An example would be the threat of the US government to impose trade sanctions against Japan unless US auto parts suppliers could get adequate access to the Japanese distribution system which is allegedly closed as a result of the lax enforcement of the Japanese AML.[6] Another case is where Motorola gained the support of the US government in its attempts to provide telephonic services in Japan. A similar issue would be where national regulations that set prohibitive and different regulatory standards for foreign firms place them at a disadvantage in comparison to established domestic producers. Another result of this 'political competition' is nation states may conflict over the differences between domestic competition laws i.e. 'System Friction' leading to the threat of extraterritorial application of domestic competition laws. These conflicts between competition policies arise as a direct result of the need for market access in services i.e. industry conditions 'create' the conflicts.

4   Where competitive advantage is determined by the ability to innovate and the speed of 'knowledge creation', domestic antitrust may be used to encourage the development of globally competitive firms through production subsidy, permissive merger policy or the exemption of R&D consortia from normal competition rules. This creates conflict in that these policies serve as effective strategic trade policy: rather than protecting 'domestic' firms from competition, they serve to give these firms a 'helping hand' in global oligopolistic competition. This may lead to 'tit-for-tat' retaliation from other governments thus further increasing conflict. An example of this relates to the complaints of US government over Airbus and West European support for this consortium. Another example would be the differences in patent laws. Thus, it is argued that Japanese patent laws discriminate against non-Japanese producers as they are administratively cumbersome for non-Japanese firms and they more closely model the Japanese firms' innovative process (Matsushita, 1993). A third example is the non-existence or non-enforcement of intellectual property rights in China and other East Asian states. It is claimed by European and US MNEs that counterfeiting is rife in China and undermines their competitive advantage as they undertake the cost of product/service development and local rivals merely copy their products and can significantly undercut the MNE prices. Thus, industry conditions i.e. the need to innovate led to conflict between nations (and trade and competition policies).

The Case Studies

This book will present case studies on trade and antitrust in two of the industry-types outlined above. These are natural resource based industries and complex-manufacturing systems. Specifically, the natural resource based industry case study will analyse trade and investment in two sectors: seafood and soda ash. While in seafood, the focus is on scarcity of natural resources, in soda ash there is the additional impact of economies of scale and hence propensity to collusion. The complex manufacturing case study will explore the automobile sector focusing on car distribution and trade policy on Japanese imports in the EU.

It is important to note that from the four industry-types developed above, there is a rich literature on internationally traded services (e.g. Tyson, 1992, Woolcock, 1993, Bar and Borrus, 1997, Bar and Murase, 1997, Vogel, 1996) and innovation intensive sectors (e.g. Baldwin, 1990, Borrus, Millstein and Zysman, 1983, Martin, 1997, Freeman et al., 1990, Hobday, 1995, Sako, 1992, Suzumura and Goto, 1997 and Yoffie, 1997). There is however relatively little research in trade and antitrust on the case studies chosen for this book. While there is a significant amount of published research on the nature of car production (e.g. Womack, Roos and Jones, 1990 as a seminal work) which is important to an understanding of the nature of complex manufacturing in the car industry, there is little work that has been done on linking trade and antitrust outcomes to the nature of car distribution.[7] In the same way, while there has been much work produced on the chemical industry in all sub-sectors, there has been relatively little research into trade and antitrust outcomes. Again, as will be highlighted in chapter 3, an exception to this is the work of Messerlin (1990). The case studies will attempt to illustrate a set of common issues in order to draw out comparative elements in the case study. First, each case study contains a descriptive analysis on the nature of production and industry conditions in each of the specific cases. Second, there is a section on the nature of trade and antitrust interventions in each of these cases. The fundamental spirit of the case study method adopted is to:

(a) illustrate how differing industry conditions create different relationships between trade and antitrust;
(b) provide a comparative study (across industry-types) in order to inform a more general discussion on the future development of the relationship between trade and antitrust.

In chapter 6, an attempt is made to see where the research insights from (a) and (b) can be used to offer solutions to the problems encountered. It is argued that one of the consequences of the conflict between trade and antitrust i.e. 'System Friction' is an increasing resort to extraterritoriality as a 'solution' in the absence of international agreements on reducing 'System Friction'.

Conclusion

This chapter developed a framework in which to explore the linkages between trade and antitrust. The approach has been that industry conditions matter in the determination of the linkages between these policy instruments – thus predicting outcomes in a particular sector requires an understanding of the industry conditions that determine trade and investment flows. Yoffie (1993) offers a useful framework in which to extend an analysis of trade and antitrust given his attempt to go beyond the narrower static trade model approach.

Given this conceptual insight, traditional notions of trade and antitrust in sectors where country-cost advantages cannot fully explain trade means that these policies may not achieve their desired ends. Thus in sectors where MNE innovative activity is high and where market share is essential in recouping the investment in R&D, a VER which attempts to blockade imports (in order to protect a domestic industry) may induce FDI and further trade flows as supply of intermediate parts used downstream in the sector (Belderbos 1998).

The following three chapters represent the main contribution of this book. As discussed above, the internationally traded services and innovation-intensive industries have been well documented and researched in the past. The two other kinds of industry classification used by this book are relatively under-researched in terms of the trade and antitrust interface. Chapter 3 explores the case of natural resource industries – it has one main case: soda ash but also details another case of scarce natural resource trade: tanner crab-meat. Chapter 4 explores the trade and competition issues in an example of complex manufacturing: automobiles. Chapter 5 examines a related issue in the global antitrust debate: the propensity towards extraterritorial application of domestic antitrust. The main case study is that of the failed global merger proposal between two US based companies: General Electric and Honeywell. In particular, the chapter focuses on the weaknesses, dangers and shortcomings of extraterritoriality as a principle for maintain market contestability.

Notes

1   A recent example of this has been the problems of excess capacity in the East Asian consumer electronics industry that has been caused by the financial crises in these countries. Prices for both components (e.g. semiconductors) and final products (e.g. VCRs) have fallen in the wake of the crisis as East Asian based producers have attempted to sell the excess capacity.

2   See Waverman et al. (1997) for detailed discussion on antitrust and research and development consortia.

3   Zenith Radio Corp. Inc., a US manufacturer of television sets alleged that Matsushita Electric Industrial of Japan had sold television sets in the US market at prices below Japanese domestic prices in order to eliminate US competitors. Once Matsushita and other Japanese producers had eliminated US firms, it was argued that the Japanese producers would then raise prices to reap monopoly profits. In 1975, Japanese market share doubled and some US manufacturers exited the market. Attempts to sue under anti-dumping law failed. The remaining firms sued under US antitrust law alleging predatory pricing. More than a decade after the first dumping claims were made against the Japanese producers, an appellate court ruled by a 5 to 4 majority that in order for predatory dumping to work, it must be shown clearly that a sustained period of pricing below cost would have led to long term profits once competition had been eliminated. The court ruled that there was no evidence that Japanese producers had gained such a dominant position for them to be able to compensate for their short run profit losses as alleged in the predatory dumping suit.

4   MNEs involved in R&D industries may prefer a situation of fragmented markets if the minimisation of competition is a desirable strategy for them.

5   An inevitable consequence for EU assemblers was that the arrival of Japanese firms would mean more competition in West Europe.

6   This type of measure is euphemistically termed 'Voluntary Import Expansion'.

7   A notable exception is the work of Holmes and Smith (1995) on more general welfare issues in trade and antitrust in the European car sector.

Chapter 3

Natural Resources

Introduction

Natural resource trade is most likely to conform to trade as explained by a static trade theory framework. As characterized by Yoffie (1993), industrial policy interventions (e.g. R&D subsidy, national regulatory frameworks) are significantly less common than in R&D intensive sectors or internationally traded services.[1] At the same time, the role of MNE strategy may also be substantially less important. This has two implications. First, trade is determined by country-cost advantages and that second, *ceteris paribus*, global market concentration will be lower than in other sectors. The source of competitive advantage for firms in these sectors is determined by access to scarce natural resources. As scarcity increases, the opportunity cost of production rises.[2] In turn, firms that can minimize costs in this traditional microeconomic sense will win international competition. Examples of this kind of industry are basic textiles, agricultural and commodity products such as coffee. In natural resource industries where firm economies of scale are important, producers are sensitive to the need to maintain output as a means of achieving (or getting close to achieving) minimum efficient scale (MES). If all the firms compete vigorously for market share, then the least cost-efficient firms will lose out (a vicious spiral in that faced with falling prices, firms with shrinking market share become less and less cost-efficient). An alternative, and certainly more acceptable one to high cost producers, is to collude on market share. Sectors such as iron, steel and basic chemicals fall under the category.

Of course, in order for the collusion to be successful, it is necessary to raise entry barriers. Thus, trade policy (if the main potential source of lower-cost competition is import competition) can serve as the necessary barrier-to-entry. Where MNEs are present, they are likely to produce where they can access the natural resources at lowest cost. Thus, multinational ownership is a function of access to scarce resources rather than other motives as may be observed in other 'globally oligopolistic' sectors. High transport costs are often a feature of natural resource industries especially if the source of the commodities are distant from the final market for the goods or the natural resource is dangerous to handle or bulky. Indeed, anything that can raise the costs of transport and storage for exporting firms is likely to substantially raise overall costs for producers.[3]

Research Questions

The chapter aims to answer the following questions:

(a) What are the characteristics of natural resource industries?
(b) How does the nature of natural resource industries determine trade and investment flows?
(c) What are the implications of this for trade policy and antitrust in isolation?
(d) What are the implications for the relationship between trade and antitrust?

Methodology and Structure

This chapter is based around two case studies. The first explores a case of how import cartelization acts as a barrier to entry for imports in a seafood sector: Tanner Crab. The persistence of import cartelization in this case is related to the lax enforcement of antitrust. Thus, inappropriate antitrust enforcement acts to frustrate international trade.

The second and main case is a detailed analysis of the EU soda ash sector. Both GATT (1993) and OECD (1998a) refer to this case as an example of the contradictions between trade and antitrust. The case illustrates the relationship between anti-dumping policy and domestic collusion. It demonstrates that where international trade is determined by access to scarce natural resources, a restrictive trade policy will lead to losses in allocative efficiency. Moreover, where there are economies of scale in production, domestic market structure will provide incentives to cartelize, especially if there is a source of lower cost competition.

The case shows that domestic manufacturers of soda ash used anti-dumping measures to facilitate domestic collusion thus demonstrating the pro-cartel impact of anti-dumping measures. This conclusion is similar to that of Messerlin (1990) whose work is explored in detail below. However, the key contribution of this case study is to go beyond Messerlin's approach which was to use official regulations and trade flows to 'calculate' the costs of protection to EU consumers and the fines imposed on EU firms for cartelization.

This case study uses a broader range of primary sources to build a detailed picture of the industry. It uses interviews with industry and government, working documents by the EU, submissions to DG I during the anti-dumping investigation, rulings of the ECJ on the EU cartel in addition to the official EU regulations and decisions. It is this detailed 'unpicking' of the case which aims to draw out the conclusions on the relationship between trade and antitrust in this sector. In a number of cases, both the documentation and especially in the interviews, it has been necessary to respect confidentiality. In cases such as anti-dumping and competition cases, both governments and firms are sensitive to the publication of commercially sensitive information and frequently request confidentiality. Moreover, EU institutions need to maintain confidentiality as a fundamental premise for their procedures. This chapter is organized as follows. The first section features the case of seafood. This sector demonstrates the classic problems of high-cost producers when faced with competition that has access to scarce resources. It details an attempt by Japanese high-cost producers to prevent the entry of Alaskan low-cost producers through an import cartel. The apparent failure of Japanese authorities to prosecute the cartel led to a US court prosecuting extraterritorially the activities of the Japanese firms. This case study illustrates that poorly enforced antitrust facilitates collusion that acts as a barrier-to-entry to import sources. It suggests that mutual liberalization of trade and antitrust is the optimal policy in this case.

The rest of the chapter forms the second and central case study for this chapter. This second case study explores the soda ash sector. It analyses the linkages between the imposition of anti-dumping measures against the most cost-competitive producers in the US and the incidence of an intra-EU cartel. There is an additional factor in this case in that although country-cost advantages were the predominant explanation for the competitive advantage of firms in the soda ash sector, the nature of production is such that economies of scale internal to the firm play a role in cost reduction. It also means that firms may have incentives to collude when faced by declining market share. As will be explained in below, successful collusion requires, among other things, the need for high entry barriers. As will be analysed below, there is a case that in soda ash, anti-dumping served to provide those barriers to entry. There is a concluding section that provides conclusions to the case studies and their implications for trade and antitrust.

Seafood: Alaskan Tanner Crab

In the *Tanner Crab* case, the US Department of Justice (DOJ) prosecuted a Japanese import cartel of crab meat which was allegedly trying to use its market power to depress the price that US seafood processing firms could sell to the Japanese firms. *Tanner Crab* arose out of a complaint filed with the DOJ by a US fishermen's union against a group of Japanese trading firms including two major trading firms (*Sogo Shosha*), C. Itoh & Co. and Mitsui & Co. who were accused of illegally exchanging price information. US fishing fleets had complained to the JFTC but the import cartel persisted. They therefore turned to the US authorities to seek extraterritorial redress. Processed crabs caught by US fishing fleets were exported to trading companies in Japan. The complaint detailed an association called the Japanese Marine Products Importers Association (JMPIA) created by the trading firms in order to exchange price information. The JMPIA was based in Tokyo and was a broad association of seafood importers that included a crab committee. The JMPIA met periodically and acted as a forum for discussions concerning the importation to Japan of processed Alaska crab. Each trading firm disclosed the price offered and details of proposed purchases offered to it by the US exporters. The primary objective was to ensure that such an exchange of price information would enable each trading firm to agree prices at which they would be prepared to purchase tanner crabs. If one firm learned that it had been offered a higher price than another trading firm had, it would negotiate the price down based on information gathered through the JMPIA.

This import cartel had the effect of lowering the import price from what it would have been in the absence of information exchange. The DOJ launched an investigation into the case to determine whether there had been a violation of US antitrust law and filed a civil suit against the Japanese trading firms. The Japanese firms proposed a consent judgment that was accepted and the JMPIA agreed to cease activities.

The graph below explains the economics of the import cartel described above. *D(dom)* is the demand curve of Japanese consumers who rely on imports of crabs. It is assumed that Japanese consumers prefer tanner crabs to domestically produced varieties. In the absence of the import cartel, Japanese consumers purchase quantity *OQc* of crabs at a price *OPc*. This is point *D* on the graph. If the JMPIA organizes the price cartel, by lowering the price that the trading firms are willing to pay *OPm*, they will lower the quantity supplied to *OQm*. In other words, the trading firms restrict their purchases up to the point where the marginal supply cost equals the marginal value of the imports at point *A*. The buying cartel gains the monopsony rent *P(dm)ABPc* at the expense of the suppliers and consumers (i.e. the amount saved due to the lowering of price) but it sacrifices the surplus *ABD* that is lost through the output restriction. ACD is the dead-weight loss.

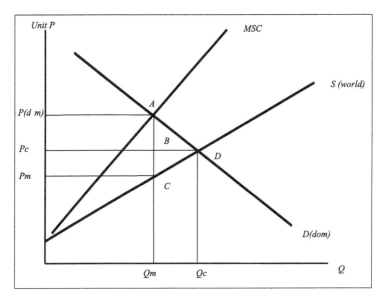

Figure 3.1   The Tanner Crab Import Cartel

Source: Author's own diagram

Matsushita (1991) is doubtful that the import restriction would have had the effect of raising the domestic price of the commodity imported into Japan. It would have been necessary to arrange a price-fixing cartel within Japan for this to succeed. This is because there would always be the possibility that the JMPIA may be unstable and break up. As with any cartel, Matsushita is arguing that there are potential gains from cheating and undercutting the cartel. The maintenance of the cartel is crucially dependent on the ability of the JMPIA to punish potential cheats and block new entry. It would be economically disadvantageous for the JMPIA cartel to sell the restricted imports of tanner crabs at the price at which they purchased them given that the cartel had successfully isolated the Japanese market. There would be considerable profit to be made in selling the imports at a higher price in Japan. Moreover, it may have made more sense in a broader context of the domestic Japanese seafood industry for the JMPIA to restrict imports of US crabmeat that would be competing with the domestic industry. In this way at least, the domestic industry would be protected from foreign competition. The condition that would allow the import cartel to capture the profits would be an ability to prevent Alaskan fishing fleets from importing directly into Japan to final customers. This is precisely what the JMPIA prevented by acting as an exclusive importer into Japan. The key assumption made here is that by lowering the price of imported crabs, the JMPIA would make it impossible for US exporters to sell in Japan independent of the JMPIA. This would have the effect of reducing the market share taken by non-Japanese sources. In Matsushita's view, the possibility that this might have occurred is remote. However, if the aim of an import cartel were to restrict foreign supply, an effective way of doing so would be to pursue a policy of price information exchange. It is considerably more difficult to monitor and prove that imports were being restricted through lower prices. If US exporters are not willing to supply at the price offered, it could be construed as a 'voluntary' exercise on the part of the exporters not to supply the Japanese market. As the trading firms concerned agreed sole import agency agreements with the US crab meat processors, then it is easier to monitor and prevent the parallel importation of the goods. Thus, the nature of import transactions in Japan through the use of trading firms could have created situations in which market access is difficult.

One problem with this case is that because it never went to a full hearing, the full facts of the case never became known. However, the judgment did outline the prohibitions on the JMPIA activities. These included the prohibition of each trading firm from 'entering into, maintaining, furthering, participating in, or enforcing any agreement, arrangement, understanding, combination, or conspiracy with any other importer or group importers to fix, maintain, establish, or adhere to the prices, range of prices, or other terms and conditions for the purchase of processed seafood.' In addition, the JMPIA members were prohibited from communicating with any other importer or group of importers to exchange information on future pricing offers for US 'processed seafood'; 'strategy, timing, or conduct of negotiations for the current season or future purchases of processed seafood'.[4] Given the consent judgment offered by members of the JMPIA, it is likely that US authorities had probably discovered an attempt by Japanese firms to maximize profits at the expense of US producers and arguably, Japanese consumers. Surely, the US authorities were correct in seeking prosecution of the Japanese firms in the interests of US firms and Japanese consumers? This is especially the case given the fact that the JFTC did not bring an end to the import cartel.

Conclusion

The findings of this case study are as follows. First, where the main source of cost-efficient competition is from imports, poorly enforced antitrust acts as a barrier to entry for import competition by facilitating domestic collusion. In other words, it allows firms to erect private trade barriers. Thus even if there are no government agreed trade barriers, the absence of antitrust policy (or the lack of its enforcement) serves the purpose of a restrictive trade agreement. Second, asymmetric enforcement of antitrust can also serve to promote extraterritorial application of domestic competition law (as with the US antitrust action in *Tanner Crab*) which undermines the multilateral trade process and increases international conflict even if the source of the inefficiency is rooted out by such action (see chapter 5).

The Chemical Industry: Soda Ash[5]

Introduction

This section explores the interface of trade and antitrust in the chemical sector. In particular, it includes a detailed analysis of the soda ash sector and this is the main research contribution to this chapter. As background, there is a brief historical section of the evolution of international cartels. This is complemented by a detailed discussion of the work of Patrick Messerlin who analysed cartelization and anti-dumping measures in low density polyethylene (LdPE) and polyvinyl chloride (PVC) in the EU. The starting point is the realization that most, if not all, chemical sub-sectors are imperfectly competitive. On a theoretical level, the industrial organization literature has contributed greatly to the understanding of competitive structures and conduct of firms in markets or sectors that are termed imperfectly competitive or oligopolistic. The analysis has tended to be focused on national or domestic industries rather than international cartels. Nevertheless, a number of the basic theoretical axioms are relevant. As discussed in chapter 1, imperfect competition implies the presence of supernormal profits for a small number of large firms producing in the market. From an antitrust policy perspective, the extent to which firms are able to exploit their market power is relevant when issues of anti-competitive practices are raised. Market contestability, a measure of the ease of exit and entry facing firms and its related costs, has become an intellectual and empirical yardstick by which markets and sectors have been examined by industrial organization. The implications for antitrust policy are that it rests on the premise that action should be taken only when incumbent firms are attempting to abuse their market power rather than the prohibition of large market share by itself. One of the primary aims of antitrust therefore has been the promotion of market contestability.

Another important characteristic of the chemical industry more generally is that with the exception of pharmaceuticals, many products in the industry are largely of an intermediate nature (being used downstream in other industries e.g. plastics for use in cars or consumer electronics). In this sense, sub-sectors of the chemical industry are vulnerable to significant cycles of demand in line with demand for downstream products. Given the nature of fixed costs and hence the need to maintain capacity and economies of scale in the industry, firms may be forced to engage in cut-throat competition in order to maintain production in the face of shrinking demand.[6] Moreover, if cost pressures rise in final goods markets, producers of these goods may seek to economize on intermediate inputs or seek lower cost alternatives.

These factors enhance the vulnerability of chemical firms and faced with such outcomes, the incentives for attempts at price co-ordination or other forms of collusion are potentially high. This is enhanced by the presence of a relatively small number of large firms. The costs of enforcing a cartel orchestrated by a relatively small number of firms who supply a large amount of the total market with a homogenous product may be less problematic than in situations in which there are a larger number of firms producing differentiated products. Under these circumstances, market contestability cannot be assured without some attempt by antitrust authorities to monitor and counter potential anti-competitive practices. The question facing antitrust therefore is whether it is possible for firms to organize successfully such anti-competitive activity.

The potential impediments to successful collusion are high across most manufacturing sectors. The dilemma facing any potential cartel is how they can successfully enforce the rules and punish any firms who decide to break the cartel without being discovered by antitrust authorities. Thus, the chemical industry should be not be regarded any differently to any other industrial sector in the economy. Yet, when a close look is taken at the history of the industry, cartelization is rife. Not only have collusive activities been successfully carried out within countries, the incidence of collusion at an *international* level is astonishingly high. For many years, the large chemical conglomerates of Germany, the UK and the US maintained agreements whereby competition between firms was minimized and geographical market divisions were set up whereby the firms involved would agree not to compete with each other. Stocking and Watkins (1946, 1948) detail late 19th and early 20th century attempts at the formation of global cartels.

Trade Policy and Collusion

In recent years, Patrick Messerlin (1990) has studied the chemical sector with a view to assessing the impact of trade protection such as anti-dumping on the ability of firms to cartelize markets. Messerlin's work on the European polyethylene PVC and LdPE market has shown that West European chemical firms exploited anti-dumping policy against low-cost East European firms for the purposes of price maintenance in the West European market by preventing the entry of lower cost competitors from East Europe. Moreover, Messerlin estimates that the benefits to producers of higher prices in West European markets as a consequence of the anti-dumping duties and the collusion far outweighed the eventual fines imposed on these producers for cartelization. The polyethylene and PVC cases are far from unique since World War II. Another example of an international cartel was in the chemical fibre sector in the 1970s. Japanese firms regarded as being competitive with their US and European counterparts in this sector and they thus represented a genuine threat to US and European producers. As a result of a trade agreement between the US and Japanese governments whereby the Japanese firms agreed to restrict their exports to the US market, European producers feared the entry of Japanese firms in their relatively sheltered domestic markets. In order for Japanese firms to maintain capacity utilization and scale economies, they would need to redirect their exports away from the US market and towards Europe. European firms successfully negotiated with the Japanese producers to restrict competition in the European market and thus maintain market share. Thus, the presence of a US-Japan trade agreement had the 'spillover' effect of encouraging collusion in Europe. More generally, this demonstrates how a restrictive trade agreement can facilitate collusion in other markets.

Another case of international collusion has been in the soda ash market, Solvay of Belgium and ICI/Brunner Mond of the UK agreed to respect each other's geographical markets – essentially, ICI/Brunner Mond kept out of the continental market in turn for Solvay's staying out of the UK market. At the same time as this long-standing cartel was active, the European Community had imposed anti-dumping measures against US producers, the most cost efficient producers in the industry. US firms were known throughout the sector for being aggressive exporters in the international market. In fact, Japanese domestic firms had successfully sheltered from US imports behind a complex web of administrative and physical barriers erected by the Japanese government and the Japanese firms themselves. Thus an interrelated set of trade barriers and markets in Asia and Europe combined with the high cost of transportation of soda ash production conspired to frustrate the US exports.

Structure of Case Study

The case study is divided into four sections. The first part reviews the economic theory that helps explain how competition occurs in this sector. The second section outlines a history of anti-competitive activity at an international level in the chemical sector. It then reviews the work of Messerlin on anti-dumping policy and collusion in the polyethylene and PVC sectors. The third part is the main section of the case study. It offers a detailed analysis of the soda ash industry. The section depicts a sector whose market structure has been prone to periods of fierce competition and international collusion and where access to key natural resources is the main factor in determining trade and investment (in the absence of trade protection).

Soda Ash: Theoretical and Conceptual Issues

The soda ash sector displays the characteristics of a natural resource industry in that firm competitive advantage is determined by access to the raw material used to make soda ash. Generally, this implies that where MNE activity occurs, it is based on a decision to locate close to the source of the raw material. Price is the main type of rivalry in this sector and where possible suppliers aim to tie in end-users to long-term contracts at an agreed price in order to reduce the risk of income fluctuation caused by price volatility. The good is homogenous. Thus, where there are pressures for protection, firms are likely to call for 'at-the-border' trade measures designed to raise the price of cost-competitive import supplies. What differentiates soda ash from the seafood case above is the imperfectly competitive nature of market structure. This is due primarily to the presence of scale economies internal to the firm and low variable costs. It should be reasonable to expect that the market be made up of a few, large producers with relatively little entry and exit activity. As the soda ash industry is also subject to swings in aggregate demand, it should not be surprising if the issue of capacity utilization in order to maintain MES is an important aspect of the producers' output decision. The need to maintain capacity in a period of falling demand can lead to the outbreak of cut-throat price competition where firms fight to maintain production and hence scale economies.

Barriers to Entry and Imperfect Competition

As suggested above, in imperfectly competitive market conditions, firms may seek collusive alternatives. There are three common barriers to entry that may enhance the possibilities of collusion. The first relates to the nature of production. If sunk costs were a significant component of fixed costs, the possibility of hit and run entry would to a large extent be ruled out. This is because a potential entrant would need to invest in non-convertible sources of capital in order to begin production. In other words, the entrant would not be able to sell on the capital invested or put it to other uses should it be forced to or decide to exit. Sutton (1991) has shown in a range of industries that as sunk costs rise, market concentration rises and thus the degree of entry and exit in industrial markets tends to fall. The second factor that could help a cartel or other collusive activity would be where a governmental policy or regulation restricts the number of entrants into a market. Generally speaking, trade policy such as anti-dumping or voluntary export restraints (VERs) are the more common form of entry barrier. By restricting the potential number of entrants on the basis of import source, the competing domestic firms would be able to capture a larger market share, thus granting them enhanced market power and enabling them to restrict output and raise prices. Import competitors are then forced to sell up the maximum quota in the case of a VER or at the minimum (non-dumping) price set under the anti-dumping regulations. A third case would be where anti-dumping measures take the form of price undertakings. This is a particularly high barrier to entry as price undertakings effectively fix import prices to a level that is so high that import sources are forced to exit the domestic market. Moreover, if domestic collusion is dependent on successful imposition of anti-dumping duties, price undertakings could be set at or above the cartel price thus aiding the stability of the cartel itself. Importantly, government induced barriers to entry may also aid collusion by reducing the potential number of entrants and thus making the organizing and administration of a cartel easier. It is more likely that domestic producers would share common objectives *vis-à-vis* importers whereas it may be difficult to persuade importers to 'play along' with the cartel. In cases where the import firms wish to avoid the imposition of anti-dumping duties, they may be prepared to agree to price undertakings. This is also likely to reduce the threat of cut-price entry strategies that could destabilize the cartel.

Antitrust and Collusion

Antitrust itself can be used to aid collusion through the allowance of 'crisis cartels'. These cartels are legal in the EU and Japan and have been used in industries prone to excess capacity such as the steel sector. These cartels have the veneer of respectability because governmental authorities sanction them frequently because the ownership of production resides in state hands. When states exempt certain kinds of cartels, they can also aid international cartels. Examples of these were extremely common in the context of Japanese exports. At one time, there were cartels in aluminium, steel, textiles and photographic equipment organized by the firms in those industries. As Japanese firms were significantly eroding market share in western markets, western firms asked them to form export cartels to reduce their exports. This would replace the threat of anti-dumping duties if the Japanese firms had persisted in their export drive. The same can be said for an import or export cartel. An import cartel can be economically justified in a situation where a particular country is reliant upon imports from one or two sources of a key raw material. The argument in this case is that the producers overseas could bid up the price of this raw material by 'playing off' each customer. If the users of the raw material can organize themselves such that the exporters have to deal with only one organization, then the subsequent monopsony power granted by the import cartel will enable the users to gain 'bargaining power' against the exporters.

By the same token, granting 'bargaining power' to users of the raw material may enable them to lower prices to the exporters' detriment as in the seafood case outlined above. An export cartel can allow member firms to co-ordinate their pricing of the good they produce thereby sharing confidential information on their customers' purchases. Information sharing would enable the cartel to raise prices and hence profits. In the US, export cartels are permitted but monitored by the authorities. However, it is not entirely clear whether it is possible to discover illicit price sharing in a situation where legitimate export administration costs are shared.

A Brief History of Restrictive Business Practices in the Chemical Industry

There is a rich and detailed history of attempts at cartelization in this sector. Interestingly the international law literature has covered a significant number of cases of international cartels. This is a statement of the prevalence of legal tribunals that have been required to prosecute chemical firms. In a work published in 1972, Heinrich Kronstein claimed:

> Standing beside the state or the international organization in the creation of [the world] order, however, is the private business economic organization. An attentive observer of the international economy is bound to notice the particular effect that the enterprises formally or informally under a unifying control have on the development and functioning of the international economy. Occasionally the activities of a single business enterprise exert influence, but more often several independent enterprises, working together under a formal agreement, or perhaps with only an informal understanding, shape the economic order. These private alliances of enterprises, which we shall call cartels [....] operate

behind the windbreak of state power. They may decide to remove a market from the ordinary economic order and subject it to their own making (Kronstein, 1972, p. 4).

Some Early Examples of Chemical Cartels

There have been numerous examples of international chemical cartels. Notable examples included pharmaceuticals where the leading producers in the US and Europe would grant each other licences to market each other's drugs in selected markets. An example of this type of cartel is the market division that existed between Hoescht and Upjohn (US) in the diabetes drug sector. Hoescht had discovered and developed an oral drug to treat diabetes called Tolbutamid. Under an agreement concluded in 1958, Upjohn exclusively supplied the market for this drug in the US and in Europe, Hoescht supplied it. In the US, Upjohn marketed the drug under the name 'Orinase' and in Germany, Hoescht traded it under the name 'Rastinon'. The effect of this market division was to charge different prices in Europe and the US.[7]

Other cartels included the urethane foam market, the west European cement market, world fertilizer markets, potash and polyvinyl chloride (PVC). From 1954, until challenged by the US DOJ, Monsanto and Bayer segmented the market for urethane foam. Monsanto supplied the US market and Bayer supplied the other importing countries.[8] The court entered a consent judgment requiring Monsanto to sell its interests in its US subsidiary that sold the urethane foam. Monsanto was also prohibited from acquiring for 10 years any facility that produced plastic foam. The role of these cartels has been to maintain the participating firms' positions in markets that are under pressure from falling demand. They were commonly geographically limited with certain sub-markets being served by specific firms and often they operated under the umbrella of various forms of government-induced protection (Kronstein, 1972, p. 30).

Nitrogen-based fertilizer producers agreed in 1962 to form an export cartel called Nitrex. The purpose of the cartel was to cope with the US and Japanese competition in third markets. However, the fact that large price differentials existed between markets of members of Nitrex suggests that there may have also been intra-European objectives behind the cartel. The syndicate's share of third markets at its peak was 60 percent (Kronstein, 1972, p. 28). Finally, the potash producers formed an international sales organization designed to allocate quotas for the European market (Kronstein, 1972, p. 29). Members of the organization included the state owned French industry, German and British potash syndicates as well as producers from Israel and Spain. An example of cartelization in the PVC sector involved several German, French, Swiss and British producers who agreed to sell PVC to Sweden at a price set by the Swedish producer thereby protecting the Swedish market from imports (Kronstein, 1972, p. 31).

The Chemical Fibres Case[9]

In 1972, five Japanese producers of chemical fibres were prosecuted under the control of international cartel provisions in the Japanese AML (article 6.1). The most famous case was the Asahi Chemical Company Case. In this case, European and

Japanese producers of chemical fibres agreed to divide the European and Japanese market for the same product. Following the United States-Japan textile agreement, Japanese firms were restricted in the amount of chemical fibre that they could export to the US. Fearing that surplus production would be consequently aimed at Europe, European producers approached the Japanese firms and agreed with them on a geographical segmentation of the market, whereby Japanese producers agreed to avoid selling in 'traditional' European markets and the Europeans offered the same assurances in the Japanese market. The method by which this geographical division was achieved was through the setting up of a Japanese export cartel that restricted exports to the European market. The first authority to act against this cartel agreement was the German Bundeskartellamt which imposed heavy fines on the German firms that were party to the agreement.[10] They then notified the JFTC who instructed the Japanese firms to desist under the terms of article 6.1 of the Japanese competition statutes. The firms accepted the decision.

This case is important for two reasons. First, it is an excellent example of the relationship between competition and trade policy. The existence of a restrictive trade agreement in one segment of the international market led to pressures for similar protection in another segment. In the absence of similar political agreement between European and Japanese governments on restrictions on trade in chemical fibres, the firms chose to seek more covert means of achieving their objectives of minimizing competition in their respective markets hence requiring action by antitrust authorities. Second, market structure fostered the conditions for successful collusion. Both Japanese and European firms were closely knit and thus were able to agree terms of the cartel. Chemical fibre production requires significant costs in capital and R&D and it is unlikely that new entry could occur easily.

Low Density Polyethylene (LdPE) and Polyvinyl Chloride (PVC): Messerlin's Tour de Force

In a seminal work on two chemical sectors LdPE and PVC, Messerlin (1990) attempted to demonstrate that restrictive or protectionist trade policies can have perverse effects on competition in domestic markets. In particular, Messerlin claims to have demonstrated that anti-dumping policy had permitted successful collusion in the EU market by blocking potential sources of competition from East Central Europe (ECE). It was only subsequent to a competition decision against EU producers that the full pro-cartel impact was appreciated. A conventional economic analysis would suggest that anti-dumping and anti-cartel decisions should have the same aims and outcomes because both deal with some form of price discrimination on the basis of market segmentation and monopoly behaviour. Messerlin demonstrates that in fact, anti-dumping policy on both counts is quite different from antitrust.

In the specific context of the EU, antitrust is governed by the basic principle that where anti-competitive behaviour affects intra-EU commerce, the use of articles 81 and 82 of the Nice Treaty should preclude and prosecute such anti-competitive behaviour. Anti-dumping rules, by contrast, are dealt with by article 113 of the Nice Treaty and concern themselves only with injury done to the domestic industry by dumped imports. Thus in terms of aims, EU antitrust has a much broader target than anti-dumping policy. The outcomes of antitrust and antidumping measures are equally different. There are few, if any, successful cases of price discrimination or predatory pricing in antitrust jurisprudence. By comparison, anti-dumping rulings are exclusively based on the concept of international price discrimination and in the majority of cases that are investigated, the plaintiffs are successful. Messerlin's main claim is that a significant proportion of anti-dumping cases have occurred in sectors where there have been attempts at cartelization in the domestic markets concerned.[11] This strong correlation led Messerlin to conclude that dumping appears only indirectly related to predatory intent.[12] In addition, the type of measure undertaken to deal with 'dumped' imports increases effective rates of protection by augmenting existing tariffs on the import goods. Messerlin even claims that in situations in which no measures are imposed on imports, this may have a pro-cartel effect by encouraging domestic industry-foreign industry private agreements.

LdPE and PVC Cartels In November 1981, the EU Commission anti-dumping authorities (DG I) initiated an anti-dumping proceeding against four ECE producers of PVC from Czechoslovakia, GDR, Hungary and Romania. Ten months later, the ECE producers (with the exception of Czechoslovakia) agreed to 'undertakings' to terminate the dumping effects of their exports. A duty of 12 percent was imposed on Czech imports. In 1983, the Czech producers agreed to similar undertakings as the three other producers. Two weeks before the 1983 decisions in PVC, DG I initiated a similar action against four ECE producers of polyethylene (Czech, GDR, Poland and USSR). The proceeding was terminated in 1983 by the 'undertakings' of the ECE producers of polyethylene to cease 'dumping' exports. At the end of 1983, the EU Commission antitrust authorities (DG IV) launched an investigation into potential anti-competitive practices in the EU LdPE market quickly followed by a similar investigation in the PVC market. Five years later, in December 1988, DG IV prosecuted and imposed heavy fines on EU and non-EU producers involved in a cartel that existed from 1976–1985 on the basis of article 85 of the Treaty of Rome. The PVC case followed the same pattern with heavy fines being imposed on the firms involved. According to Messerlin, the DG IV rulings provided ample evidence that as DG I was acting against 'dumped' imports of LdPE and PVC from ECE countries, the complaining EU firms were themselves involved in concerted attempts to fix prices and market share at regular meetings.

Tables 3.1 and 3.2 below outline the level of fines imposed on the firms involved in DG IV's actions and those firms involved in the anti-dumping petition. The striking feature of both cartels was that they involved a large number of firms and controlled a large percentage of industry capacity. In LdPE, Messerlin estimates that the cartel controlled 75 percent of industry capacity. Consumption was provided by 50 percent imports of which intra-EU imports were three-quarters of the total imports.[13] The majority of the remaining imports came from West European sources (non-EU members of the cartel). Thus, around 80 percent of LdPE consumption in the EU was under the cartel's control. The reach of the cartel in the PVC case was even more remarkable with roughly 95 percent of total EU capacity in the hands of the cartel firms. Imports supplied 30 percent of consumption in the EU of which two thirds of imports originated in the ECE countries subject to anti-dumping measures. Consequently, over 90 percent of EU consumption was controlled by the cartel.[14]

As discussed above, large cartels by their nature tend to be difficult to orchestrate. Evidence from the anti-cartel cases suggested that although the origins of the cartels can be traced back to 1976, there were no explicit attempts to fix market shares before 1981.[15] Messerlin suggests that because of the difficulties the firms had in undertaking collusion, it was necessary to seek public policy support for the cartel. This was evidenced by the EU LdPE producers' unsuccessful attempt to lobby for a crisis cartel policy for the industry. Both PVC and LdPE producers sought anti-dumping actions at about the same time as they began to organize the collusion. Messerlin points out that according to the competition investigations, the PVC anti-dumping case was initiated in December 1981– only a few months after the original proposals for collusion (August 1980). In the LdPE case, collusion began in January 1992 followed 8 months later by the anti-dumping action.

EU producers and other West European producers involved in the cartels turned to anti-dumping as the means by which they would enforce their cartel. In the LdPE case, the investigation was initiated in late 1982. Immediately following the initiation, the steadily declining price for LdPE (a decline that began in 1980) ended. Prices leveled out. Following the imposition of measures, imports from the ECE producers concerned fell away and prices rose. In this sense, according to Messerlin, the anti-dumping measures served their useful purpose for the cartel. The arrival of rising ECE imports in 1980 created problems for the cartel producers as this occurred at the time that the plans to impose the cartel were hatched according to the anti-cartel case. A similar story is borne out in the PVC case. According to Messerlin, this change in import competition necessitated the imposition of anti-dumping duties.

This for Messerlin, at least, is evidence of the anti-competitive impact of trade policy in international markets. Messerlin estimates that the anti-dumping measures, by increasing the effective rate of protection on the products *and* by allowing collusion to occur cost the EU consumer 600 to 650 million DM. Moreover, because the anti-cartel fines were imposed after four years of protection, the benefits reaped by the EU firms far outweighed the costs of the fines. Messerlin believes that these conclusions are robust enough to 'send a very powerful message in terms of policy making'.[16] He argues that the first-best policy is to abolish anti-dumping regulations altogether. Second best for Messerlin is to subordinate anti-dumping rules to competition rules: '[I]t makes little sense to have two types of rules, one for domestic competition and one for external competition' (Messerlin, p. 1990, p. 48).

Soda Ash

This chapter now turns to our second case. Soda ash is a chemical used to make plate glass. It can occur in two forms: natural soda ash (called *trona*) and soda ash produced synthetically using electrolysis. Extraction of soda ash is significantly cheaper than the production of synthetic soda ash. *It is this difference in cost that is the overriding source of efficiency and competitive advantage of firms.*

Table 3.1   The PVC Anti-Cartel Case: Fines, Capacities and Location

Firms	Plaintiff in AD cases	Plant Locations	Production capacity 1981 and (1986) in M. Tonnes	Anti-cartel fines M. ECU
Atochem	Yes	France	615 (485)	3.20
BASF	Yes	Belg., FRG	280 (230)	1.50
DSM	Yes	Netherlands	170 (180)	1.35
Enichem	No	Italy	650 (700)	4.25
Hoescht	Yes	FRG	240 (240)	1.50
Huels-Veba	Yes	FRG	410 (380)	2.20
ICI	Yes	France	603 (657)	2.50
SAV-ECM	Yes	France	150 (160)	0.40
Shell	Yes	France, FRG, UK	575 (460)	0.85
Solvay	Yes	Belg., FRG, France, Italy	772 (768)	3.50
Wacker-Hoescht	Yes	FRG	345 (350)	1.50
Norsk Hydro	Yes	Norway, UK, Sweden	125 (125)	0.75

Source: Modified table taken from Messerlin, 1990 p. 12

Global production patterns are such that on the one hand, the US producers benefit from naturally occurring mineral sources that require relatively low costs of processing to transform into soda ash while European, Japanese and other Asian manufacturers produce soda ash using energy-intensive salt electrolysis. A fall in US prices would have a significant impact on the ability of other producers to cover fixed costs and maintain capacity. In a world of liberalized soda ash trade, it would be likely that US producers would be the main producers and suppliers of soda ash given their inherent cost advantages. In common with many similar sectors in the chemicals industry, the market and firm structure in soda ash is also imperfectly competitive: economies of scale, high fixed costs, and cyclical demand patterns. Transport and storage are an important component of variable costs because soda ash is both bulky and toxic. A result of this is that soda ash manufacturers are frequently located near to their customers (for the most part flat and plate glass producers). Japanese production has been vertically integrated into glass production through ownership of synthetic production by glass manufacturers. One of the central demands made by glass manufacturers is a reliable and steady supply of soda ash. Supply bottlenecks caused by slower than expected delivery must therefore be minimized.

Table 3.2   The LdPE Anti-Cartel Case: Fines, Capacities and Location

Firms	Plaintiff in AD cases	Plant Locations	Production capacity 1981 and (1986) in M. Tonnes	Anti-cartel fines M. ECU
Atochem	Yes	France	350 (350)	3.60
BASF	Yes	FRG	593 (218)	5.50
Bayer	Yes	FRG	150 (150)	2.50
BP	Yes	Belgium, FRG, France, Italy	400 (570)	0.75
DSM	Yes	Netherlands	430 (430)	3.30
Enichem	Yes	Italy	680 (595)	6.50
Hoescht	Yes	FRG	160 (145)	1.00
ICI	Yes	France	485 (100)	3.50
Orkem	Yes	France	570 (400)	5.00
Shell	Yes	France, FRG, UK	575 (460)	0.85
Neste Oy		Fin., Swe.	165 (465)	1.00
Norsk Hydro		Norway	125 (125)	0.50
Chemie Holding		Austria	115 (250)	0.50
EMP		Spain	232 (312)	0.10
Dow Chemical		Netherlands, Spain	320 (550)	2.25
Monsanto		UK	50	0.15

Source: Modified table taken from Messerlin, 1990 p. 11

Structure of the Global Industry

The following section provides a detailed survey of the world soda ash sector. It focuses on production, product type, the number and location of sellers.

Product Characteristics   Soda ash is described by most industrial classifications as a bulk, low value, and high volume chemical product. Soda ash can be produced through an energy intensive salt electrolysis (the *Solvay* method – patented by Solvay and is known as synthetic soda ash). This is the method used by EU and ECE manufacturers as well as Japanese producers. By contrast, there are 'virtually inexhaustible' natural sources of trona found in Wyoming in the US. Trona is a mineral that is essentially the same as synthetic soda ash and is thus processed and used in the same way as soda ash. An alternative classification for soda ash is between 'light' and 'dense' soda ash. Dense soda ash is a free-flowing powder with low dust content. This makes it suitable for glass production. Light soda ash, by contrast, is less free flowing. It needs to be handled in closed systems due to problems of dusting.

Production Technology   Synthetic soda ash production requires very high fixed costs of production: both in terms of capital machinery and energy cost (particularly electricity). Low variable and marginal costs and high fixed costs imply extensive economies of scale in production. Capital depreciation is relatively fast and significant investment is required to maintain processing machinery, to minimize corrosion and thus to maximize production efficiency.

Natural soda ash is relatively inexpensive to process. Due to the low salt content of natural soda ash from the US, it 'is particularly suitable for the manufacture of glass, and some glass manufacturers who purchase mainly synthetic ash may seek to mix it with US soda ash to achieve the required concentration'.[17] However, in relation to the EU market, Wyoming sources of soda ash face transport and storage costs that tend to reduce the production cost advantage that US soda ash has over EU and ECE production. By reducing transport or other variable costs, US producers are capable of providing a significant export threat to any producer of synthetic soda ash. In particular, 'at current exchange rates it is possible for these producers to sell in Europe at prices substantially below the market price levels without dumping'.[18] This is a crucial point that will be dealt with in this chapter's analysis of the causality between anti-dumping policy and pro-cartel effects. It is necessary however to differentiate between land transport and sea transport. The latter form of transport is relatively cheap, so exports from the Eastern Seaboard of the US to Europe incur relatively low costs. However, the cost of land transport is higher. Industry experts estimate that for every 200 kilometres of distance from a soda ash plant or port, the price of soda ash increases by around 20–30 ECU per tonne.[19] Nevertheless, US producers' incentives for exporting are enhanced by the possibility that export targeting could gain significant market share as synthetic producers may be forced to exit the market faced with lower variable cost competition if US producers are able to cover the shipping costs.

The US market furthermore has a substantial excess of capacity over domestic demand and a surplus of 2.5 million tonnes is typically available for export annually.[20] This possibility is, of course, tempered by the fact that end-users need a steady and reliable supply of soda ash. In the US market, US producers have been selling at substantial discount from official list prices. In 1989, the official price was $93/ton FOB but was being sold at $73/ton.[21] In order to illustrate the comparative cost advantage that US firms benefit from, one of the most commonly cited reasons for preventing 'unfair' imports of synthetic soda ash from East Europe has been that the considerable costs of electricity used were offset by state subsidy in ECE. Furthermore, labour costs in East Europe compared to West Europe and Japan are likely to be much lower thus further lowering variable costs. In terms of labour and capital intensity, a combination of high labour, capital and energy costs, which are the hallmark of synthetic soda ash production, are likely to raise the total costs of EU and Japanese suppliers. Compared to US extraction methods, which while being still relatively capital intensive, are not as high as the capital costs of electrolysis equipment. Moreover, Japan has one of the highest energy costs of any of the OECD economies – this suggests that Japanese production of synthetic soda ash was also likely to be highly costly. Taken together, this suggests that US firms benefit from a 'natural competitive advantage' over their rival producers of synthetic soda ash.

Number of EU Firms   At the time of the case study, the EU industry had 6 firms operating synthetic soda ash plants. These were Solvay (Belgium), ICI/Brunner Mond (UK), Rhone-Poulenc (France), Akzo (Netherlands), Matthes and Weber (Germany) and Lars Christensen (Germany). Solvay and Brunner Mond are, by a considerable margin, the largest producers. Solvay produces in 7 of the EU member states (Austria, Belgium, France, Germany, Italy, Portugal and Spain). Solvay established a *Direction Nationale* for Austria, Belgium, Luxembourg, France, Germany, Italy, the Netherlands, Portugal and Spain. Its Brussels' headquarters supervised and co-ordinated each national subsidiary.[22] The west European soda ash market is highly segmented along national lines. There is no competition between Solvay and ICI.[23] Solvay has a complete monopoly of sales in Italy, Spain and Portugal. In Belgium, its market share is 80 percent and in France and Germany, its market share exceeds 50 percent.[24] For its part, ICI/Brunner Mond has about 90 percent market share in the UK.[25]

Non-EU Competitors   Other than US, ECE and EU production, Japan is the last major consumer (and producer) in the global market. There are five synthetic plants in Japan and ownership is spread among four companies: Asahi Glass, Central Glass, Tokuyama Soda and Tosoh.[26] Production costs in Japan are the highest compared to other industrialized countries due to high costs of energy, raw material and labour costs. EU domestic firms face potential import competition from primarily ECE[27] and the US. In the former instance, competition from ECE has been as a consequence of significant subsidy from ECE governments given that the former centrally planned economies owned all soda ash capacity in these countries. In the US, 6 firms extract trona soda ash. The chief wholly US owned firms are FMC Wyoming, General Chemical Corporation and North American Chemicals Corporation (NACC). Rhone-Poulenc, Solvay and Asahi Glass (Japan) own or partially own extraction facilities in the US. These firms account for almost 50% of total production in the US. This can be explained by two reasons.[28] First, ownership of Wyoming capacity acts as risk reduction strategy for EU producers in that they can more easily control a potential source of market disruption in the EU. Second, as noted above, natural soda ash when mixed with the synthetic variety is preferred by end-users. Thus ownership of US natural soda ash is for captive use.[29] US firms are organized for export to non-EU countries under an export cartel called ANSAC (American Natural Soda Ash Corporation) formed in 1981 and granted exemption from US antitrust law under the 1918 Webb-Pomerene Act (US Export Trade Act of 1918).[30] US producers of soda ash have also been active in non-EU markets.[31] In terms of global production scale, the US and West European firms are the largest followed by their Japanese and ECE competitors.

Demand in the EU Market   Over 65 percent of total soda ash output in the EU market is destined for use by glass manufacturers.[32] Soda ash represents 60 percent of raw material costs for the production of glass.[33] As glass manufacturers operate continuous process plants, they require an assured supply of soda ash. The fixed costs of plate glass manufacture are high and require a minimum capacity utilization. As with steel production, glass manufacturers suffer from problems of falling demand and excess capacity.

Competition, Collusion and World Trade in Soda Ash

Two attempts at cartelization have occurred in the major markets for soda ash. The first was orchestrated in Japan and the second in the EU. In Japan, there was an import cartel that sought to block entry of US imports until the early to mid 1980s. After an investigation of the cartel and subsequent desist order from the Japanese Fair Trade Commission (JFTC), US imports of trona soda ash rose. This change of fortunes for US exporters is alleged to have led to further collusive agreements[34] between US producers and Japanese producers whereby US firms agreed not to target the Japanese market in return for a share of Japanese domestic monopoly profits. This is further enhanced by the fact that the US firms also benefited from monopoly profits in Latin American markets where there is little domestic production to act as competition to US imports.[35] The second cartel took place in the EU market. There is a great deal more evidence in the public domain given that the firms alleged to have been responsible for this cartel were investigated and prosecuted by DG IV in 1990 and 1991. The central allegations were that Solvay and ICI colluded to restrict intra-EU trade in soda ash and were offering unfair commercial inducements to large consumers of soda ash.

The Japanese Market: From Domestic to International Collusion

In the ongoing debate on Japan's allegedly closed market, soda ash was an industry that was singled out by US trade negotiators in the 1980s and 1990s for being unduly closed because of collusive activities by Japanese domestic producers. Even during the oil crises of the 1970s Japanese imports never exceeded 70,000 tonnes per year. This was despite a number of cost factors that would have mitigated Japanese competitiveness. All inputs to make soda ash in Japan must be imported. These include naptha for the production of ammonia (Pugel, 1986, p. 28). Many years there was an export surplus. Japanese prices for soda ash in 1981 were $250 to $290 per tonne compared with US landed prices including the trade tariff of $185 to $200 per tonne (Pugel, 1986, p. 28). US producers approached the US government asking to investigate suspicions of collusive behaviour in controlling imports. Indeed, given US firms' comparative advantage, Pugel (1986) argued that the only explanation for the US firms' failure to capture market share in Japan must be due to the presence of some form of import barriers.

The US Department of Commerce (DOC) conducted a survey which showed that despite a price advantage for US soda ash, US producers had succeeded in capturing only 5 percent of the market in Japan by 1981. It was alleged that co-operation among Japanese firms and MITI served to limit access for imports. The DOC investigation concluded that Japanese producers of soda ash agreed to four actions. First, they formed an association called the Japanese Soda Ash Importers Association (JSAIA) that agreed to jointly import all soda ash from the US and that this amount would be equal to the difference between domestic demand and supply. In 1980, each US producer was assigned an import level of 12,000 tonnes each (Pugel 1986, p. 28). Second, the JSAIA entered into an import agreement with US exporters through a trading company of the Japanese firms' choice. There were seven trading companies involved and despite the fact that they handled different amounts of soda ash, each of them had identical profits of 20 million yen in 1980 (Pugel 1986, p. 28). Third, the amount imported was shared among the firms who were party to the agreement in Japan and fourth; they jointly operated the only silo in Japan specializing in soda ash storage.

The DOC study concluded based on the evidence above, that there was indeed some form of cartel limiting imports of soda ash into Japan. If US soda ash manufacturers could have competed directly with Japanese counterparts, it was likely that the US firms' lower costs would have ensured considerable market share. According to the DOC study, the JSAIA held annual meetings to decide the amount of soda ash to be imported in the following year and an appointed trading firm distributed it to all four firms along the lines of fixed quotas. The crucial step in the cartel's formation was to agree upon operating the soda ash silo. Given that it was the only one in Japan, in order to import soda ash, it was necessary to go through JSAIA. JSAIA would only allow imports of soda ash up to the agreed quota. Thus, it was virtually impossible to undercut the JSAIA buying cartel.

The DOC requested the JFTC to investigate whether there was an infringement of the Japanese antitrust law. Following an investigation, the JFTC concluded that there was indeed an import cartel arrangement that violated Japanese antitrust law and ordered the JSAIA to abolish the agreement. In March 1983, the JFTC introduced a cease and desist order. The firms accepted the recommendation and the JFTC ordered them to revoke the agreement. US imports began to rise to almost two-and-a-half times the previous import volume. In 1983, the total amount of US imports was 140,000 tonnes (Pugel 1986, p. 29). It is worth emphasizing the role of the trading firm, which on behalf of the JSAIA operated the silo that stored the soda ash. Given that the trading firm in this case possessed a monopoly in distribution and given that it was party to the agreement between the JSAIA, it was difficult, if not impossible, to distribute soda ash imports any other way. One US exporter was allegedly told by the trading company that they would handle more US imports if the US firm could get MITI approval. It would be interesting to explore whether it was feasible whilst the cartel was in operation for US firms to set up their own facilities in Japan to distribute the soda ash. In fact, this is probably one of the greatest impediments that faced US firms. The costs of building an import facility were likely to be prohibitive given the cost of land and the necessary safety requirements under Japanese rules for soda ash.

Thus, the only way US firms could have gained market access to Japanese markets would have been to negotiate a market share 'cartel' with Japanese producers. Given that US firms had successfully captured market share in Japan, is it possible to argue that supernormal profits in the Japanese market (by selling at Japanese prevailing domestic prices) enabled the US firms to cross-subsidize exports to the EU? The allegation of Japanese and US firms' collusion rests on the belief that the US firms could only substantially enter the Japanese market if they were prepared to eschew aggressive behaviour in the Japanese market. This allegation could be supported by the fact that Japanese firms own capacity in ANSAC. By acquiring ownership of the ANSAC supply, Japanese producers of synthetic soda ash could influence ANSAC's behaviour in relation to the Japanese market. Second, that US producers' natural comparative advantage in soda ash production ensured that, in the absence of trade barriers, they faced little or no competition in the Japanese market from other non-Japanese sources. Third, the aim of ANSAC is believed to be to increase export prices obtained by US firms. Prices in Southeast Asian markets are believed to have risen by the end of 1993.[36] This would lend credence to the view that there was the possibility of profitable exporting to Japan.

A Closer Look at the EU Market: Import Competition and Collusion

Over a period from 1982 to the present day, EU producers have been protected from imports of soda ash from major competitors in the US and ECE through the imposition of anti-dumping duties or equivalent measures. The argument for protection by EU firms has been that they are faced with 'unfair' competitors who have been dumping their imports at below their costs of production. This was an attempt in a couple of cases, they alleged, to eliminate EU production and thereby create a monopoly position for exporters to the EU.[37] The EU Commission, with one important exception, agreed to investigate injury and imposed anti-dumping duties on imports from the US and ECE.[38] Imports of soda ash from the US are already subject to a tariff of 9.1 percent. At the same time as these anti-dumping duties were put in place, an investigation by the EU antitrust authorities (DG IV) concluded that there were a series of anti-competitive and concerted practices taking place in the EU. DG IV alleged that the two main EU producers (Solvay of Belgium and ICI/ Brunner Mond of the UK) were at the centre of the conspiracy.

An analysis of the decision of EU Commission's Competition Directorate (DG IV) to prosecute EU producers of soda ash point to the existence of geographically-orientated restrictive measures whereby Solvay and ICI tacitly agreed to not export into each other's markets. Among a list of anti-competitive practices, the EU Commission alleged that Solvay would buy soda ash from ICI i.e. 'purchase for resale' without telling its customers before selling it to them. The objective of this policy was to ensure that any excess capacity produced by ICI could not enter the continental market without the agreement of Solvay. ICI benefited from this policy by being guaranteed a sale and Solvay could control supply to the continent and hence price for soda ash. In addition, EU firms allegedly offered secret rebates to big customers in order to encourage them to take on extra volumes. This system was called the 'top slice rebate system'. This pricing mechanism consisted of a price discount on the last 10 percent of the end-users purchases. The Commission believed that this was an attempt by Solvay and ICI to ensure that its major end-users did not switch to a second supplier.[39] The firms concerned claimed that in fact that the non-competition agreement had been defunct since the early 1970s and that

EU markets remain segmented because soda ash is a low value product that incurs large costs of transportation.

Nevertheless, following DG IV's investigation and decision, the EU Commission had successfully broken up one of the EU's 'tightest, longest-standing and most pernicious cartels'.[40] The cartel resulted in Solvay gaining 70 percent share of the European continental market and ICI maintained a 90 percent share of the UK market.[41] In the above case, ICI made it clear about its relationship with Solvay, confirming DG IV's allegations: '[o]ur relationship with Solvay is crucial as to volume, price and limiting the intrusion of others into our market'.[42] In one specific case,[43] Solvay attempted to control tonnage on the German market. It did this by preventing Kalk, a producer in Germany, from cutting prices in the German market. If Kalk was unable to sell its capacity, rather than allowing Kalk to lower prices to clear its excess production, Solvay would buy it directly from Kalk. This was an attempt by Solvay to ensure that the price levels were not pulled down by competitive sales of surplus tonnage. Indeed cross-shipments of soda ash were very low until the anti-dumping measures on US imports were lifted and DG IV imposed fines on Solvay and ICI. DG IV noted that despite a 20% higher price in the UK when compared to the continent, there had been an absence of cross-border shipments between the UK and the continent. In fact,

> [n]o material has been sold by Solvay (or indeed any Community producer) to customers in the United Kingdom, although price calculations found at the producers themselves show that even after the relatively high cost of transport from locations in continental western Europe the final delivered price to major customers (particularly in the south east and east of England) would have been comparable to or even lower over a considerable period than ICI's price.[44]

DG IV discovered an agreement entitled 'Page 1000' between Solvay and ICI/ Brunner Mond that had been in existence since 1945. The agreement was rescinded when the UK joined the EU in 1973. Yet, from DG IV's investigation, it had discovered that ICI had kept Solvay informed of its policy in Sweden. According to DGIV, '[t]o all intents and purposes the respective commercial policies of the two producers in soda ash have been maintained exactly as they were set out in 'Page 1000''.[45] The home market principle of the agreement limited sales where firms would only sell where (a) they had established production facilities and where (b) there was no domestic producer. Meetings to enforce the agreement appeared to have taken place every two months since 1985.[46] Despite protestations by ICI/ Brunner Mond and Solvay that the meetings were not held in secret, DG IV found that 'Solvay informed ICI of general price trends and planned price increases in continental Western Europe'.[47] During the court hearings, the Business Manager of ICI Soda Ash products, 'while asserting that he had never seen "Page 1000", admitted that he knew of its existence'.[48] Moreover, the same manager stated that the 'traditions which existed in the past' were something that ICI/Brunner Mond had to take into account when making its decisions.[49] DG IV's analysis of the cartel was fairly clear: ICI/Brunner Mond and Solvay, when faced with the possibility of competition with each other, chose to collude. To quote DG IV's analysis:

In addition ICI and Solvay point to the risk of 'retaliation' in the event of a competitive incursion by one into the market of the other. If one producer displaced the other at a particular customer, the affected supplier would have no alternative but to seek the lost tonnage elsewhere, the most likely being the aggressor's own home market; ultimately each would end up selling the same tonnage but both would incur greater costs and generate lower profits. The reason the two producers do not aggressively market in each other's home markets is thus said to be an awareness that such an exercise would generate a price war from which neither would gain.[50]

As DG IV was imposing fines[51] on the firms alleged to have cartelized the EU market for soda ash, a decision was taken by the EU Commission not to renew the anti-dumping duties on imports from the US which were due for reappraisal and possible renewal. Anti-dumping duties remained in force on imports from East Europe.

One issue surrounding this case concerned whether DG I had lifted anti-dumping duties on US imports in the light of the anti-cartel actions. There is no evidence of any explicit link between the two investigations because DG I, responsible for anti-dumping investigations and DG IV, in charge of antitrust, do not communicate on a regular basis.[52] However, both the competition decisions to prosecute EU producers and lift the anti-dumping measures against US exporters occurred within three months at the end of 1990. This possibility is supported by an interpretation of the same case by the GATT/WTO. The soda ash cases were highlighted by the GATT/WTO secretariat in its *Trade Policy Review* of 1993:

> A recent case in which the EC authorities intervened to restore competitive conditions concerns in soda ash, where domestic procedures had sought anti-dumping protection to defend cartel rents against competing imports. The companies involved were convicted under EC competition law and the anti-dumping measures repealed in 1990/91 (GATT, 1993, p. XII).

The causation implied by the GATT/WTO is that *as a consequence* of the anti-cartel actions, the EU Commission lifted anti-dumping duties. Confidential industry sources[53] point to the fact that falling prices, a direct result of the anti-cartel action according to US exporters, forced EU firms to begin shipment across borders in order to try to maintain capacity utilization. In its investigation, DG IV noted that as a consequence of the antitrust proceedings 'Solvay has started quoting to customers in the United Kingdom from Germany at prices that are competitive with those of ICI'.[54] The moment that the cartel was broken up, there was a significant increase in intra-EU trade suggesting a more competitive market and the ending of the rigid market structures imposed by the cartel firms.

The EU Soda Ash Market: An Anti-Dumping and Competition Chronology

October 1982:   EU imposes anti-dumping duties on ECE soda ash imports from Bulgaria, the German Democratic Republic, Poland, Romania, and the Soviet Union. Becomes definitive in February 1983.

November 1982: EU first imposes anti-dumping duties on US soda ash imports and accepts undertakings from other US soda ash producers. Becomes definitive by March 1983.

April 1984: In response to a complaint by CEFIC, EU reopens the anti-dumping proceeding against US soda ash imports. CEFIC's request was based on evidence showing a recurrence of dumping at an alleged level of at least 20 percent causing injury alleged to be a depression of prices which prevented the Community industry from recovering its costs, in addition to an increasing threat of market penetration.

July 1984: EU imposes further anti-dumping duties on US soda ash imports and accepts further undertakings. The outcome of this decision is that duties are increased on US imports on the basis of increased dumping margins. The duties become definitive in November 1984 leading to a 67.49 ECU per tonne duty.

June 1986: EU extends the scope of anti-dumping on ECE soda ash imports from Bulgaria, the German Democratic Republic, Poland, Romania and the Soviet Union.

June 1988: EU decides to review the anti-dumping measures concerning ECE soda ash imports from Bulgaria, the German Democratic Republic, Poland, Romania and the Soviet Union.

March 1989: EU decides to review the anti-dumping measures concerning US soda ash imports.

May 1989: Following a review, the EU re-imposes anti-dumping duties on EU soda ash imports from Bulgaria, the German Democratic Republic, Poland and Romania.

September 1990: EU terminates the review of the anti-dumping measures concerning dense sodium carbonate originating in the US leading to the lifting of measures.

December 1990: EU decides to ban the activities of ANSAC under Article 86 of the EEC Treaty related to the abuse of a dominant position of the export cartel.

December 1990: EU prosecutes ICI/Brunner Mond and Solvay for the orchestration of a cartel under article 85 of the EEC treaty and for the abuse of a dominant position under article 86.

August 1993: Following a complaint by EU soda ash producers, EU opens a new investigation into US soda ash imports.

April 1995: EU imposes provisional anti-dumping duties on US soda ash imports. Becomes definitive in October 1995.

June 1995:   EU overturns the decision to prosecute Solvay and ICI/Brunner Mond on procedural grounds.

The Role of Import Competition from the US

While the anti-cartel investigation and subsequent prosecution may have broken up the cartel and increased intra-EU trade, the lifting of anti-dumping duties in September 1990 may also have contributed to the shake-up in the industry. This section explores the role played by US exporters in the competitive changes in the soda ash sector.

In marketing terms, the UK market is easier to sell in because rules for storage, transportation and labeling are less strict in the UK than in other markets in the EU. As noted above, US producers had been attempting to enter the market since the 1970s. By 1982, US imports had reached 100,000 tonnes of which 80,000 tonnes were destined for the UK market.[55] The most striking element in the data is that between 1988 and 1992, there was a significant increase in imports to the EU as a whole and that the UK again bore the brunt of the most significant increases in imports. However, the most significant change in export activity was that US firms were now for the first time in this period selling into EU continental markets. Table 3.3 below outlines the evolution of US imports in selected EU member states (1990–1992).

What is clear from the data is that the UK was initially and disproportionately affected by the activity of ANSAC. This corroborates the view that the UK was relatively easier to export to given the existing regulations in the UK. What is also important to note, however, is the fact that even continental Europe experienced an increase in imports (especially Germany, France and the Netherlands). As discussed later in this chapter, there is a possible correlation between the emergence of US imports and the intra-EU cartel losing its cohesiveness – one of the standard predictions of cartel theory is that increased competition is likely to lead to price cutting and hence the collapse of the cartel. The ability of US firms to sell on the continent shook up the continental European producers of soda ash and offered alternative sources of supply for glass manufacturers.

Anti-Dumping Decisions and Soda Ash   The three-year 'window' when anti-dumping measures were not imposed was applied only to US sources with ECE sources remaining subject to anti-dumping measures. For the purposes of the EU anti-dumping instrument, DG I need only demonstrate that first, the EU industry has been injured by changing fortunes in the industry. Second, the injury was caused by imports. Third, these imports were being sold at prices in the EU market below their 'normal value' and fourth, that it would be in the 'Community Interest' to impose these measures in the industry concerned.

Table 3.3   US Imports of Soda Ash into the EU (000Kg)

	1990	1991	1992
Belg./Lux.	2	16860	170196
France	11559	60805	95236
Denmark	0	1239	0
Germany	24	22312	31909
Ireland	1	1	0
UK	36676	108481	36090
Italy	0	0	21116
Netherlands	7	23813	84079
Portugal	0	0	0
Spain	0	35714	179843
Total	48269	269225	618469

Source: CEFIC Anti-dumping Complaint, June 1993, Appendix Table 1, p.12

The 1995 Decision   In June 1993, a request for an investigation on imports of soda ash originating in the US was lodged by CEFIC, the European Chemical Industry Council. CEFIC is the umbrella organization for the chemical industry that acts on behalf of EU chemical producers. DG I promptly launched an investigation in August 1993 covering the period January 1st 1992 to June 30th 1993. In its deliberations, the EU Commission concluded that US imports had been imported at prices significantly below production cost (i.e. normal value). Normal value in EU proceedings is calculated on the basis of the fixed and variable raw material and manufacturing costs for the product exported to the Community, together with any reasonable amount for selling, administrative and other costs as well as a reasonable margin of profit. This constituted dumping as defined in the EU Anti-Dumping Regulation (No. 2423/88/EEC). DG I found the dumping margins allegedly caused by US companies in Table 3.4 below.

There are three points to note. First, the margins ranged from as high as 14.3 percent for FMC and as low as 0.1 percent for Texas Gulf. Second, that two EU owned subsidiaries (Rhone-Poulenc and Solvay) had been found to be selling below normal value. Both latter producers based in the EU were not excluded from the anti-dumping proceeding *as complainants* because the DG I concluded that although they themselves were exporting from the US, the quantities that they were exporting were not large enough. Furthermore, in one case, Solvay was using the export for its own captive use. Third, the dumping margins in the 1995 decision were lower than the previous cases involving US exporters (please see Table 3.4 for dumping margins in the previous cases).

Table 3.4   Dumping Margins of US Soda Ash Firms (1995)

US Firm	Dumping Margin
AG Soda	10.5%
FMC	14.3%
General Chemical	8.1%
NACC	9.4%
Rhone-Poulenc of Wyoming	13.9%
Solvay Minerals	9.7%
Texas Gulf	0.1%

Source: EU Commission Regulations 1995

Evolution of Market Conditions[56]

During the period covered by the 1995 decisions, there was a significant cyclical downturn in the economy. This had a marked effect on the glass industry and the soda ash industry. DG I figures state that consumption fell from 6.4 million tonnes in 1990 to 5.96 million tonnes in 1992, falling further to 5.6 million tonnes in 1993. A second factor that may have accounted for the drop in consumption was the increased use of glass recycling and switching from soda ash to alternative alkali feedstock for glass manufacturing. In its investigation, DG I noted that US imports had increased by 183,000 tonnes between 1990 and 1993. This, in market share terms, represented an increase from 0.8 percent in 1990 to 8.27 percent in the first six months of 1993.[57] This in isolation could not represent sufficient justification for imposing anti-dumping measures. However, DG I attempted to compare prices of US imports and EU domestic production in the most important markets in the EU during the investigation period. DG I calculated that US imports were approximately undercutting EU firms by 20 percent. EU firms reduced prices by approximately 10 percent during the period in order to deal with the downward pressure on prices. DG I analysis showed that during the period of investigation, the EU industry had experienced the following changes in production, capacity utilization, sales, market share, profits, employment and investment.

Table 3.5   Economic Indicators used in Anti-Dumping Case (1995)

Indicator	1990	1991	1992	1993
EU Production (Mn tonnes)	6.8	N/A	5.9	5.5
EU Capacity (Mn tonnes)	7.3	N/A	N/A	6.9
EU Capacity Util^n(%)	93	N/A	N/A	81
EU Sales (Mn tonnes)	6.1	N/A	N/A	5.2
EU Market Share (%)	96.1	91.8	85.2	86.9
EU Profits (%)	13	N/A	3.5%	4.6%

Source: EU Commission Decision 1995

Overall, there was an important downturn in industry fortunes. However, it was not entirely clear what were the principal causes of the downgrading of industry performance. In order to decide whether to impose duties, DG I turned to the issue of causality. It claimed that, *prima facie*, there was a correlation between rising imports from the US and falling market share, falling prices and profitability for EU firms. For DG I, this amply demonstrated that the change in fortunes of EU firms must have been related in some way to the increased export success of US firms. Moreover, US exporters had gained at the expense of EU firms not through 'fair' competition but by artificially lowering prices i.e. dumping. While DGI can claim that the correlation between falling prices and increasing US imports represents unfair competition, this is neither a necessary or sufficient condition. Indeed, in order for DGI to show that the US exporters were 'unfair', it would be necessary for them to show that the US firms were 'selling below normal value'. In its calculations, DGI derives cost information from independent industry sources as well as submissions from the firms involved in the investigation both complainants and exporters. Based on their investigation, DGI found that US exporters were selling below 'normal value' and therefore dumping.

Other Factors

Both the US exporters and the EU glass industry claimed that there were a number of mitigating factors that could account for the downturn of fortunes for the EU soda ash industry other than through US exports. First, there was a significant economic recession that had affected all industries in the EU. Second, there had been an increase in imports from ECE given the collapse of the centrally planned economies and that of East Germany in particular. Third, there had been a shift in the glass industry away from the use of soda ash and towards the use of other alkalis such as cullet and caustic soda. Fourth, technological change has occurred in the glass industry such that bottles and jars consume less glass. Fifth, exchange rate fluctuations at the time were such that US dollar exports were favorably priced in EU markets. Sixth, the increase in imports from the US should have been seen as a temporary and unique because of the necessity of US importers needing to set up long-run relationships with its customers.[58] Seventh, EU producers were less productive than US producers owing to the higher production costs that synthetic production entails. Finally, and the central focus of this discussion, the shaking out of the EU industry caused by the anti-cartel actions had a significant impact on the competitive situation in the EU and led to lower prices and improved market access for imports. As far as the recession was concerned, DG I noted that while this had an effect in absolute terms, it was adamant that the loss of market share faced by EU firms 'mirrored' the gain of market share by US exporters. In DG I's view,

> Should the downturn of the Community industry have been caused exclusively by the unfavorable trend of the general economic conditions, the United States imports could not have remained unaffected.[59]

DG I ruled out the issue of substitution between soda ash and other feedstock because alternatives to soda ash were priced higher and that 'no substitution between soda ash and caustic soda took place'.[60] A similar rejection was put forward concerning the issue of technology improvements.[61] On the link between ECE imports and injury to the EU industry, DG I argued that an increase in market share from 2.6 percent in 1990 to a peak of 4.3 percent in 1992 and a subsequent decline to 3 percent in 1993 could not 'be considered to have had a measurable impact on the Community industry'.[62] According to the DG I, exchange rate fluctuations did not affect prices charged by US firms because prices appeared to be decreasing continuously despite the temporary fluctuations alleged by the US producers and even when the dollar appeared to be appreciating against EU currencies.[63] As for the transient nature of US imports to the EU, DG I rejected this claim arguing that dumping 'at significant levels' had been detected since the 1980s. Moreover, '(the 1984 measures were only terminated in 1990 in consideration of the low market share of the United States imports, though the United States producers were found to have dumped)'.[64]

Given that the US firms were still dumping, why did DG I lift duties? A first explanation would be that US imports at that time were not injurious. A second possible explanation, explored in more detail below, may lie in the anti-cartel actions against EU firms coinciding with the lifting of anti-dumping measures. Finally, productivity differences between the US and EU firms was not an issue as far as DG I was concerned because any difference in costs between US and EU firms was less than the price undercutting that US firms were engaging in.

Appraisal of DG I's Arguments

DG I's central argument that injury was caused by US imports being dumped can only be based on a number of important facts that they were not explicit in their Decisions or on a series of assumptions about the nature of US import competition. Some clues to DG I's thinking can be derived from recital 42 of Commission Regulation (EC) No 823/95. It is quoted below.

In this connection, the Commission notes that the United States exports have a clear interest in extending their position in the Community through active price competition. [...] the United States domestic market is only partly profitable. As a consequence of stagnating domestic consumption, considerable quantities are available for export. Following the set up of new production facilities in China and South Africa however, the United States has practically lost these traditional export markets and encounters increased Chinese competition in the Far East.[65]

The use of the word 'active price competition' has a number of implications for the EU industry. DG I appeared to be arguing that US strategy seems to be orientated around the objective of increasing market share. Price competition by itself could not have been the reason why the DG I was prepared to pursue the US producers. By way of contrast, in a competition law case, active price competition cannot be regarded as a harmful *per se*. Rather, there must be some kind of predatory intent in order for competition authorities to prevent the competition from occurring. In the case of anti-dumping measures, there is no need for complaining firms to demonstrate predation in order to have anti-dumping measures imposed. While on the one hand consumers ought to welcome price competition as it brings down prices and leads to an improvement in allocative efficiency, consumers may be worried if 'active price competition' has predatory intent. In order for a predatory strategy to be feasible, US firms would have to cross-subsidize their operations from some other revenue source i.e. 'long pockets'. These sources of revenue which are used to finance an export drive may come from two sources. First, the firms may have supernormal profits derived from another of their markets that they use to cross-subsidize their operations. Some evidence of cross-subsidy can be elucidated from the role of ANSAC. ANSAC is widely believed to have been set up in response to difficulties that US firms were facing in their attempts to access the Japanese market as analysed above. Total annual sales for ANSAC world-wide amount to $250 million.[66] The early result from the formation of ANSAC was a significant increase in prices, sales and profits in Japan. ANSAC is also active in the rest of the Far East, Latin America and the Middle East.

According to a confidential industry source,[67] their main export markets are in Japan, China and Latin America. Given that DG I notes that US firms appeared to have lost market share in China, then by elimination, the only export markets where US firms could have cross-subsidized their EU operations would have been in Japan and Latin America. In this context, it is interesting to note that Asahi Glass Soda Corporation was mentioned as a US producer/exporter in the anti-dumping regulations. Thus it could be argued that in the Japanese and Latin American markets, the US firms may have been deriving supernormal profits that they were using to subsidize an export assault on the EU market given that at the time, anti-dumping duties had been lifted. A second possibility for cross-subsidy could be derived by convincing owners of the firms that shareholder profits may have to fall for a temporary period in order to finance an export drive to capture new markets. The fact that DG I claims that the US market is only partly profitable suggests that owners of US soda ash manufacturers may have been prepared to take lower profits in order to support an export drive in the EU. While the cross-subsidy argument is frequently forwarded, informally, by anti-dumping legislators as a means of 'proving' the existence of 'unfair competition', the necessary conditions for such a strategy to succeed are numerous.[68] One argument against a cross-subsidy argument is that if an export drive to capture new markets represents a sound strategy in itself, it should not necessarily be difficult to acquire finance from shareholders or banks who would view the future profitability of the strategy as worth the investment – hence the second explanation for financing an export drive.

Competitive Structures in the EU Industry and the Role of Anti-Dumping

The strength of competition in the EU market is a source of great controversy. One of the central claims of Solvay and ICI/Brunner Mond is that the 1990 anti-cartel decisions did not seek to break the monopoly stranglehold on soda ash production in the EU because users were not obliged to rely upon Solvay and ICI/Brunner Mond exclusively for supplies. They argued that first, there were four other firms producing in the EU market and second, that sources of competition from ECE also allowed for diversity of supply – despite the fact that ECE sources of soda ash were subject to anti-dumping duties. End-users of soda ash and US soda ash exporters claimed that the fringe producers in the EU had inadequate capacity in order to act as substitutes for Solvay and ICI/Brunner Mond. Furthermore, ECE supply was unreliable both in terms of supply regularity and quality.[69] DG IV points to the fact that EU soda ash producers abused their market power by forcing yearly contracts on users whereby prices were fixed for that year. EU soda ash producers could impose such restrictions safe in the knowledge that given the need for local and secure sources of supply, glass manufacturers could do little to re-negotiate the terms of their contracts. Moreover, 'a large number of Community in the glass sector have indicated their intention to take a substantial part of their business away from the Community producers and to buy from the United States'.[70] In this context, it important to note that excess capacity in the US has created pressure on the US producers 'penetrate the European and other markets'.[71]

This led to EU producers to argue for anti-dumping duties and price undertakings such that 'the undertaking price for Germany, France and other markets was substantially above the market price so no sales were commercially feasible under the undertaking outside the United Kingdom'.[72] Only when DG IV "discovered market share agreements designed to restrict competition'[73] and then the anti-dumping duties on US soda ash were lifted that glass manufacturers were able to seek alternative sources of supply and hence imports rose considerably. The glass manufacturers and US soda ash producers referred to this in the anti-dumping regulations as the consequences of 'competitive forces [that] were unleashed through the breaking-up of mechanisms that had maintained prices at high levels'.[74] Indeed as mentioned above, these arguments were central to the case put forward by the US exporters and the glass producers concerning the causes of injury to the EU soda ash firms. One of the hallmarks of a successful cartel is its ability to maintain stable (and high) prices.

Thus if the arguments of US soda ash producers were to be rejected, it would have to be shown that price stability was due to factors other than cartelization. DG I's methodology in dealing with the allegations raised by EU glass firms and the US firms was to look at price evolution. DG I noted that there was no immediate decrease in prices following the 1990 anti-cartel decisions. This may be due to the fact of 'the usual practice of negotiating prices on an annual basis'[75] in the industry. DG I argued that another reason for the relative price stability of soda ash was because 'the users' market [was] concentrated within a few large glass producers who have considerable bargaining power'.[76] DG I's reasoning is at odds with pricing theory that would suggest that it is economically irrational for a powerful group of firms to not put downward pressure on prices especially if they have, in the words of DG I, 'considerable bargaining power'. Moreover, DG I appears to make a factual mistake by attempting to show that prices fell as the major wave of US import surge struck the EU market and defend the causality arguments they forwarded previously: '[h]owever, in early 1993, the price decrease was substantial (10 percent) and this coincided with the large increase of imports from the United States of America throughout 1992 *and the first half of 1993* at prices which undercut those of the Community producers [emphasis added by this author]'.[77]

This contradicts the facts that as soon as the anti-dumping investigation was launched, US imports fell back in 1993. This is evidenced by the increase in market share for EU firms during the period of six months to which DG I refers. Market share for EU firms in 1992 was 85.2 percent but by June 1993 had reached 86.9 percent. Imports from ECE had remained stable over this period thus the EU firms' gain must have been at the cost of US firms. Indeed given that, according to DG I, it is normal 'world-wide' practice to set yearly contracts, it is hardly surprising that US firms were unable to cut back imports even more as the investigation was launched. The arguments on price stability offered by DG I are also opposed to those of DG IV's competition investigation. DG IV claimed that price stability was not a consequence of glass monopsony practices but due to the cartelized west European market. Thus there is a clear contradiction between DG I and DG IV's analysis. As mentioned above, one of the central arguments put forward by the glass manufacturers and US firms was that as a consequence of the competition decisions and increased import competition, the usually low level of intra-EU shipments began to rise.[78] However, DG I denies the importance of this, instead claiming that '[t]he position of the different Community operators on the national markets barely changed in relation to each other. [...] No major trend indicating an increase of the tonnage involved in intra Community 'exports' is discernible from the statistics for the period 1990 to the end of the investigation period in 1993'.[79] Again, this runs contrary to DG IV's assertion that as a consequence of its investigation, Solvay starting taking orders from UK customers.

Conclusion and Evaluation

Having outlined the series of events in this sector and offered the views of US firms, their EU competitors, DG IV and DG I, it is necessary to evaluate these arguments. Above all, there is a clear divergence of opinion between the two EU authorities investigating the trade and competition issues in the soda ash sector. DG IV appeared convinced of the existence of anti-competitive practices engaged in by Solvay and ICI/Brunner Mond. DG IV is also convinced of the fact that US producers could sell into the EU market 'at prices substantially below the local market prices without dumping'.[80] This, in itself, is evidence of the barrier to entry created by anti-dumping and its pro-cartel effect. Thus in DG IV's view, there can be little doubt that soda ash cost advantages determined trade patterns. The US manufacturers had clear competitive advantage in the production of soda ash. They thus faced resistance from higher-cost EU manufacturers. Their main competitive handicap arose from the cost of land transport of soda ash. The contrast between the cartelized EU market and the US market could not be starker. To quote DG IV: 'There is no competition between ICI and Solvay, each limiting its Community sales to its traditional "spheres of influence" in continental western Europe and the British Isles respectively [...] Given the over-supply and the presence of a number of producers with similar costs, the US domestic market has been marked by strong price competition'.[81]

While DG IV does not make this clear, it is likely that anti-dumping measures had succeeded in reducing the role of import competition from US exporters. This was achieved by effectively blocking EU firm's main source of competition hence facilitating collusion in the EU. Thus, trade policy had an effect on competitive structures by eliminating a source of lower cost competition. This argument is especially compelling given the statement of DG IV that European glass manufacturers were actively seeking to replace EU sources of soda ash with US imports. Moreover, the effect of anti-dumping and price undertakings was such that 'no [US] sales were commercially feasible [...] outside the United Kingdom'.[82]

There have also been import cartels in Japan; export cartels in the US in addition to the concerted anti-competitive practices in the EU market. The anti-dumping measures in the EU served to segment international markets while the collusive agreements within the EU sought to create market segmentation between the UK and mainland EU markets. Possibly, the JSAIA attempts at restricting competition in the Japanese market formed another segmentation in the international market. The key aspect in all of these incidences of anti-competitive conduct was that the main source of cost-competitive soda ash was blocked. Thus, does this case provide evidence that backs up Messerlin's crusade against anti-dumping measures? There can be no denying that EU firms were engaged in anti-competitive practices. EU anti-dumping measures had also kept US import competition at bay. The question thus is to what extent in the soda ash sector did the anti-dumping measures facilitate collusion in the EU market? As noted above, the GATT/WTO appears to be convinced of the Messerlin-type argument. Moreover, on economic theory grounds, the claim that anti-dumping serves to aid collusion is feasible as long as the cartel is able to create sufficiently high barriers to entry that all potential competition is eliminated through the imposition of anti-dumping measures.

In the soda ash case, this argument is compelling. EU producers had successfully argued for measures against US and ECE competitors it was unlikely that new sources of competition could emerge to threaten the EU producers' position. In theory, cartels are easier to orchestrate if there are relatively few firms producing. Again in soda ash, this precondition for successful collusion was present as the EU market was a virtual duopoly with ICI/Brunner Mond and Solvay controlling significant shares of the market. In the UK, ICI/Brunner Mond controlled 90 percent and in the continental market, Solvay controlled 70 percent. Thus, the co-ordination and monitoring costs were likely to be substantially lower than in instances of cartels where the number of participating firms would be higher.

Thus, a combination of high entry barriers, few potential competitors and a small number of domestic producers creates the necessary conditions for successful collusion. The crucial point is therefore that the high entry barriers were created by the imposition of anti-dumping measures. As the evolution of the industry in the EU suggests, when anti-dumping measures were lifted, the ability of ICI and Solvay to maintain their cartel was significantly undermined as evidenced by an increase in US imports which led to an increase in intra-EU trade. It would thus appear, as the GATT/WTO suggests, that a combination of DG IV's actions and the lifting of anti-dumping duties served to restore competitive conditions in the EU market: Messerlin's arguments seem to hold in the soda ash case.

Implications and Solutions for Trade and Antitrust Conflicts

The soda ash case is as an example of where international collusion has been undertaken, and to a degree, been highly successful. It has demonstrated how domestic industries have managed to capture the trade policy process in order to facilitate their collusive aims. The soda ash case also demonstrates how conflicting antitrust policies both in substantive and enforcement terms can aggravate the situation. In the US, ANSAC was given legal immunity from prosecution even though it may have been the forum to launch the export drive into EU markets. In Japan, the JSAIA was allowed to block imports because of a lack of enforcement of the Japanese anti-monopoly law. In the EU, the inappropriate imposition of anti-dumping measures may have prevented the efficient working of antitrust in the EU. The next question is therefore what alternative policies could be pursued to eliminate or reduce the conflict between trade and antitrust? While in the LdPE and PVC cases, Messerlin's analysis may suggest that anti-dumping rules need radical re-orientation (see chapter 5), *Chemical Fibres* suggests that with adequate co-operation between national competition authorities, solutions can be reached. This is an example of successful joint action by the German and Japanese authorities. The Bundeskartellamt could have resorted to extraterritorial application of its law on Japanese producers but chose not to and relied upon the goodwill of the Japanese authorities to stamp out the illegal conduct.[83] Even though the Bundeskartellamt could have acted on the grounds that the activities of Japanese firms had a direct impact on commerce within Germany, it took the comity[84] route and chose to avoid potential friction. The case itself provides two main conclusions. First, the chemical fibres sector is an example of where international collusion can take place. Second, the co-operative route taken by the German and Japanese authorities provides a possible blueprint for future successful action to deal with attempts at cartelization at an international level.[85]

Soda ash suggests that if DG IV and DG I could co-operate more regularly, then the problems of the EU soda ash market may be solved. If DG IV and DG I were to formally notify each other of their ongoing investigations into the activities and events in particular sectors, they may be able to find situations in which trade policy measures (DG I's remit) would not impact adversely on the monitoring and maintenance of competitive conditions in the EU single market (DG IV's task). However, institutional procedures hamper formal contact as in a competition case DG IV must act fully independent from other organs of the EU Commission. A similar problem would occur when DG I was investigating an anti-dumping case. A more radical solution would be to make anti-dumping rules subject to antitrust code disciplines, thereby implying that the burden of proof would shift.[86]

Conclusions: Scarce Natural Resources and the Implications for Trade and Antitrust

Through the cases above, the central analytical relationship between industry conditions, trade and antitrust has been analysed. The OECD argues that competition policies and trade policies are 'in general, mutually reinforcing' (OECD, 1998a, p. 4). In other words, if the policy emphasis in trade policy is liberal, then antitrust should follow a similar path and vice versa.

This chapter has detailed the existence of two concerted attempts to cartelize natural resource markets. In the tanner crab case, the JMPIA sought to bid down the prices of Alaskan seafood in order to gain excess profits by reselling the product at higher prices to Japanese consumers. The poor enforcement of antitrust in Japan acted as a trade barrier to imports by allowing the JMPIA import cartel. Only when US antitrust authorities sought prosecution of the JMPIA members and the case was heard in a US court were the actions of the cartel ended.

In the soda ash case, anti-dumping duties prevented significant import penetration from US exporters – the most efficient source of soda ash. Moreover, the duties served to facilitate an intra-EU cartel. Evidence of the frustration of price competition emerged when anti-dumping duties were lifted for a short period and US imports rose, driving down prices. This occurred at the same time as the Solvay-ICI/Brunner Mond cartel was broken up. Thus, 'mutually reinforcing' liberalization of trade restrictions and enforcement of antitrust led to a more competitive and more efficient market.

Thus, this chapter suggests that in scarce natural resource industries, trade policy and antitrust should act as complementary policies of liberalization. Free trade in the absence of enforced antitrust is unlikely to ensure contestability. Nor is a rigorously enforced antitrust likely to maintain contestability given the interdependent nature of trade and investment in the contemporary international economy especially if the source of competitive advantage resides in importing firms who have access to natural resources which higher-cost domestic producers do not possess.

This chapter further argued that where exploitation of scarce natural resources are the source of competitive advantage for firms, there will be strong pressures for protection from competition on behalf of those firms which are relatively cost-inefficient. In isolation, this is the classic political argument of protection if the sources of competition are from imports.

In this kind of industry, the location decision of firms will be dictated by access to those resources. In soda ash, although US firms' major markets were overseas, US firms needed to produce in the US by virtue of the availability of scarce resources in the US and not in Japan or Europe. A similar explanation holds for the presence of Japanese and European firms in Wyoming.

In the case of seafood in Japan, through their domestically-linked fishing fleets, the JMPIA purchased Japanese seafood. Due to the scarcity of crab off the coast of

Japan, the cost of fishing for crab in Japan was substantially higher than in Alaska. If the Alaskan crab companies could have sold direct to Japanese consumers, they would have significantly undercut the price of Japanese competitors and hence the need for protection.

However, in the more interdependent economy as depicted in chapter 1, the links between traditional policy boundaries have become blurred and thus as Ostry (1997) and Jacquemin and Sapir (1991) suggest, a restrictive trade policy effectively acts as a barrier to entry into an oligopolistic domestic market. In the starkest terms, anti-dumping facilitates domestic collusion.

By the same token, poorly enforced antitrust allows firms to erect their own trade barriers e.g. the JSAIA import cartel. A similar argument holds for the Tanner Crab case – the JMPIA were able to orchestrate their import cartel by virtue of inadequate investigation by the JFTC. It required US legislators to impose US law (rightly or wrongly) in order for the cartel to be broken up and to allow the Alaskan producers to exploit their competitive advantage. Thus, it was necessary for the JMPIA to orchestrate the cartel to erect a trade barrier: private actors imposing their own protectionism. Moreover, in scarce-resource industries, there are few arguments to support the pursuit of strategic trade policy or derogations from antitrust on the basis of the existence of external economies or learning economies of scale as in the case of innovation intensive industries. Competitive advantage can only reside among those firms who have access to those scarce resources.

Notes

1   Although the decision of the US government in 2002 to impose trade tariffs of 30 percent on steel imports is an exception to this rule.
2   Scarcity increases as non-renewable resources are used up. In general, as scarcity increases, the macroeconomy shifts away its usage of these resources. The speed with which that occurs is a function of the availability of substitutes. For those factors of production that remain in the increasingly scarce natural resource sector, the opportunity cost of production rises.
3   This does not deny that certain natural resource industries such as certain agricultural commodities resemble this.
4   Ibid. (Both citations in paragraph).
5   I am indebted to Toshihide Kasutani (MITI) and Hiroshi Kanai (Mitsubishi Kanai Petrochemical) for the expert advice on the economics and 'science' of the chemical industry.
6   See Sutton (1991) for a detailed discussion of this issue.
7   U.S. Congress Senate Committee on the Judiciary, Subcommittee on Antitrust and Monopoly, *Hearings on Administered Prices*, 86th Congress, 2nd Session, Part 20 pp. 11065, 11257 (1960).
8   United States v. Monsanto Co., Farbenfabriken Bayer AG and Mobay Chemical Co., Trade Case ¶ 72,001, p. 83,553 (W. D. Pa. 1967).
9   JFTC Decision 27 December 1972, *Shinketshusu*, 19 (1973), 124 *et seq.*
10 *Bundeskartellamt* Decision, 1972, *Wirtschaft und Wettbewerb* 525–48, Bkart A 1393, 1407, 1411 and 1915.
11 Messerlin claims that in the 1980s, 23% of all anti-dumping cases have been in cartelized sectors in the EU.

12 Although the revised anti-dumping code of the EU requires a 'Community Interest' test, it is not entirely clear that the most recent cases (and the soda ash case reviewed in section 6 of this chapter) have shown that the EU Commission has produced a workable and credible definition of the 'Community Interest'.
13 Messerlin (1990), p. 10.
14 Ibid.
15 Ibid. p. 13.
16 Messerlin (1990), p. 47.
17 Commission Decision of December 19 1990 relating to a proceeding under Article 85 of the EEC Treaty IV/33. 133 – A: Soda-Ash – Solvay, ICI (91/297/EEC), recital 3 (OJ L 152, 15/06/1991).
18 Ibid. recital 5.
19 Isonex Inc. is an engineering consultancy who specializes in soda ash. Website: www.isonex.com.
20 Opcit., 28, recital 12.
21 Ibid.
22 Opcit., 49, recital 2.
23 Ibid.
24 Ibid.
25 Ibid.
26 Source: *Japan's Chemical Industry 1996* produced by the Japan Chemical Industry Association.
27 These are the national state-owned producers predominantly in the Former Yugoslavia, Bulgaria, Romania and (the then) Czechoslovakia.
28 Source: Isonex Inc.
29 In addition, Elf Acquitaine own Texas Gulf Chemicals Corp.
30 ANSAC was originally formed by three US producers to enter the Japanese market. By December 1983, all six soda ash producers had joined ANSAC.
31 The EU soda ash manufacturers and the EU Commission point out that part of the increase in US exports to the EU may be explained by the loss of market share in China. This would be probably due to the necessity for US firms to avoid capacity cuts and hence rising costs.
32 Opcit., 28, recital 3.
33 Ibid.
34 It is a common view held by EU Commission anti-dumping administrators that in cases involving firms in market economies, dumping occurs because of forms of cross-subsidy. In the official documents used by the EU Commission in the administration of this case, a strong theme was on the US firms' positioning in other markets (especially Asian ones).
35 Commission Regulation (EEC) No 823/95.
36 A confidential industry source.
37 The views of a confidential industry source that expressed dismay at the activities of US firms, describing them as 'cowboys'.
38 See following pages for a chronological list of the anti-dumping actions taken by the EU Commission in this industry.
39 Ibid.
40 *Financial Times*, December 21 1990.
41 Ibid.
42 The Community v. Solvay et Cie SA and Imperial Chemical Industries Plc, Case IV/ 33.133–A, 4 CMLR, p. 468.
43 The Community v. Solvay et Cie and chemische Fabrik Kalk (Case IV/33.133–B) [1994] 4 CMLR p. 482.
44 Opcit., 29, recital 1.

45 Ibid. Recital 4. As noted by DG IV, it is interesting to contrast the caustic soda market with that of soda ash. Like soda ash, caustic soda is costly to transport given the corrosive nature of the chemical. Yet in a market where both ICI and Solvay produce significant quantities, ICI produces in Germany and operates distribution facilities in France and the Netherlands. Solvay also sells in the UK from stocks held on Merseyside.
46 Ibid. recital 6.
47 Ibid.
48 Ibid.
49 Ibid.
50 Ibid, recital 8.
51 7 million ECU in fines for ICI/Brunner Mond and Solvay respectively.
52 Point made by Hannes Welge, Head of Unit, DG I. It is vital from a legal procedural view that the Commission is not exchanging confidential information used in one investigation for the purposes of aiding another separate investigation.
53 It is important that the reader is aware that the confidential sources are from industry (CEFIC and Chemical Industries Association) and from the EU Commission.
54 Opcit., 48, recital 51.
55 Ibid, recital 12.
56 For the uninitiated reader, the EU Commission services send out questionnaires in order to derive the data that they use in their regulations.
57 It is important for the reader to note that table 3.3 has data from 1990 to end 1992 whereas the period of investigation undertaken by the DG I was until June 1993. The data used by this author is the same as that of the Commission but the additional six month data (January to June 1993) used by DG I was available only in a confidential submission by CEFIC whereas the data used by this author was from the non-confidential submission from CEFIC.
58 Thereby implying that once US soda ash firms had captured long-term customer loyalty, they would raise prices.
59 Recital 48, Commission Regulation (EC) No 823/95.
60 Recital 50, ibid.
61 It is important to note that the Commission, in its official regulations, is not required to explain its claims.
62 Recital 49, ibid.
63 Recital 51, ibid.
64 Recital 53, ibid.
65 Recital 42, ibid.
66 Opcit., 48, recital 3.
67 An official at the Chemical Industries Association.
68 Refer back to the Zenith-Matsushita case discussed in footnote 18 above.
69 This may further indicate a motive on behalf of EU glass manufacturers to source elsewhere as a 'discipline' on excessive price rises that may have been imposed by Solvay and ICI (Brunner Mond).
70 Opcit., 48, recital 4. It is interesting to note that glass manufacturers were not immune from anti-competitive practices themselves having been prosecuted for import sharing agreements: 81/881/EEC: Commission Decision of 28 September 1981 relating to a proceeding under Article 85 of the EEC Treaty (IV.29.988 – Italian flat glass). OJ L 326, 13/11/1981. They have also been involved in market sharing in the Benelux markets: 84/388/EEC: Commission Decision of July 23 1984 relating to a proceeding under Article 85 of the EEC Treaty (IV/30.988 – Agreements and concerted practices in the flat-glass sector in the Benelux countries) O J L 212, 08/08/1984.
71 Ibid, recital 4.
72 Ibid.

73 Recital 44, Commission Regulation (EC), 823/95.
74 Ibid.
75 Recital 45. ibid.
76 Ibid.
77 Ibid.
78 Recital 30. Council Regulation (EC) 2381/95. It is also interesting to note that ICI/ Brunner Mond's submission to the EU Commission in response to a request for information for investigation was sent in two forms, a confidential and non-confidential type. In the non-confidential type, on which this dissertation chapter is based, the data relating to intra EU cross-border movements of soda ash was removed from the Annex.
79 Recital 45. Commission Regulation (EC) 823/95.
80 Opcit., 48, recital 3.
81 Ibid, recital 4.
82 Ibid.
83 See chapter 4 for a detailed analysis of extraterritoriality in the field of antitrust.
84 Comity is the principle in international public law of the respect for state's legal jurisdictions.
85 The issue of co-operation in antitrust is dealt with in chapter 5.
86 See Holmes and Kempton (1997) for a discussion of the issues on anti-dumping reform.

Chapter 4

Complex Manufacturing Industries

Introduction

In complex manufacturing, the implications for trade and antitrust are somewhat more complicated than for the natural resource industry type. This is due primarily to the existence of market externalities and the presence of MNEs in the explanation for trade and investment. Additionally, and probably implicit in the analysis is the perception that industry conditions may encourage an activist role for government policy above and beyond the classic case of trade protection as explained in chapter 3.

Given that even in natural resource industries, there are strong linkages and conflicts between trade and antitrust given the emergence of 'System Friction' (e.g. in asymmetric enforcement of competition policies between nations), it should not be surprising therefore to expect even more complicated relationships emerging in complex manufacturing systems. Unlike the case study on natural resources (chapter 3), this case study illustrates that sources of both competitive advantage for firms and production complexity emerge from a range of external economies (e.g. value-chain linkages, transaction cost minimisation through vertical supplier-producer-distributor relations), and firm strategy. Thus, if the source of Japanese producer competitive advantage comes from the implementation of inter-firm linkages or the flexible production/managerial system, then competition and trade policies that are orientated towards maximising these benefits may be optimal. This is beyond the traditional static conceptualizations of economic efficiency (as argued in chapter 1).

Theoretical Implications for Trade and Antitrust

This section explores the implications of complex manufacturing systems on the interface of trade and antitrust. It is interesting to explore first, how MNE strategy and the sources of externality that arise from the nature of complex manufacturing are linked and second, how national competition and trade policies could be employed to capture the externalities that flow from this type of industry condition.

Dunning (1998) suggests that with imperfect competition, trade and investment (and hence the relationship between relevant policy domains) could be explained by considering three factors. First, the significance of micro-organizational costs and benefits (e.g. transaction costs). Second, the growing mobility of firm-specific assets and third, the role of national governments in the determination of the location and type of economic activity.[1]

(a) The minimisation of transaction costs in a complex manufacturing system is probably one of the most important aspects in explaining trade and investment outcomes. In a multi-tiered production system, the sources of transaction costs are potentially great. In markets that are international, the challenges to minimize transaction costs increase. This leads to a consideration of,

(b) The growing mobility of firm specific assets: MNEs respond to international transaction/co-ordination costs by locating assets in order to minimize these costs. Thus, if marketing is a crucial aspect in the success of a product that is sold in several markets internationally – it makes sense for the MNE to 'get close to the customer' by locating production and distribution close to the final market. This enables the MNE to respond more effectively to consumer tastes for example through production customisation.

(c) Successful MNE production strategy relies in part upon the necessary level of incentives and infrastructure provision by government:[2] this implies an enhanced role for government policy making (see below).

Where and How to Produce: A View from the MNE

Porter (1986) is one of the seminal contributions on understanding the nature of competition and production where the role of the MNE is important. In his analysis, he notes that one of the sources of comparative advantage is factor-cost or factor quality differences. However when dealing with industries that Yoffie (1993) terms 'global oligopolies', Porter claims:

> The global competitor can locate activities wherever comparative advantage lies, decoupling comparative advantage from the firm's home base or country of ownership. Indeed, [this] suggests that the comparative advantage story is richer than typically told, because it involves not only production activities [...] but also applies to other activities in the value chain, such as R&D, processing orders, or designing advertisements. Comparative advantage is specific to the activity and not the location of the value chain as a whole (Porter, 1986, p. 37).

Unlike natural resource industries, location and nature of production in complex manufacturing is not dependent on access to these natural resources. Thus the decision on how to and where to produce is determined a range of other factors. Table 4.1 adapted from McGee and Thomas (1988) helps to explain the 'causes' of trade and investment in complex manufacturing. There are several variables that determine the nature of complex manufacturing systems. To some degree, while all the variables determine and are determined by the strategy adopted by firms, it is possible to differentiate between predominantly exogenous and predominantly endogenous variables. Thus, complexity involves both controllable variables such as marketing, financial and production decisions and 'uncontrollable' variables such as government policy and the process of 'globalization', itself related to intensified competition at a global level. Within complex manufacturing, it is possible to have a range of sub-sectors depending on the relative importance of these different variables. If public procurement is an important part of a company's total revenue, then gaining access to government circles will feature considerably in MNE strategy. Alternatively, if technological change (and responding to it in a broader sense) is a source of competitive advantage, then investment in R&D may be important. If relationships along the supply chain require large amounts of information exchange, then minimising the transaction costs of information exchange will figure clearly in the minds of MNE strategists. Lastly, if the company is owned through the stock market, the objectives of the firm may not be the same as if the company was privately owned. In particular, the problems of principal-agency relations may emerge where the objectives of managers may be different from those of shareholders. Porter finds that:

> Many forms of competitive advantage for the global firm derive less from where it performs activities than from how it performs them on a world-wide basis; economies of scale, proprietary learning, and differentiation with multinational buyers are not tied to the countries but to configuration and the co-ordination of the firm's world-wide system (Porter, 1986, p. 37)).

Moreover, Porter claims there are two kinds of competitive advantage that a firm may possess: low cost or differentiation. In Porter's words,

> Competitive advantage is a function of either providing comparable buyer value more efficiently than competitors (low cost) or performing activities at comparative cost but in unique ways that create more buyer value than competitors and hence command a premium price (differentiation) (Porter, 1986, p. 20).

Dunning depicts the complexity of these kinds of industries,

> [A]s societies become more sophisticated, not only are markets likely to be less perfect (i.e. in a Pareto-optimality sense), but any imperfection is reflected in increasing co-ordination costs of using this organizational mechanism. Such endemic failures [...] reduce to the presence of uncertainties, economies of scale and externalities, and the increasing public good characteristics of intermediate and final products, which contain a high ingredient of created (as opposed to natural) assets (Dunning, 1998, p. 128).

To the last line of this quotation it is worth adding that the created assets require significant degrees of sunk investment for firms and their creation is a highly complex process in itself. For example, access to capital may be limited because of capital markets' inability to supply adequate amounts of venture capital for investment in new production systems. Another example would be the need for significant outlays in marketing due to the fact that firms compete not on price but on product differentiation.

Thus complex manufacturing is not based on a perfectly contestable model – the presence of sunk costs and market externalities undermine or deny this possibility. In the presence of apparent market failure, the argument that governments can intervene in these sectors becomes theoretically plausible. If, as suggested in this book, the classic aim of antitrust policy is the maintenance of market contestability, in a world in which this is not likely to occur independent of government intervention, then antitrust policy should be reoriented in the light of this. Similarly, if international free trade occurs in an imperfectly competitive world, it is unlikely that the predictions of welfare gains in a static trade theory framework are likely to occur in practice.

Table 4.1   Key Sources of Complexity

Causal Factors	Issues	Aims of Firm
Organization and Management	Ownership Capital Structure *Organization* Structures: design of organization systems and procedures	Firm aims to develop firm-specific skills e.g. reputation, image, patents, production system
Competitors and Markets	*Competitors*: number, type, location *Markets*: Geographic Coverage of Markets: global/local segmentation	Firm aims to develop a sense of competition and of sources of competitive advantage in market niches
Product Initiation and Development	Value-added chain; substitution patterns; vertical integration; horizontal linkages; Scale effects; R&D capability	Firm aims to capture rents, value added where appropriate
Internationalization	'Globalization'; Competitive Advantage	Firm aims to assess the effect of the linkage between national base and need for global strategy.
Technology	Inventions, innovation, technological change	Firm aims to assess the effect on the value chain of changes in technology.
Government/ Public Policy	Policy formulation, regulation, ownership/ procurement	Firm aims to assess effect on the value chain of government intervention.

Source: adapted from McGee and Thomas, 1988, p. 68

Picking or Finding Winners

Where there is an objective to develop complex manufacturing industries for the positive spillovers that they bring (e.g. an increase in skilled employment, potential for R&D spillover), governments can use both trade and antitrust tools to encourage such activity.[3]

(a) Domestic authorities can exempt complex manufacturing sectors from standard antitrust rules e.g. offer subsidy, merger or joint venture exemption. The exemption itself would depend on first, the type of complex manufacturing and second, in the case where vertical value-chains are important, on the particular part of the chain that may offer the external spillover.

(b) If it is unlikely that domestic sources of capital could develop the kinds of industries that are the object of development policy, then attracting foreign-owned firms into the national economy may bring the requisite benefits. Of course, ownership would not reside in domestic hands but nevertheless, employment, technology and managerial know-how transfer may occur. Policies that offer special tax concessions may encourage FDI. There is evidence to suggest that trade policy measures e.g. VERs or anti-dumping may serve to encourage FDI through 'tariff-jumping' (Belderbos 1998).

(c) If existing domestically owned complex manufacturers are suffering from a loss of competitive advantage, temporary protection may offer them the opportunity to adjust production to meet the competitive threat of more efficient producers elsewhere. If, in the process of protecting these firms, FDI is encouraged, 'learning' effects may further stimulate managerial and technological 'best practice'. Thus, the imposition of a VER may offer domestic firms the necessary breathing space required for successful adjustment.

(d) Lastly, even if the case for capturing externalities in complex manufacturing is difficult to implement in practice, then employment considerations may play a role in pursuing protective policies. Thus if Korean semiconductor producers are likely to emerge as winners in a competitive game with US producers, surely it is preferable to encourage Korean companies to hire US workers to manufacture semiconductors then to allow other nations to gain the employment benefits of Korean MNEs? If Japanese auto assemblers rely crucially on innovative parts suppliers for their assembly operations, then surely it is preferable to encourage Japanese assemblers to Europe in order to 'shake out' inefficient and outdated parts supply chains in Europe? Trade policy that encourages FDI may help achieve that objective.[4]

Even if the arguments outlined here do not apply in practice, if governments believe they do apply, they will pursue policies that seek to 'pick winners'. Thus if the Japanese government did support their manufacturing sector by allowing certain business practices, then whether or not they were successful, the nature of 'System Friction' is that there will be a 'spillover' on international competition.

Summary

This section has outlined the argument that in sectors where there are international market externalities, traditional comparative country-cost models cannot adequately explain trade and investment patterns. Thus, in the presence of these externalities, it is possible to account for forms of firm organization and strategy that would not exist in a traditional framework. In complex manufacturing, three issues emerge. First, FDI and strategic alliances may well offer alternatives to trade as the main source of international transaction. Second, 'arms-length' transactions are less important than intra-firm, network or hierarchical transactions e.g. the prevalence of vertical integration in the supply chain in sectors such as electronics and automobiles (Sako 1992, Womack, Roos and Jones 1990). Third, the argument that governments can (and should) attempt to influence the disbursement and location of productive activity in complex manufacturing has gained currency. The implication for trade and antitrust is well summed up in the words of Dunning (1998) when he claims,

> National macro-organizational policies may be increasingly deployed by governments to promote domestic economic interests, which have negative externalities for the rest of the world – and thus promote a vicious circle of retaliatory action on the part of other governments. This is leading both economists and politicians to urge for the widening of the rubric of existing supranational regimes, and/or the creation of new regimes to embrace such issues as competition, FDI technology and environmental policies (Dunning, 1998 p. 139).

Thus ironically, the presence of market imperfections may require the multilateralisation of policies that would, if left to national governments, engender 'beggar thy neighbour' industrial policy. The following section explores a case of internationalized complex manufacturing: cars. It is a sector in which aspects of global oligopoly are important. Government intervention in this sector is high. On this last point, the case study illustrates that externality arguments for government intervention are present as well as the more traditional rent-seeking political arguments for trade protection and antitrust exemption. Above all, the trade and antitrust linkages are significantly more complicated than those in scarce natural resource industries.

The Car Industry

Structure, Method and Contribution

The principal objective of this case study is to relate the nature of complex manufacturing in the car industry to the relationship between trade and antitrust policy. It analyses EU policy on car distribution in the period 1985–2002 and the 'Elements of Consensus' agreement between the EU and Japan concerning imports of Japanese cars. It shows that although, using traditional neo-classical approaches, it may be possible to criticize the policy adopted by the EU on car distribution and trade with Japan, the nature of complex manufacturing offers arguments related to the presence of micro-organizational and international transaction externalities: both hallmarks of complex manufacturing. This suggests that conventional emphases on the promotion of competition and trade liberalization may be misplaced. However, it does not deny that the industry has been subject to strong regulatory capture in a traditional sense related to the resistance to trade liberalization.

Mattoo and Mavroidis (1995) and Holmes and Smith (1995) have explored the conflict between trade and antitrust in the car industry. They made explicit the issues of trade policy and 'weakened' antitrust. In particular, Mattoo and Mavroidis (1995) focused on the 1985 (Block Exemption) BE and its links and with the EU-Japan 'Elements of Consensus'.[5] Mattoo and Mavroidis (1995) claimed that there might be legal problems if the EU attempts to organize trade along the lines set out in the EU-Japan agreement.

While trade policy and antitrust policy in the car industry has been extensively analysed both as separate issues and in their relationships, there has been no detailed 'unpicking' of the development, formulation and evolution of policy in this sector. The key contribution of this chapter, therefore, is to provide detailed analysis of the evolution in the sector with an aim of highlighting how industry conditions relate to trade and antitrust. As with chapter 3, this chapter makes use of evidence from policy documents from industry and government related to both the current trade policy and antitrust decisions. There is a detailed discussion of the arguments for and against the renewal of the BE using documents from various main sources in the car industry including assemblers, distributors and consumer groups. In addition, the chapter makes use of the official regulations from the EU – especially the BE and the Commission's arguments for its renewal. In addition, a series of in-depth interviews with staff in MITI in Japan, staff of Toyota in Japan and the US, industry representatives in the EU, officials of the Japanese Automobile Manufacturers Association (JAMA) and the *Keidanren* were undertaken. The principal objective of using the range of sources is to build as broad as possible an analysis of the sector.

This case study goes further than the work of Mattoo and Mavroidis (1995) in that they ignore the complexity of the nature of car assembly and provide a conventional neo-classical refutation of derogation from liberalization. They do not attempt to explore the counter arguments in detail. While Holmes and Smith (1995) analyse the industrial policy issues in the car sector, they focus predominately on the issue of subsidy rather than the issue of distribution and the BE. Thus this case study offers a detailed positive analysis of the policy formation in this sector and attempts to analyse systematically the arguments related to trade and antitrust in this sector.

This chapter is organized in the following sections. The first part presents a discussion on the economics of complex manufacturing in cars. This is in order to set up an analysis of the relationship between industry conditions and the nature of the trade and antitrust interface. The second section outlines the development of the EU car industry. The third part explores the EU-Japan 'Elements of Consensus'. It will look at nature of the agreement and draw out the theoretical mechanisms and effects underlying the accord. A fourth section presents some theoretical propositions relating to the economic effects of exclusive and selective distribution (SED) as well as a presentation of the current regulatory framework for car distribution in the EU.

Lastly, a fifth part brings these two separate policy instruments together by examining the linkages between them both from a perspective of policy aim as well as policy outcome in the light of the 1995 renewal and the progress of the EU-Japan accord. It also contains a detailed analysis of important case law that highlights the complementarities and conflicts between trade and antitrust in this case study.

The Economics of Complex Manufacturing in Cars

The production and distribution of a finished automobile involves a multi-stage process. At one end of the value-chain are the parts manufacturing that make up the finished vehicle. As automobiles have become more sophisticated, the technological requirements placed upon parts manufacturers have increased enormously ensuring that the Model T Ford of the 1930s is a technologically simple car compared to the advanced luxury vehicles produced today.

At the other end of the value chain is the distributor and maintenance service. On the one hand, the improved quality of today's cars has meant that the modern car requires relatively less servicing than cars in the past. However, the level of technological and diagnostic expertise that mechanics require today is without doubt greater. Moreover, the marketing of the modern car has become ever more sophisticated requiring greater outlays in promotional investments. This is due, partly, to increased competition that has forced an increased need for product differentiation. Moreover, in an increasingly competitive industry, marketing and advertising are crucial features of the competitive game between assemblers. Both marketing and advertising are costly and carry significant risk to suppliers in the industry.

In between these two end-stages is the process of assembly. It is arguable that the co-ordination of these multiple stages of elaboration is probably the single most important factor in determining the competitive advantage of car manufacturers. This is the hallmark of 'lean production' pioneered by Japanese car assemblers which is crucial in determining competitive advantage in the car sector. In economic theory, Williamson's transaction cost analysis sought to explain why firms prefer to set up complex intra-firm or intra-network exchange relationships rather than acquire the necessary intermediate goods in spot, arms-length markets. Essentially, arms-length markets are risky when both the quality and timing of provision of intermediate goods is crucial in determining a company's competitiveness. First, this is due to the possibility of the firm being 'cheated': the problem of opportunism. Second is the reality that a complex manufacturing system has a sufficiently high information requirement that imperfect or incomplete information becomes a problem: it is simply not possible for managers to know everything especially in risky market transactions. Thus, firms will seek to replace the market transaction with less-costly internalized or strongly linked transactions.

Thus while neo-classical theory of the firm ignores the role of transaction costs, the very nature of complex manufacturing requires an understanding of the consequences of these micro-organizational costs. A firm that can minimize these costs is likely to emerge as a highly competitive entity. Another crucial aspect of complex manufacturing is the relationship between quality and trust. Casson (1997) has attempted to develop a framework for the economics of trust and Sako's (1992) empirical study on the UK printed circuit board industry have aided an understanding of this relationship. Essentially, where trust between supplier and user can be maximized, it is likely that the quality of intermediate or final goods will rise. This is because both parties to the transaction are aware of the interdependence of their commercial success and they understand that both parties will lose should one of them decide to shirk or renege on an agreement.

It is unlikely therefore that in spot markets, the necessary kind of trust that comes from frequent exchange is likely to develop. If anything, market transactions engender adversarial behavior with each side trying to gain the most and probably at each other's expense. Trust, therefore, can only be fostered when non-market transactions occur. Taken together, the issue of transaction costs and trust imply strongly that forms of vertical integration are necessary steps in achieving competitive advantage.

There is however a paradox in this analysis: that non-market transactions can become cosy and opportunistic too. This is one of the central messages of Womack, Jones and Roos (1990). Where car assemblers become too closely integrated, the disciplining nature of markets is removed and the pursuit of quality can be weakened as laziness becomes an issue. Moreover, even though the supply chain has become strongly integrated, there is still the tendency for one stage of the chain to regard itself as being in a negotiation with another rather than seeking to develop a harmonious relationship. Thus for Womack et al., the key is to capture the benefits of non-market transaction through long-term contracting and at the same time avoid the laziness and opportunism that may arise when fully integrated elements in the supply chain seek an 'easy life'.

Womack et al. (1990) claim that, in the past, it has been the failure of European and US auto manufacturers to achieve the latter approach and by comparison the incredible success of Japanese (and latterly Korean) assemblers to harness these benefits which has strongly determined the competitive advantage of East Asian producers. By implication, the source and direction of international trade and investment is determined by this difference. They point to evidence that the 'Big Three' US automakers still have large amounts of the parts for assembly built 'in house' whereas the Japanese assemblers purchase over 70 percent of their parts from independent but closely linked suppliers in the vertical keiretsu that characterize Japanese car assembly. This factor contributes significantly to the result that defective parts in US and European-owned assembly remain considerably higher than Japanese manufacturers – all over the world.[6]

Another factor in determining the competitive advantage of automakers is the system of co-ordination of production and the 'Just-in-Time' (JIT) delivery process developed by Toyota in Japan. The principle of JIT is that the assembler requires parts in minimum quantity at the exact time that they are required in the assembly process. It means that assemblers can reduce the costs of inventory by keeping very low stocks of unused parts. In a country such as Japan where land costs are high, the successful implementation of a JIT programme means significant cost reduction. The parts suppliers are aware that failure to achieve the targets will probably lose them their long-term contract.[7] Again, the superior management and personnel policies of Japanese assemblers which seek to involve workers in all stages of the manufacturing process are argued to be a source of competitive advantage. Taken together, these are the hallmarks of 'lean production'.

A similar process has occurred in the final stage of the supply chain: the advent of lean distribution. As the demands of final consumers for a highly customized vehicle increase, the availability of stock to meet the consumer's demands becomes a problem. Thus, the use of direct ordering from the manufacturer, where the retailer orders the vehicle to the customer's specifications has become increasingly important. Again, the concept of transaction costs minimization is crucial. The internet is also becoming an increasingly important feature of car retailing where sales costs are minimal for the assembler.

As Japanese firms emerged as the most competitive assemblers, they were able to gain significant market share in world car trade. From the mid-1970s onwards, their success was also in part due to the oil price shock which made the costs of driving significantly higher and therefore the demand for smaller, more fuel efficient engines – the hallmark of Japanese cars – grew. A direct response to the competitive threat posed by the Japanese firms was for US and West European manufacturers to seek import protection. A series of VERs was imposed in the US and across several West European states in an attempt to curb the import flow. In addition to the other reasons why complex manufacturing may internationalize, this increased protection encouraged the decision of Japanese assemblers to pursue an FDI strategy. For Japanese MNEs, the benefits of local presence could not be underestimated in a market where marketing and after-sales service were crucially important – there were important learning effects of marketing which could be better captured through local presence. Moreover, as they were no longer subject to import restrictions, they would be able to achieve a higher level of scale production that, in turn, would lower their costs. Probably their main dilemma was the process of 'transplanting' their production chain in a non-Japanese location; especially the parts supply chain given the importance of the assembler-supplier relationship.

For foreign host governments, the arrival of Japanese MNEs posed a serious problem: they could not treat Japanese firms in their country as foreign firms which would be subject to the same restrictions as import trade. The EU member states had discussed the possibility of introducing a local content rule on FDI. However, this would have contravened GATT/WTO rules. Moreover, as different member states had received varying degrees of FDI, opinions differed between them. At the same time, they recognized the employment gains that FDI brought to their country. They also probably recognized that although difficult it might be for US and West European-owned assemblers, the arrival of Japanese firms might provide the necessary restructuring impetus that these sectors required. However, they were under severe pressure from domestically owned assemblers for protection from the new competition. Moreover, the initial problems of maintaining the JIT supply chain for Japanese firms was achieved by (a) bringing their parts suppliers with them to the foreign location and (b) importing parts from Japan. Thus, the arrival of 'lean suppliers' from Japan and induced trade flows of parts from Japan further threatened the parts supply industries in these countries.

The EU Car Industry in the 1980s and 1990s

The start of the 1980s brought with it a difficult period of adjustment for the West European car industry. Assemblers were recovering from the two oil price shocks and the emergence of increased competition from Japanese producers. The downturn in industry fortunes led to calls for 'temporary' support. Specifically, West European assemblers needed support against increasing competition from Japan and financial support from governments to facilitate the process of structural adjustment in the industry.

The downturn in the early 1980s forced significant rationalization in the industry. Despite the view of producers and their closely allied governments that capacity was the secret to maintaining the position of the 'national champions', the early 1980s brought the stark realization that excess capacity in the industry would have to be reduced. There were three major sources of competitive disadvantage among European assemblers: outdated capital equipment, over manning and problems with the managerial and supply chain systems used by these producers. Moreover, as several of the producers in the West European industry were state-owned, inappropriate strategic incentives ensured that rather than adopt profit maximizing strategies producers relied upon subsidy from governments for their financial survival. In the first half of the 1980s, capacity to produce one million vehicles was taken out (Jones, 1999, p. 308). This led to a reduction in employment in the industry between 1980 and 1986 by 420,000 (Jones 1999, p. 308). In the UK, wholesale privatization of the industry took place. Jaguar was sold in 1985 and was followed by the sale of Rover in 1988. In France, there was greater resistance to privatization as a method of rationalization. This was in part due to the election of a Socialist government in 1981 and the strong resistance among organized labour. However, the French government sold some shares in Renault to Volvo in 1990. A similar series of events occurred in Italy where Alfa Romeo was sold in the 1980s. Of all the major assemblers, German producers fared the best as their reputation for quality and reliability enabled them to sell beyond their European markets.[8] Table 4.1 below shows the evolution of car production 1981–1996.

Another important aspect of the West European car sector is that when domestic rationalization occurred, a similar process occurred in overseas markets with assemblers closing down plants abroad.[9] This meant that of the major producers (US, Japanese and West European), the latter became most dependent on domestic production. Exports to the rest of the world (excluding the US and Japan) fell from 979,000 units in 1979 to 409,000 in 1996 (Jones 1999, p. 309).[10] An exception to the retrenchment abroad has been the ability of luxury car producers such as BMW, Mercedes, Porsche, Jaguar, Volvo and Saab to sell considerably in the US. This is evidenced by the fact that over the period 1979 to 1996, exports to the US remained relatively stable (Jones 1999, p. 309). One of the most notable impacts on the West European sector has been the arrival of Japanese imports first through exports and lately through FDI. Between 1979 and 1989, Japanese imports into the EU rose by 438000 units.[11] Since 1989, most of the imports have been replaced by local production such that in 1996, the EU imported fewer Japanese cars than in 1979 (from 780,000 units in 1979 to 714,000 units in 1996).[12]

Despite the rationalization of the industry in response to global pressures, West European producers still rely heavily on their domestic national markets. Table 4.3 below illustrates this point.

One explanation for the relative strength of producers in the domestic market might be the persistence of national barriers which maintains national market segmentation.[13] The trend however is downwards for the producers and the recent merger wave in the industry may be a response to the decline in domestic market shares for the producers. In terms of trade policy in the car sector, before the 'Elements of Consensus' agreement, member states had their own national rules on Japanese imports. Pre-dating the Common Commercial Policy in the 1960s and the SEM (i.e., before 1993), Italy sanctioned restrictive quantitative measures against Japanese imports through article 115 of the Treaty of Rome. Article 115 of the Rome Treaty allowed member states to impose unilateral import measures that may run contrary to the Common Commercial Policy. The article enabled member states to introduce trade barriers if they were in 'economic difficulties'. However, as Jovanovic (1997) points out, there has been a steady decline in the use of the 'bolt hole' measure. In 1980, there were over 300 measures introduced by member states. By 1989, the number of these measures had halved (Jovanovic 1997, p. 281). While Italy formally applied article 115 measures, other measures in member states have been more covert and subsequently of a highly questionable legal nature. In particular, non-GATT approved QRs in France and in the UK existed where, in the UK case, export restraint agreements were made between the Japanese and UK producers.

Table 4.2   Car Production in the EU 1981–1996 (000s)

Year	D	UK	E	I	F	B	Nl	A	Swe	Total
1981	3897	1184	987	1434	3019	237	101			10859
1982	4062	1156	1070	1453	3149	278	109			11277
1983	4154	1289	1288	1575	3336	285	122			12049
1984	4045	1134	1309	1601	3062	249	129			11529
1985	4445	1311	1418	1573	3016	267	128			12158
1986	4578	1203	1307	1913	3195	295	142			12633
1987	4634	1389	1704	1913	3494	352	152			13637
1988	4625	1545	1866	2111	3678	398	149			14372
1989	4852	1626	2046	2221	3920	389	149			15203
1990	4661	1295	1679	1875	3295	313	121			13258
1991	4677	1237	1774	1633	3188	253	85			13129
1992	4864	1292	1791	1477	3329	223	94			13386
1993	3794	1376	1506	1117	2836	374	80			11404
1994	4094	1467	1822	1341	3175	409	92			12798
1995	4360	1532	1959	1422	3051	386	100	59	388	13258
1996	4540	1686	1942	1318	3148	368	145	97	368	13611

Source: Jones 1999, p. 307

Table 4.3   Market Shares of West European Firms (percentage of total domestic market)

	1979	1988	1996
French	71	63	56
German	47	46	42
UK	20	15	11
Italian	62	52	44

Source: Table adapted from Jones 1999, p. 310.

Some argue that the most recent EU-Japan trade accord has had spillover effects on the nature of intra-EU competition (Mattoo and Mavroidis, 1995, Holmes and Smith, 1995). In particular, the EU Commission has permitted the current regime of SED in cars within the EU because it is indispensable for the successful control of Japanese imports. This question is explored in more detail below.

EU car producers have also faced a different antitrust regime when compared with their US and Japanese based counterparts. In the EU, sales and distribution of finished cars have been subject to exemptions from antitrust rules under the terms of the Treaty of Rome. Car producers and their related distributors in the US and Japan do not have the legal right to impose restrictions on the nature of branding and sales in car distribution.

Market Structure and Policy Objectives

In the car sector, there are essentially four sub-markets: production of finished cars; distribution and sales of finished cars; production of car parts; and sales and distribution of car parts for the purposes of repair and servicing. Trade and competition policies have had both direct and indirect impact on each of these sectors.

Trade policy has been aimed primarily at influencing finished car production in the EU. Both member states and the EU have sanctioned trade policy measures. In turn, trade barriers have, in part, encouraged the arrival of Japanese FDI and production in the EU with Toyota, Nissan and Honda having production bases in the EU. Thus an important side effect of restrictive trade policy has been to increase domestic competition and because of the nature of complex manufacturing, to induce further trade through the importation of car parts used by foreign producers based in the EU. The encouragement of FDI through the imposition of import restrictions provides important employment, productive and innovative benefits to the domestic industry (Trebilcock and Howse 1998, p. 280).

Antitrust policy, by contrast, has had a broad ranging direct effect on the sales and distribution of cars and car parts as well as an impact on the geographical spread of production both of finished cars and car parts. Antitrust policy in the EU has diverged from a traditional liberalization approach. It recognizes arguments that in complex manufacturing industries, it may be necessary to consider dynamic efficiency considerations such as discovery of the best processes and products for meeting changing consumer tastes and hence the need for product differentiation (OECD, 1998a, p. 12). In this light, antitrust has allowed for exemptions from the rules on competition based on arts 85 and 86 of the EU treaty through a Block Exemption (BE). It allows for the SED of automotive products. The BE is a legal instrument granted where in the EU Commission's view, there are grounds for exemption from competition. The criteria for exemptions from normal competition rules are broad (ranging from technical progress to public morality). In the case of cars, the Commission's arguments for the BE are related to the necessary investment in distribution and retail facilities that car manufacturers have to undertake. This is in order to ensure that consumers can obtain the best possible information when purchasing a vehicle and maintaining safe and reliable after sales-service for their customers. The economics of the BE is analysed in detail later in this chapter. When originally introduced in 1985, the BE allowed car manufacturers to impose exclusive distribution contracts on their dealerships whereby dealers were granted territorial exclusivity. Given the nature of SED, the dealers found themselves in a situation where they couldn't advertise outside their own 'region' and importantly, they were unable to sell competing brands of cars on the same site. It will be shown that with the 1995 renegotiated variant of the BE, some of these stringent measures were slightly liberalized giving more freedom to dealerships.

There are a number of effects of the BE that relate to intra-EU trade. Arguably, the BE in distribution has to a considerable extent sanctioned the persistence of national and segmented markets. This has led to difficulties for consumers who have tried to make cross-border purchases of cars (see 'Key Case Law in the Car Sector' for a detailed discussion of case law related to the operation of the BE and cross-border purchases within the EU). Moreover, they may be a link between the persistence of considerable price variations for finished cars and the BE at a time when the creation of the Single European Market (SEM) has been the primary economic policy agenda at the EU level prior to monetary union. An indirect consequence of this antitrust instrument has been that the adjustment process, in the face of market liberalization both at a global and national level has been significantly affected (Flam and Nordström, 1995). Servicing and repair of cars and the production of car parts have been directly affected by the BE due to clauses creating a monopoly in production of certain types of parts. This had arguably led to higher prices of parts and difficulties faced by independent parts producers in their attempts to supply the repair market with non-original parts of equal quality. The 1985 BE was renewed in 1995 to remain in force for another seven years. However, the 1995 BE contained a number of important liberalization measures concerning the flexibility that dealers would have to multifranchise; the provision of spare parts and servicing; and the discretion that the EU Commission will have in removing the exemption.

Intra- and Extra-EU Trade in Cars

Until 1991, the EU car industry was protected by a series of national quotas on car imports from Japan. Member state preferences varied considerably on the need for trade protection. They varied primarily as a function of the relative strength of the domestic industries (i.e. between net exporters versus net importers). Thus although France and Germany have been net exporters of cars, Germany always had a more liberal view of Japanese competition because of the strength of its own national producers whereas France, whose 'national champions' have been largely state-owned, has consistently sought protection. Successive UK governments have accepted the restructuring but have sanctioned covert industry agreements with Japanese producers. This is evidenced by a long running and revealing litigation between the EU Commission and BEUC which highlighted the role of the UK industry VER.[14] Nevertheless, the Conservative government, 1979–97, realized that the shift of car industry ownership from state to private has raised issues of competitiveness and efficiency. Arguably, the UK government encouraged a process of significant adjustment through attracting Japanese FDI into the UK car industry.[15] Ownership of the EU industry is concentrated.

Table 4.4 below details market share by producer group in the European Car industry in 1998 and 1999. The VW group along with the PSA group, GM, Renault, Ford and Fiat are the largest producers accounting for 75.2 percent of the total EU market in 1999. The Japanese producers account for 11.4 percent of the market with Toyota and Nissan being the largest Japanese producers in the EU. Concentration has increased with the Daimler-Chrysler merger (May 1998) and the Ford take-over of Volvo (January 1999). With the Nissan-Renault tie-up announced in March 1999, the EU market will be further concentrated. These changes further justify an analysis of a global oligopolistic market in which firms respond to each other's policy. It is arguable that the Daimler-Chrysler merger was a strong influence on Ford's decision to tie-up with Volvo. There are also justifiable claims that the current concentration process in the world car industry is related to the development of 'global strategy'. In particular, ownership and market concentration enhances a firm's ability to influence the market – fewer competitors imply that the monitoring costs of a firm will decline. Competitors may have specific assets which a merger could capture and which could considerably reduce costs.[16]

Industrial organization theory may also suggest that this raises the possibilities of collusion – it is easier to orchestrate a cartel in an industry dominated by a small number of large firms. Furthermore, the consolidation process may be a risk-reduction strategy (Yoffie 1993) by the major assemblers ahead of the phasing out of trade protection in the EU and the potential for further trade liberalization under the forthcoming WTO 'Millennium Round' trade talks. Table 4.5 shows the change in Japanese sales structure in the 1990s. What is clear from this table is that the Japanese have considerably increased their local production in the US and EU. The reasons for this have been discussed above namely, there are arguments related to the benefits of local production for a complex manufacturing system and local production may also be part of a necessary strategy to overcome trade barriers.

All of these pressures were increasing at a time in the EU that the completion of the internal market was a priority of the policymakers in the EU institutions. This policy implied the elimination of all barriers to trade between member states and the liberalization of factor movements. This left the West European manufacturers with a major dilemma. They were likely to (or they feared that they would) lose import protection imposed by national governments and would need to lobby the EU Commission for a new policy on Japanese import competition (see below).

Whether the EU's trade and competition policies on cars were a tool of cozy protectionism or necessary policies to capture the benefits of marketing externalities, the implications for trade and antitrust were clear. First, a restrictive EU-Japan trade agreement may ease and slow-down the necessary restructuring of the West European car industry. Second, the agreement might also aid the existing market segmentation by reducing import competition. Third, that in order for a VER with Japan to work in the context of an Internal Market, it may be necessary to maintain the BE i.e. it may be necessary to use antitrust to make a restrictive trade policy work.

Table 4.4   Market Shares in the Western European Car Industry (1998–1999)[17]

Firm	Market Share 1999 (%)	Market Share 1998 (%)
VW	19.8	18.6
GM	11.6	10
PSA	11.4	11.7
Ford (incl. Volvo)	11.3	11.3
Fiat	10.3	11.9
Renault	10.8	11.2
BMW	5.0	5.5
Daimler-Chrysler	5.4	4.9
Nissan	2.3	3.1
Toyota	3.1	3.1
Mazda	1.6	1.5
Honda	1.3	1.3
Mitsubishi	1.3	1.3
Other Japanese	1.8	1.6

Source: ACEA Press Release April 20, 1999 (1999 figures included forecasts for future sales in 3rd and 4th quarter

The EU-Japan Elements of Consensus

The Agreement

In July 1991, Mr. Andriessen, Vice President of the EU Commission and Mr. Nakao, the MITI minister made declarations to the effect that Japanese car imports into the

EU were to be restricted up to and including the end of 1999. The details of this agreement were laid out in an unpublished text entitled 'Elements of Consensus' (Economist Intelligence Unit, p. 1994, p. 31). The agreement called for monitoring of this 'consensus' throughout the EU by the EU Commission and by MITI in Japan. It allowed the EU Commission and MITI to agree 'forecasts' on imports into France, Italy, Portugal, Spain and the UK. The agreement noted that restrictions have been historically applied in Italy, Portugal, Spain and France but made no mention of previous arrangements in the UK. The 'monitoring' process supersedes these agreements. In addition to the monitoring process, restrictions on 'indirect' imports into Italy, Portugal and Spain were lifted i.e. the member states concerned no longer had resort to article 115. Nevertheless, the EU-Japan agreement stated:

> The guiding principle to this understanding is that growth in the market is assumed and both the Japanese and European manufacturers should have sufficient participation in that growth. The market share concept is based upon a sharing of growth on the basis that a third of any market growth should be available to European suppliers and two thirds to Japanese manufacturers. If there is a decline in the market, Japanese manufacturers should accept a reduction in exports by 75% of the deviation (Economist Intelligence Unit, 1994, p. 35).

Table 4.5   Japanese Car Production in the US and EU

	Japanese Sales in the EU		Japanese Sales in the US	
	Made in Japan	Made in the EU	Made in Japan	Made in the US
1990	1750497	76190	1719324	1320368
1998	1254879	573249	1274785	1930283

Source: JAMA: *The Motor Industry of Japan 1998*, ACEA (www.acea.be), and SMMT data

Furthermore, the Commission undertook not to restrict FDI and the free circulation of European assembled Japanese brands. Finally, the Commission undertook not to request any further co-operative measures on January 1 2000 or thereafter (Economist Intelligence Unit, 1994, p. 32). The official aims of the agreement are to achieve progressive and full liberalization of the EU market; avoidance of 'market disruption' by exports from Japan; a contribution to the necessary adjustment of EU manufacturers 'towards adequate levels of international competitiveness' (Economist Intelligence Unit, 1994, p. 31). The annual level of exports was calculated based upon demand variations and relaxation and abolition of restrictions. Vehicles covered by the arrangement included passenger cars, off-road vehicles, light commercial vehicles and light trucks (up to 5 tonnes) including complete knock down kits (CKD). Abolition of national restrictions started on

January 1 1993. Monitoring of the agreement was in accordance with the forecasts set out in Table 4.6 below.

MITI agreed to convey to Japanese producers that specific national markets were not to be targeted. The agreements established meetings between MITI and the EU Commission on a half-yearly basis in order to assess overall market conditions and to establish guidelines for the six months following the market (Economist Intelligence Unit, 1994, p. 31).

Table 4.6   Forecast of Imports from Japan and Total Demand by Country (1999) (000s of Units)

Country	Forecast 1999	Total Demand
France	150	2,850
Italy	138	2,600
Spain	79	1,475
Portugal	23	275
UK	190	2,700

Source: EU Commission, Table adapted from Economist Intelligence Unit, 1994, p. 33

The 'monitoring' process itself was a 'grey' area. Indeed, according to confidential sources in the industry,[18] MITI had no power to enforce quotas but the quotas were allocated to firms as the result of a process of discussions between MITI and the Japanese producers. These negotiations generated 'forecasts' for six-month periods. These forecasts were effectively export quotas for Japanese producers since should Japanese firms decide to sell more in the EU through exports, at the next meeting, the EU Commission could have requested MITI to reduce the size of Japanese firm's quotas in the next six month 'forecasts'. This clearly had a number of consequences for the quota allocation process. If MITI did not suggest quotas for each firm and left the allocation process to the Japanese industry, then there was the possibility that Japanese firms could be prosecuted under EU competition law for distorting intra-EU trade. The Japanese firms could not claim sovereign immunity in this case. If MITI dictates the quotas then the Japanese firms are safe from prosecution under EU law. MITI does not assume that there will be a conflict between Japanese producers and MITI over the allocation of firm quotas. MITI believed that such problems would jeopardize the 'political situation' between Japan and the EU. Furthermore, pressure to increase a firm's share would hinder the process of structural adjustment in the EU market. MITI would actively explain to a Japanese firm of the consequences of the political situation if indeed there was indeed conflict between Japanese producers and MITI over the allocation of quotas. Not surprisingly for the Japanese and EU authorities, this agreement was extremely sensitive. The EU member states had resisted an EU-Japan deal in the past – some fearing that an EU-wide policy might have been more liberal than their national regimes. It was however difficult to argue for the maintenance of national regimes in the light of the completion of the Single Market. It would have been problematic to remove all barriers to trade within the EU but to maintain national restrictions on imports. For example, how could the UK prevent parallel shipments of Japanese vehicles imported into Germany?

Neither Mattoo and Mavroidis (1995) nor Holmes and Smith (1995) believe that the official aims of the agreement were the actual aims of the agreement in practice. In fact, Mattoo and Mavroidis (1995) believe that there was a possibility that the agreement itself could be challenged on legal grounds for the following reasons. First, the Uruguay Round negotiations stated that the EU has one VER that it can keep until 2000. This rule is a consequence of the GATT/WTO Agreement on Safeguards.[19] Given that the EU-Japan consensus acted as a set of national quotas, it was arguable that these agreements contravene GATT/WTO rules.[20] Second, the agreement was not a legal document and therefore there were no strict legal obligations imposed to ensure observance to the national 'forecasts'. Third, Japanese firms may have found it difficult to argue that they should have respected the national 'forecasts' because there was no compulsion to do so. This is particularly the case if the Japanese authorities refused to act to impose the 'forecasts'.

While these arguments, from a legal point of view, may be intriguing, industry experts and government officials interviewed for this research indicated strongly that it was unlikely that Japanese firms or government would have caused problems for the agreement. The political stakes were too high. None of the interested parties would have wished to create a difficult situation. Although a first best situation for the Japanese would be unlimited exports and segmented national markets[21] the reality was that they could ill afford to create a political dynamic that may lead to future protection. Given that Japanese producers had already set up production in the EU, it made considerably more sense for them to accept the restrictions as they stood. The fact that their production facilities were not explicitly included in the agreement allowed them to expand production in the EU independent of their import quotas.[22]

Mattoo and Mavroidis (1995) claim that based on newspaper reports in France, Toyota and Nissan have offered assurances that they will not use their production facilities elsewhere in the Community to ship into France. Of course, if the BE remains intact, it might frustrate the attempts of parallel importers to sell Japanese vehicles into countries that have import quotas and the Japanese producers need not offer such assurances. The French government throughout the management of the current agreement claimed that Japanese local production should be included in the agreement. This is very similar to the situation that the Japanese faced in the US where today, they supply the bulk of the US market with US produced cars. It is possible that the higher priced ranges of cars will be produced in Japan for export. This can be explained by virtue of a combination of understanding the nature of complex manufacturing and an awareness of the politics of car production. As discussed above, local production enables the Japanese MNE to capture micro-organizational externalities. At the same time, it is a risk-reduction strategy in that it is less probable that west European governments would be able to impose restrictions on production based in west Europe. If however, the Japanese maintained export led sales, then the use of anti-dumping could be used with more political acceptability by west European states. From the EU side, neither the authorities nor the producers had any interest in quarrelling over the terms of the agreement, legal or otherwise. The producers were very happy that despite an extremely powerful lobby to resist a new trade agreement from within the EU and increasing pressure in the WTO for further trade liberalization, they still maintained some form of import relief.

The Role of FDI and The EU-Japan Consensus

Neither MITI nor the EU Commission drew an explicit link between FDI and the agreement. The Commission insisted levels of transplant production and exports would not be linked in any way. Yet it was clear that Japanese producers were fully aware of the consequences and sensitivity of transplant production and were likely to 'promote (increased) local content and restrain production growth during the transition period to 1999' (Economist Intelligence Unit (1994:34)). After the agreement expires, they could expand local production significantly – this is corroborated by the decision of Toyota in 1998 to build a new 'greenfield' facility in France. Any increase in transplant production in the EU might tend to increase market share for Japanese producers in the EU assuming little substitution between exports and local production. Toyota, for example, stated that its strategy is to increase its transplant production and the promotion of local content in the UK as part of a general strategy to increase its dependence on local production. This policy is in line with what would be expected in a complex manufacturing sector beyond the political imperatives of protectionism. Given the discussion above the nature of production is such that Japanese firms would gain through increased local market share. It is likely that other Japanese producers will follow Toyota's policy as a means of a localizing strategy both from a marketing strategy perspective and in order to lessen trade friction.

Commitment to local production can also pre-empt future trade restrictions by ensuring a well-established local production base. However, it is important to note that significant increases in local production could have an impact on the 'forecasting' involved in the EU-Japan agreement. Thus if Japanese market share begins to rise to an 'intolerable' level through local production, EU member states may negotiate a downward revision of the import 'forecasts' as a means of controlling Japanese market share growth. Therefore, transplant production should be, de facto, counted for the purposes of monitoring. This is important given that the 'forecasts' are revised every six months. This allows the EU member states most opposed to liberalization to place constraints on the extent to which the Japanese could promote European production during the term of the agreement.

Competition, Market Structure and Efficiency

Complex manufacturing conditions in combination with import restrictions can result in domestic firms taking a higher share of industry profits at the expense of import competitors. Smith and Venables (1992) constructed a model of oligopolistic competition and applied it to the EU car industry in order to calculate the effects of lifting the VER on Japanese cars. They showed that lifting the measures would have an unambiguously positive net welfare effect for the EU.[23] How Japanese producers were likely to respond to European producers is clearly important. If they use their production facilities in Europe to lower prices in the EU and force European producers to follow suit. Alternatively, they could attempt to foster co-operative agreements. Increases in co-operative activities between European and Japanese producers could raise issues of antitrust concerning anti-competitive co-operation and market sharing especially where joint sourcing of Japanese and European brands are concerned.[24] There is a risk that these activities could result in price co-ordination of car brands that ordinarily would be competing with each other. This is likely to serve as a means of pacifying European producers who fear circumvention of trade restrictions on imports from Japan but may prove costly to the consumer in higher prices as well as offering Japanese producers with reduced competition and increased monopoly profits.

Given the 'forecasting' process, this may lead to collusion among the Japanese producers in the allocation of shares and markets. OECD (1987) has shown that in the US case, the process of quota allocation leads to rigidity in import shares because allocations are based on past performance. This is an implicit barrier to entry for new firms and disproportionately favours larger producers. Smaller firms may need to enter into alliances with domestic firms in order to gain market share and this action again raises issues of potential collusion.

The above analysis has been based on a traditional concept of allocative or static efficiency. If dynamic efficiency is taken into consideration, the existence of a VER and the arrival of FDI in the EU can have other effects. First, in the case of input providers, the arrival of FDI transfers competitive advantage to parts suppliers. This is because '[w]here a firm is unhappy with the quality of domestic inputs but must use them to circumvent the tariff wall through foreign investment, it may still be in the firm's interest to produce locally but also to work with domestic input providers on quality control' (Trebilcock and Howse, 1998, p. 280). Second, as the foreign firms have invested substantial resources in setting up a new production facility, they may have little choice but to stay and in doing so may increase consumer welfare. This is due to the fact that some of the rents from protection against competing foreign firms that accrue to the investing firm are clawed back in the form of boosted sales for domestic providers of inputs (Trebilcock and Howse, 1998, p. 280).

The Industry's Response

There were few dissenters on the European side of the agreement particularly because European manufacturers were given an extra year than was originally envisaged for the transition period to the new agreement. (Economist Intelligence Unit, 1994, p. 35). This was due to the willingness by all parties to make the agreement work and the avoidance of trade friction being a top priority on all sides of the agreement. However, ex-Chairman of the PSA group, Jacques Calvet, did not support the agreement because it was his view that the agreement ought to cover Japanese transplant production in the EU. Calvet's view diverged from Renault's view in that Renault appeared to accept that without some sort of trade agreement at an EU level, it was unlikely that the French government could do any better on its own. Calvet's isolation was further enhanced by the fact that a number of EU producers had forged business alliances with Japanese producers.[25]

Nevertheless, there was sufficient agreement among EU producers that the EU-Japan consensus was a better option than no agreement at all. On the Japanese side, it was expressed, of course, that Japanese producers would prefer a situation of full liberalization in cars. However, they recognized the political sensitivity of the car industry in Europe and the potential losses in employment from 'market disruption'.[26] But as the Economist Intelligence Unit pointed out:

> Longer term, beyond 1999, the opportunities for the Japanese in Europe are significant and it is reasonable to assume that the consensus will be made to work without disruption as it will be in the interest of the Japanese to ensure that it does (Economist Intelligence Unit, 1994, p. 35).

A point raised by officials and managers[27] during interviews was that their experience of trade protection in the US was that although US government and the public at large were generally unsympathetic towards Japanese import competition, job creation that came about through Japanese FDI was more welcome. This was because it placated the view that Japanese competition meant a loss for the US citizen and voter. As the Japanese FDI presence increases in the EU, even hard-line sections of the French government and public may have to accept that employment considerations and the dynamic of the internal market can no longer be overridden by the defence of 'national champions'.

This change was typified by the decision of the French Government in December 1997 to allow Toyota to place its second major production facility in Europe in France. Japanese firms and government are aware of this. The efforts that these firms have made to incorporate their production in the US and now in the EU suggests that market disruption from the Japanese side will be minimized in the future as it has been during the life of the current 'Elements of Consensus'.

Summary and Research Findings

Experience of the agreement's operation confirmed the insights gained from discussions with MITI, JFTC, JAMA and Toyota. Based on the primary research interviews for this case study, the following areas can be highlighted. First, the agreement has been made to work by the relevant parties in Europe and Japan as it was in all their interests for it to work. Japanese firms realize that after 1999, there are considerable benefits to be gained from European markets. It made little sense, from a political point of view for Japanese firms to have pursued aggressive strategies during the period of the agreement and increase the influence of European interests opposed to presence of Japanese competition in European markets that after 1999 are supposed to be fully liberalized. Second, the impact on European consumers is likely to be affected by the rate at which Japanese producers are able to shift their production from export led to transplant production. On the issue of Japanese exports from the US to the EU, Japanese industry sources were skeptical of Japanese producers' readiness to increase exports from the US to the EU.[28] By restricting Japanese exports only, the agreement allows for the expansion of Japanese FDI in the EU and makes no restrictions on increases of import penetration from third country producers. Third, it may have negative consequences for the competitive process by reducing the number of independent suppliers. Through covert agreements of the type alleged in the UK market preceding the 'Elements of Consensus', market sharing may increase monopoly power of the European producers.

The following section turns to the issue of the regulation of competition in car distribution in the EU. Additional conclusions from the analysis of the EU-Japan agreement include the impact of increases of imports from third country producers (notably Taiwan, South Korea and Malaysia)[29] and how the West European producers use the 'breathing space' offered by the agreement to begin to bridge the productivity gap between them and the Japanese suppliers.

The Economics of Car Distribution

Views and analyses differ as to the benefits of SED systems. There are two principle aspects of SED: selectivity i.e. the ability of manufacturers to allocate sales territories and exclusivity i.e. the right of manufacturers to restrict its dealerships to selling only its brand. Overall, the main argument in favour of allowing selective distribution is that sales of certain brands require a particularly a specific level of technical expertise to fully inform a prospective customer. This is an illustration of micro-organizational externalities for firms involved in complex manufacturing. The predominant counter argument is that SED systems restrict consumer choice and maintain geographical price differentials between dealerships and between regions for different brands. This is because consumers are unable to exploit the price differentials through inter-regional or international goods arbitrage. This is due to the nature of SED whereby only one dealer can only sell a single brand in a given area. An additional criticism of SED is that manufacturers impose exclusivity in repair and after-sales service too. In the following section the effects of selectivity i.e. intra-brand competition is analysed followed by an analysis of exclusivity.

Intra-Brand Competition

Selective franchising places limits on the amount of competition a dealer would have to face from other outlets distributing the same product normally through some form of geographical restriction. For a dealer, this selectivity is attractive because by reducing competition in the dealer's area, it permits wider price-wholesale cost margins than would be permitted in the absence of geographical restrictions. For the manufacturer that grants the restrictions on distribution to the dealer, the wider margin provides incentives for the dealer to spend more on advertising and promotional activities as well as provide quality maintenance and repair services. This phenomenon is sometimes referred to as a horizontal externality (Telser 1960).

From an antitrust perspective, the main issue is whether competition in retailing may prevent the provision of the services mentioned above. A retailer who incurs the cost of providing the specialist sales information must charge a higher price than the retailer who does not provide this service. In the absence on restrictions on intra-brand competition, consumers then have the incentive to visit the 'specialist' retailer, acquire the knowledge for free and then purchase the same product from the 'non-specialist' retailer. The second retailer is thus 'free-riding' on the public good provided by the 'specialist' retailer. In this sense, it could be argued that there are grounds for the manufacturer restricting intra-brand competition and thus capturing this information externality. If the retailer could not capture this externality, they would not supply the service thus harming consumer welfare. Although capturing the externality ensures the social benefits of providing the specialist information are maximized, the higher prices that consumers may be forced to pay when the retail system shifts from a competitive to a monopoly situation may outweigh these benefits.

An essential issue is whether services can be un-bundled from the purchase of the product. In other words, does a dealer need to offer these pre-sales and after-sales services? Thus, it is necessary to differentiate between pre-sales service and after-sales service. In the former case, it is difficult to un-bundle the 'test drive' and the actual sale of car. The most effective way a consumer can appreciate the product's performance prior to purchase is to 'test drive' it. In this case, the arguments for the horizontal externality are strong.

By contrast, it is possible to separate car sales and after-sales service and provision of repairs. In the latter case, car assemblers would need to licence independent mechanics and repairers. However, the practice has been that customers are 'encouraged' to visit their approved dealer/maintenance site for their car. There are theoretical monopoly concerns that argue against restrictions on intra-brand competition especially where the restrictions on competition relate to the provision of repair services goods. Suppose that a manufacturer imposes territorial restrictions on a group of repairers. Further suppose that the repairers and manufacturers together create a set of 'trademarks and standards' on products and services that the group of repairers provide. This allows the manufacturers and repairers to impose a minimum retail price by preventing non-trademarked repairers access to parts for the purposes of repair. This vertical restraint thus aids horizontal collusion between repairers who can co-ordinate their provision of services to maximize their geographical monopoly. It is thus harder to argue that some form of restriction on intra-brand competition should be allowed in the after-sales part of the value chain. The larger the territorial area covered by SED, the more difficult it is for consumers to compare prices for the same brand. It also means that there are fewer distribution outlets and it may therefore facilitate price co-ordination.

A closer look at actual sales and distribution practices in other complex manufacturing sectors (e.g. audio-visual) shows that there is the possibility for the co-existence of small 'specialist' retailers and large discount outlets that provide a minimalist sales service. In the US, the development of large retail chains in home electronics and computer technology has not led to the elimination of the 'expert' providers of similar products. Smaller specialist retailers can benefit from the existence of large competing outlets. They receive customers for more specialist, higher priced equipment based on recommendations of the large 'generalist' retailers.

Inter-Brand Competition

It is important to stress that as long as inter-brand competition is intense enough there will be the possibility for consumers to choose between brands. Thus if one producer overprices their product in comparison with similar products, the latter will be selected by consumers.

Exclusive dealing can also have implications for inter-brand competition because the imposition of exclusivity prevents the retailer from selling competing brands on the same premises. If a retailer is allowed to sell competing brands of the same good, the promotional activities that a manufacturer who grants the retailer a licence to sell their product might lead to enhanced sales for a second brand of product. This is due to the fact that simply enticing a consumer onto their premises may encourage the customer to buy the second brand. Exclusivity is then a means by which a manufacturer can create a property right in her promotional expenses. The main argument against exclusivity contracting is a strategic one. This is because this type of contract creates a barrier to entry for new entrants. New manufacturers who may wish to enter the market would need to set up their own distribution networks which is a costly and possibly sunk investment and this may thus discourage new entry. A second motive for exclusivity is that it can help competing manufacturers to collude by preventing the possibility of a 'retail price war' that, in the presence of inter-brand competition, may not be orchestrated by the manufacturers themselves but by their dealer networks.

The EU Block Exemption Concerning Selective Distribution of Cars

The theoretical discussion above provides a backdrop to the nature of the selective distribution regulation for cars in the SEM. The aim of this section is to contrast the original 1985 BE which imposed an extremely restrictive policy on the distribution of cars and parts as well as the provision of servicing and the 1995 BE that came into effect in 1995. There have been some interesting and possibly important liberalization measures introduced in the 1995 BE and these changes may have consequences for the control of Japanese imports. The 1995 BE imposes significant distribution restrictions where a dealer, while not being legally prevented from multifranchising, is required to show a number of 'objective' reasons why it should be allowed to encourage inter-brand competition. However, as explained below, the BE forbids any activities other than certain forms of advertising outside the geographical scope of the dealership agreement. In practice, this prevents intra-brand competition.

The 1995 Block Exemption: Its Components and its Proponents

In 1985, the EU Commission introduced its article 85 (3) exemption on the distribution of cars allowing manufacturers to impose a number of restrictions on the sales and distribution of finished cars and auto-parts. This BE was re-negotiated in 1995 and extended for a further 7 years. In most respects, the revised BE was the same as the 1985 variant. However, there were some differences introduced in the revised BE relating to the ability of dealerships to negotiate with manufacturers on the possibility of multifranchising; the situations in which the Commission has the discretion to lift the BE; and the provision of car parts.

The manufacturers were keen to maintain the rules of the 1985 BE while dealers called for liberalization of the BE in respect of multifranchising. Consumer groups called for a major re-writing, if not full liberalization of the distribution of cars and spare parts. The three major interest groups involved in the negotiations have been ACEA[30] for the manufacturers, CECRA[31] for the dealerships and BEUC[32] for the consumer. ACEA and CECRA provided arguments that supported the case for market externalities in complex manufacturing systems that have been outlined in the early sections in this chapter. BEUC focused more directly on the anti-competitive impact of the BE offering more traditional welfare arguments against the exemption based on static welfare considerations e.g. loss in consumer surplus caused by higher prices and efficiency losses caused by a lack of competition.

The Manufacturers   At the start of the consultation and renewal process, it was clear that the manufacturers understandably were looking for maintenance of the *status quo* and for a renewal of at least 10 years. The manufacturers were keen to ensure that they could enlist national support for their renewal campaign and UK dealers were encouraged to send letters to their MPs persuading them to lobby the DTI and the UK government for renewal of the BE. The main set of arguments for a renewal of the BE are to be found in a position paper that they produced in July 1993. Their central conclusion was unequivocal: the SED system had led to an increase in consumer benefits and a reduction in any 'possible anti-competitive side effects' caused by the SED itself. The manufacturers claimed that the car was not like other consumer goods. Competition as it is understood in the standard economic textbook could not be reasonably applied in this case. Implicitly, the manufacturers were drawing a contrast between complex manufacturing in cars with other industry types. Aside from housing, the car represents the second largest investment for a consumer. Moreover, the manufacturers argued that safety and regular maintenance are essential features of the car that can only be guaranteed through a carefully drafted regulatory regime. The manufacturers argued that the demands of safety required significant investments in safety equipment, electronic and mechanical diagnostic tools as well as training of staff. All these investments, the manufacturers claimed, could not be made without adequate financial security and a return on their investment.

> The cost for advanced repair equipment is high and financial returns are unattractive. [...] The only way the manufacturers can guarantee the continued existence of a competent network is based on the Block Exemption [...]. If manufacturers were no longer permitted to operate on this basis, dealers would only concentrate on the profitable elements of the business and nobody would take responsibility for the financially unattractive service related to emissions and service for which sophisticated high tech equipment is indispensable.[33]

In any case, ACEA maintained that competition in car retailing is fiercer today than it was in 1985 especially since there has been new entry from imports from Japan, Korea and the US. Even more reason, they argued, to ensure stability through the renewal of the 1985 BE. The manufacturers claimed that an over emphasis on a model of competition based on 'perfect contestability' at the retail level tended to mask the harsh reality that inter-brand competition between manufacturers was fierce. They pointed to low margins on car sales as evidence of a highly competitive industry. In order to provide attractive retail facilities for consumers, the manufacturers stated that their dealer network needed to invest time and money and again, the provision of the state-of-the-art retail facilities could not be guaranteed in the absence of a regulatory regime which encouraged the sale of one particular brand. All in all, the existence of a SED system was indispensable for the maximizing of welfare for consumers and producers alike. On the issue of price differentials, ACEA claimed, supported by a quotation from Sir Leon Brittan, Commissioner for Antitrust at the time, that although the BE may have maintained price differentials between member states, it was not the *cause* of price differentials. Moreover, the manufacturers poured scorn on the causal link from SED to the existence of price differentials claim by placing emphasis on exchange rate fluctuations, and differences in national registration and insurance formalities all of which created a significant barrier to trade between member states. In short, ACEA made great play of the reality that there has never been a SEM in the car industry. EU policy makers cannot expect a single market without a single currency and an end to national restrictions. The manufacturers, ACEA asserted, had repeatedly sent letters to their authorized dealerships reminding them of their obligations regarding cross-border sales. On the question of exclusivity, ACEA stated that there has never been a court ruling against the manufacturers that condemned them for refusing a request for a multifranchise agreement. In this context, one industry analyst pointed out that although there has been no litigation on the part of dealers to promote multifranchising, it is unlikely that dealers would wish to confront their manufacturers for fear of their exclusive contract being terminated.[34]

Territorial and brand exclusivity, according to ACEA, has no restrictive impacts on competition. This is because every dealership is faced with competition in other brand dealers in its vicinity. Indeed, ACEA asserted that brand exclusivity is pro-competitive in that concentrating on one particular brand prevents the spillover of competitively sensitive information and acts as a safeguard against 'tactical interaction and co-ordination of competitive behavior'. Moreover, there is a pro-consumer effect whereby dealers are forced to concentrate on one brand and therefore enhances sales and after-sales service provided to consumers. ACEA pointed to evidence from the US that suggested that multifranchising is 'well below' the performance levels of single-brand dealers.

> Multi-make dealers also have a greater number of vehicles to deal with and as a consequence they do not always possess the in-depth product knowledge that is required to provide high quality service for goods of an ever increasing technical complexity.[35]

Spare parts supply should also remain exclusive according to ACEA. The major fear forwarded by the manufacturers was that allowing authorized dealers to use parts of 'inferior quality' would result in lower repair standards. It would threaten emissions standards and make it more difficult for manufacturers to recycle vehicles in an 'orderly' way because manufacturers would not be aware of the recyclable nature of the parts. The 1985 BE did not offer complete exclusivity and so ACEA recommended that the EU Commission should consider full exclusivity in order to promote parts quality. This issue was much contested by the consumer groups and is explained in more detail below.

The Dealers   Generally speaking, the dealers, represented at the European level by the umbrella organization CECRA, took the same position as the manufacturers on the issue of price differentials pointing out that exchange rate and national regulatory differences were the cause of continuing price differentials between member states. The Commission had been sympathetic to the views of the dealers as evidenced by an early draft of the 1995 BE in which the Commission recognized that the previous BE had failed to take into account the demands for greater economic and financial independence (Groves 1995, p. 100). The main points of contention for the dealers were the nature of contractual obligations imposed by manufacturers, the issue of direct sales and the possibility for multifranchising. The 1985 BE gave little power to dealers to influence the terms of the contract. Dealers could have their contracts terminated by manufacturers without sufficient notice CECRA claimed that '[a] dealer agreement should recognize the dealer's substantial investment in premises, equipment and personnel. Unless, therefore, there is an established substantial continuing breach of the dealer agreement by the dealer [...], the [manufacturer] should be liable to indemnify the dealer in respect of obligations incurred [...] and to pay adequate compensation to the dealer'.[36]

Moreover, this created an adversarial climate between manufacturer and dealer and provided little economic security to the dealer. CECRA wanted to ensure that dealers could have greater freedom to advertise outside their assigned territories. As far as direct sales were concerned, CECRA feared that greater use of direct retailing method by manufacturers was a serious threat to dealers. They wanted restrictions on this practice because sales to fleets represent important sources of revenue for dealers. Direct sales also undermined territorial control for the dealer and contributed to the asymmetric relationship in favour of the manufacturers. The dealers claimed that '[i]n many cases, the delivery of vehicles sold to manufacturers direct are entrusted to authorized Dealers, and Dealers reasonably seek adequate remuneration for their involvement [in after-sales service]. Sometimes manufacturers pay this compensation, but not in the majority of instances'.[37]

The UK Ford Dealer Associations circulated a paper on the issue of the renewal of the 1985 BE.[38] They were more categorical about the issue of direct sales. They called for a regulation forbidding direct sales except at national level public procurement and sales to manufacturer owned outlets. Discounting was also criticized by the UK Ford dealers where manufacturers offered higher discounts to leasing fleet companies than to their dealers. They called for a restriction on such activities and where possible, all sales to fleets should be through the dealer networks. Dealers were unhappy that manufacturers wished to maintain exclusivity of brand in the contractual terms and called for the possibility of multifranchising. Again, multi-brand sales would broaden the dealer's portfolio and allow a dealer to spread his/her risk and investment should one particular brand of car prove unpopular. Of course, being able to negotiate with at least two manufacturers would allow the dealer to regain an element of bargaining power. He or she should be able to bargain for better terms by playing one manufacturer's terms off with another.

Dealers and Manufacturers: Brothers in Arms? Given these major differences in expectations between the manufacturer and dealer groups, the greatest challenge faced by dealers and manufacturers was how they were going to be able to form a united position in the consultation process with the Commission. Early communication between ACEA and the dealer networks attempted to form an alliance to tackle the consumer groups. Industry producer interests were rather worried that Karel Van Miert, the Commissioner in charge of antitrust at the time would be sympathetic to the consumer groups' views.[39] In other words, the EU Commission may take a pro-liberalization stance. Thus it was imperative that the combined might of manufacturers and dealers were brought together to counter this possibility. A document authored by the EU car producers was to form the basis of all the manufacturers' lobbying activities regarding the BE.[40] However, when ACEA suggested that this paper should be adopted as a joint CECRA/ACEA paper, it received only lukewarm support from dealer groups. UK groups pointed out that the claim of the paper that the BE of 1985 struck the correct balance between the interests of manufacturers, dealers and consumers was unacceptable.[41] Equally unacceptable to the dealers was the claim by ACEA that high tech service operations could only be provided by exclusive dealerships. Finally, UK dealers could not agree with ACEA's claims that direct sales have a minimal impact on dealer interests.[42] Further questions were raised by dealers concerning the concrete advantages for consumers of SED. They pointed to the necessity to tackle consumer groups' claims that there is no evidence that consumer welfare would be worsened under free competition. This question will be addressed in more detail below when the consumer groups' positions are explored. Another issue that the dealers raised with ACEA was whether the manufacturers could put forward a convincing argument on the supposed link between market segmentation and 'excessive' price differences. Van Miert was believed to be looking at the renewal of the 1985 BE in a 'pragmatic' way implying that manufacturers and dealers would need to seek a detailed response to consumer groups.

The Consumer Groups BEUC represented the national consumer groups and their central contention was that there was no evidence offered by manufacturers and dealers at all that a liberalization of rules on distribution would worsen the consumer or the industry at large. Thus the 1985 BE should not be renewed. They claimed that the onus of proof should be on the industry to show that the necessity for the BE. BEUC claimed the 1985 BE had a number of directly and indirectly restrictive effects on competition. BEUC further claimed that that 1985 BE had been drafted and administered in such a way as to be 'much too permissive [....] Which has subtly shifted the burden of proof from those who favour restrictions on competition to those who are opposed to such restrictions'.[43] The Commission was accused by BEUC of not being tough enough on price differentials, parallel imports and for their lack of active investigation of claims against manufacturers and dealers. BEUC claimed that ACEA formed a concentrated oligopoly and the 1985 BE served to weaken the willingness of the manufacturers to compete with each other. BEUC argues that 'partly because of an attachment to the *status quo* (and the benefits that they derive from it), and partly for fear of "rocking the boat". In these circumstances the aggregate behavior of the parties in the system can (and in this case does) produce anti-competitive effects similar to those produced by explicit arrangements not to compete outside the scope of the application of the block exemption'.[44]

BEUC placed an important emphasis on the broader consumer interest in the car distribution sector: in particular BEUC asserted that attempts to restrict availability of spare parts on the grounds of safety and quality was a spurious argument. In BEUC's view, there was no reason to suggest that given an enforceable regime on part standards, independent parts suppliers and repairers should be prevented from servicing cars.

BEUC asserted furthermore that if the 1985 BE was so effective, it would be reasonable to expect three effects of the operation of the BE. First, consumers could expect a high standard of after-sales services, spare parts and repairs from franchised outlets. Second, there should be freedom for consumers to buy cars and obtain repairs anywhere in the EU. Third, and most controversially, there should be only negligible price differences for cars between different member states. There was no evidence to suggest that on the basis of BEUC's research that any of these advantages had manifested themselves during the period of operation of the BE. On the central question of SED, BEUC claimed that this system in itself acts as a non-tariff barrier and that '[t]he system as a whole has also led to a market that is dominated by very strong manufacturers, who are heavily reliant on branding, and very weak retailers, who are unable [...] to strike advantageous deals on behalf of their consumers'.[45]

BEUC criticized the link between sales and service as unnecessary – despite claims by the manufacturers that this link was indispensable for the safety and quality of service provided. Two further areas were covered by BEUC's detailed report. The first relates to the role of intermediaries in cross-border purchases and the second was the issue of price lists compiled by the Commission. On both counts, BEUC argued that the Commission's actions were insufficient despite the regulatory controls that the Commission possesses. The Commission submitted a communication on intermediaries in December 1991 restricting the number of cars that can be sold by a dealer to a single parallel importer. This figure was set at a 10 percent ceiling. The communication also precipitated the *Eco-System* action (see below). This was incompatible with the Single Market, BEUC claimed. The 1985 BE granted the Commission powers to withdraw the rights of the exemption if it considered price differentials between member states as excessive. Following a complaint filed by BEUC in January 1990, the Commission acted by sending letters to all major manufacturers reminding them that they should inform their dealers that they should not prevent parallel imports. Moreover, every three months, manufacturers would be obliged to compile price lists across member states for the five top-selling cars as well as a six-monthly list of prices of one standard, low-equipment model in each of the various market segments applied to the car industry. Although welcoming the action by the Commission, BEUC still claimed that it fell short of what the consumer really needed – without specifying exactly what it was they did need.

In summary of their report, BEUC stated that the Commission was faced with two extreme options: maintaining the *status quo* or abolishing the 1985 BE altogether. BEUC claimed that '[i]t is not acceptable for the industry, the European

Commission or the national competent authorities simply to assert that benefits exist. They must provide evidence that they do. [W]e submit the Commission in its review, should not look simply at ways of making the current block exemption "workable" or "less bad". [It] must ask the fundamental question of whether it is needed at all'.[46] Table 4.7 summarizes the positions the different groups in the renewal process.

Table 4.7   The Block Exemption Renewal: The Groups' Positions

Issue	ACEA	CECRA	BEUC
SED	Indispensable	Necessary	End
Renewal?	Yes, 10 years minimum	Yes, at least 10 years	No
Manufacturer Direct Sales	OK	Restrictions to protect dealers	No position
Length of contract between manufacturer & dealer	No legally binding rules	Legal protection	No position
Spare Parts Distribution	Parts must supplied by manufacturers. Must also protect IPRs of parts manufacturer	Parts must be of matching quality as manufacturers	Freedom of suppliers to sell parts to dealers. A separation of sales and service
Reselling	Only authorized resellers.	Only authorized resellers.	Right enshrined in SEM
Price Differentials	Not caused by BE. Caused by fiscal distortions; and national registration rules	Same as ACEA	BE segments market causes price differentials
Cross-border sales	All manufacturers recognize the right to buy anywhere in EC. Have sent letters to dealers to instruct them to sell. National rules cause problems.	Dealers accept the right of consumers to buy cross-border. National rules cause problems.	Cases of consumers being prevented from buying a car and getting service from another dealer – due to BE.

Source: Author's own table

Analysis: Competing Models of Competition and Efficiency

The above analysis of the different interest groups in the EU car sector highlights the differences in analytical models used to explain the nature of production, competition, efficiency and welfare outcomes in this sector. Both ACEA and CECRA stress the importance of understanding the nature of complex manufacturing. In particular, the role of market externalities and vertical integration is highlighted.

According to ACEA and CECRA, it is not possible to view the car industry in terms of a standard model of competition as this may miss the role of managerial and strategic aspects in production. On the other hand, BEUC's model of competition that underpins their claims to the anti-competitive nature of car distribution is based on a model of contestability that would regard SED as a barrier-to-entry and unambiguously harmful to consumers.

This is manifested in part by the persistence of significant price differentials for cars across the EU.[47] They claim that SED is simply a means by which producers and retailers can segment the market and reap increased profits. Following BEUC's reasoning, it should be the case that where there is no legal protection for SED, a liberalized market should function on the basis of strong intra- and inter-brand competition, no restrictions on after-sales service and the car retailing sector should function as any other retail good. However, the practice of SED is widespread. In both the US and Japan, this retail method is pervasive (Harbour et al., 1994). This suggests that there must grounds for this practice to exist other than on political economy arguments. In other words, there might be efficiency arguments for the existence of this practice as in a liberalized market, it should be expected that anti-competitive, inefficient market practices should be rooted out by new entry. This may also support the case for the renewal of the 1985 BE that came in to force in 1995.

The 1995 Block Exemption

Following these submissions, the Commission proposed to the Council of Ministers to renew the BE for a further seven years.[48] This section will explore the 1995 BE and analyse changes that have been made in the areas of multifranchising, spare parts, terms and termination of dealerships and restrictions on cross-border trade.

Multifranchising   CECRA's central claims were that dealerships should have the right to multifranchise. Not surprisingly, BEUC agreed with this principle (Locke and Bovis (1994)). Interestingly, the UK Mergers and Monopolies Commission (MMC) agreed with the views of the dealers and consumers, arguing that some liberalization of the tied/exclusive dealership system would be beneficial to the EU consumer (MMC 1992). According the Commission, however, it would be difficult for a dealership to offer complete technical expertise on more than one brand of car and thus if liberalization were to occur, the consumer would suffer because of sub-standard information and service. As the Commission in the 1995 BE stated:

The exclusive and selective distribution clauses can be regarded as indispensable measures of rationalization in the motor vehicle industry, because motor vehicles [...] at both regular and irregular intervals require expert maintenance and repair, not always in the same place. Motor vehicle manufacturers co-operate with the selected dealers and repairers in order to provide specialised servicing for the product.[49]

Nevertheless, the 1995 BE did not exclude multifranchising. There was however a number of conditions that applied as outlined in article 3(3) of the 1995 BE. First, sales of different brands are allowed if they are carried out on separate premises. Second, these premises must be under separate management (in the form of a distinct legal entity) and third, that there must be no 'confusion' between brands. Fourth, the dealer would be required to show 'objective reasons' to prevent a manufacturer from imposing exclusivity restrictions.[50] Brown (1994) suggested set-up costs for new state-of-the-art franchises are considerable. This implies that it may be difficult for a prospective dealer to be able to multifranchise without significant sources of capital that possibly could only be provided by a manufacturer. (Groves 1995, p. 99) points out that an earlier draft of the 1995 BE originally allowed dealers to show objective reasons for the multiple distribution of brands and still remain under contract with a particular manufacturer.

As with the 1985 variant, the 1995 BE imposed territorial restrictions on dealerships' activities. The manufacturer continued to benefit from the right to restrict advertising that a dealership may wish to carry outside of its territorial scope. Moreover, the 1995 BE still banned dealers from setting up branches outside its assigned territory. This effectively minimized intra-brand competition. Harbour et al. (1994) argued that in fact, the restriction on intra-brand competition was not that important as the real issue for competition was the promotion of inter-brand competition. Research by these authors suggests that consumers frequently visit more than one dealer selling the same brand before buying and thus they are able to 'shop around' in this way. Second, a consumer is free to visit competing brand dealerships within similar geographical constraints.

Termination of the Franchise Agreement Where 'objective reasons' are offered by dealers, they can be released from the service agreement with manufacturers (article 5 (2)(1)) in 1995 BE. The 1985 BE variant placed the dealer in an extremely weak position by allowing for indeterminable contracts, which in reality turned into one-year renewable contracts (Groves 1995:101). The 1995 BE restricted the ability with which a supplier could unilaterally reorganize the dealer's territory or appoint an additional dealer. However, the manufacturer may terminate a dealership agreement with half a year's notice if there was an urgent need to reorganize sales activities. Interestingly, there was no mention of 'objective reasons' concerning the right of manufacturers to terminate the contract in this case!

The BE and Spare Parts This distribution issue was equally contentious as that relating to finished cars. Looking at the 1985 BE, the Commission allowed manufacturers to impose exclusive purchasing obligations on the dealers whereby dealers were forced to purchase 'parts of matching quality' to those supplied by the manufacturer. Figure 4.1 below shows how this practice works. Instead of offering the dealership the possibility of purchasing what is essentially a second input in the downstream sale of a car (i.e. a spare or replacement part), the dealer is obliged to a form of tie-in in that it must purchase parts from an approved supplier. This meant that dealers were frequently buying parts with the manufacturers' name on them and that these parts were also the same ones that went into finished vehicles at the time of assembly (Groves 1995, p. 99). This restriction was maintained in the 1995 version of the BE because an alternative forwarded in earlier drafts allowed dealers to use competing parts as long as an independent authority had scientific proof that they were of equivalent quality (Groves 1995, p. 99). Nevertheless, the 1995 BE stated that if a manufacturer prevents a dealer from using parts contracted from alternative suppliers, then the exemption will be lifted on that manufacturer. The same would occur if the independent parts manufacturers were denied access to the network. Whether a dealer would be prepared to challenge a manufacturer is unlikely because he may lose favours with the assembler (see *Automec* below).

Prohibited Restrictions   In addition to the changes outlined above , the 1995 BE prohibited the following actions by manufacturers. First, practices designed to inhibit parallel imports whether by intermediaries or by established by members of the network. Second, any attempts to impose parts exclusivity other than those provided for in the BE itself. Third, discrimination between members of the

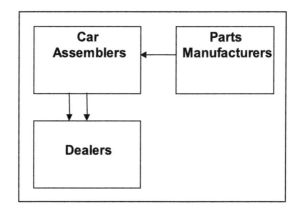

Figure 4.1   The System of Parts Purchase in the BE Rules

Source: Author's own diagram

manufacturer's authorized dealer network.

Unlike the 1985 BE, the 1995 version explicitly states the sanctions that will be imposed on manufacturers or dealers who attempt to contravene the BE in their agreement. According to the regulation, if both parties include clauses that are prohibited by the terms of the BE in their agreement, then the BE will be lifted entirely (Groves 1995, p. 192). If one of the parties to the agreement attempts to impose prohibited restrictions, then the loss of the exemption will fall only on that party.

In addition to these specific sanctions, the EU Commission reserves the right to withdraw the exemption where there is no competition in a substantial part of the internal market; prices or conditions of supply differ substantially between member states over a considerable period. As is explained in more detail below, whether the Commission actually carries it threat to withdraw exemption should price differentials remain as high as they do at present is not clear.

Key Case Law in the Car Sector

An analysis of key decisions and cases is also important in understanding the development of trade and antitrust in the car industry. The chapter will now explore key case law that deals with import competition from Japan, distribution of Japanese cars in the EU and the restrictions imposed by the BE. The cases illustrate three main points. First, they highlight the contradiction between restrictive trade policy and the pursuit of contestability-based concepts of competition in the EU in a highly internationalized, complex manufacturing sector. Second, the case law highlights the competing models of competition that underlie the analysis of distribution in car retailing. The ECJ is convinced of arguments based on a standard model of competition while the European Commission regards the externality arguments for SED as important. Third, due to these differences in the underlying model of competition, there is conflict between the different institutions over trade and competition regulation in this sector.

Asia Motors This case referred to the sale and distribution of Japanese cars in France. First, the existence of an agreement between the importers into France of cars of the Japanese brands – Toyota, Honda, Nissan, Mazda and Mitsubishi, and the French government. Under this agreement, French importers of the Japanese brands above agreed to limit their aggregate share of the French domestic car market to 3 percent. This was in return for an undertaking on the part of the French authorities that the market in vehicles of Japanese origin would be reserved to them exclusively, and existence of an agreement between the undertakings in question allocating between themselves their aggregate market share.[51] The second agreement was between the dealers of the same Japanese brands in Martinique and the French government under which those dealers allegedly agreed to limit their share of the Martinique car market to 15%. Again, this was in return for an undertaking that the market in vehicles of Japanese origin would be reserved to them exclusively, and existence of an agreement between those undertakings allocating as between themselves their aggregate market share.[52] The EU Commission rejected the claim that these agreements were a breach of article 85 of the Treaty of Rome. The arguments offered by the Commission were first, that the dealers were under orders from the French government and therefore could not reject its orders i.e. sovereign compulsion and second, that the allegations referred to a national agreement over which the EU had no authority. Moreover, the Commission argued that the restrictions referred to French national rules pertained to road safety in which foreign made cars required special registration. This policy was best administered through recognized French importers even if this frustrated parallel imports of identical brands from other EU member states according to the Commission.

The complainants took the case to the ECJ, and unlike the EU Commission, the ECJ ruled that on a procedural and substantive level, the Commission had misunderstood the status of the national restrictions.[53] First, the rules related to the registration of cars and their entry on to French roads did not cover the importing of identical brands. Thus, there should be no presumption that France could restrict parallel imports of cars *per se*. Second, the Commission failed to exercise due and fair examination of the facts and documents submitted by the complainants. In particular, it did not pay due attention to a document which explicitly showed that the authorized French importers agreed to administer the market sharing agreement among themselves – thereby implying an element of choice on their part and thereby denying the sovereign compulsion argument.

This case highlights that the EU Commission was not willing to enforce the rights of independent dealers and was prepared to sacrifice free movement of goods in order to ensure that the sensitivities of the French government and its allies in the French car industry could be taken into account. The agreement between the authorized French dealers and the French government was a clear illustration of trade policy, in the form of a technical non-tariff barrier, distorting competition in the internal market.

BEUC/NCC   Similar to *Asia Motors*, this case involved allegations of a restrictive agreement this time between SMMT and JAMA in which they agreed to restrict the total annual car sales of Japanese brands in the UK to no more than 11 percent of the total UK market. This agreement had been in force for many years before the EU-Japan 'Elements of Consensus' agreement. In a letter from SMMT to the EU Commission in July 1994, the SMMT confirmed that talks between SMMT and JAMA had been taking place for 17 years and ended in 1992. However, SMMT denied that any formal arrangements to restrict Japanese exports to the UK had been in existence during this period. However, in this letter, it was noted that 'both sides recognized that thereafter any question related to Japanese exports to the UK as part of the EC would have to become part of the EC/MITI discussions and would not be discussed at all by SMMT and JAMA'.[54] BEUC and the National Consumer Council (NCC) alleged that this agreement breached article 85 of the Treaty of Rome. BEUC and NCC requested that a formal investigation by DG IV of the EU Commission be undertaken.

The Commission replied that given that the EU-Japan agreement was in force at the time of BEUC and NCC's request and that the former had superseded the SMMT-JAMA agreement, it was not necessary to enter into an investigation. The Commission did not see a 'Community Interest' claim on a UK agreement that did not greatly affect intra-EU trade and was therefore not a matter for EU competition law (articles 85 and 86). Only if BEUC and NCC could show that the SMMT-JAMA agreement was still in force after the EU-Japan agreement came into force, would the Commission investigate. On the substantive issue of the coming into force of the EU-Japan agreement and the lapsing of the SMMT-JAMA agreement, the ECJ's Court of First Instance (CFI) ruled that the Commission did not provide sufficient evidence to suggest that the SMMT-JAMA agreement would lapse once the EU-Japan agreement came into force. This is because an analysis of the EU-Japan declaration announcing the deal did not make it clear that any existing agreements would be monitored to ensure that they had been phased out. To quote the CFI,

> Finally, the Commission's representative stated at the hearing, in reply to the questions put by the Court, that the commercial consensus between the Community and Japan was not recorded in writing and that it was not an official agreement [....] but rather a political commitment. In those circumstances, and in the light of all that has been said above, the Court considers that an unwritten commitment, purely political in import and not made within the context of the Common Commercial Policy, coupled with a transitional period of application expiring at the end of 1999, did not entitle the Commission to reply that the commitment would necessarily put an end to the agreement complained of by the applicants.[55]

On the issue of the impact of the SMMT-JAMA agreement on intra-EU trade, the CFI rejected the Commission's claims to the trivial impact of a UK market agreement. Again to cite the CFI,

> The Court considers that, as the applicants maintain, [the SMMT-JAMA] arrangements are by their very nature, liable to impair the functioning of the common market. As measures restricting imports into the Community and affecting the entire territory of a Member State, they are liable to interfere with the natural movement of trade, thus affecting trade between Member States, and to reinforce the compartmentalization of markets on a national basis, thereby holding up the economic interpenetration which the Treaty is intended to bring about....[56]

Despite the condemnation of the ECJ, the Commission did not investigate and in fact refused to release documents to BEUC in order for them to take the matter further. Faced with these difficulties, BEUC decided to drop the case.[57] As with *Asia Motors*, this case emphasizes the linkages between trade policy and antitrust, i.e. it is unlikely that antitrust can maximize a pro-competitive impact if trade policy serves to restrict market access for competing firms. The maintenance of a restrictive trade agreement in this case took precedence over the legal requirements of free movement of goods within the EU. This is highlighted by the Commission's denial of the 'spillover' of trade policy on competition within the EU.

Automec   This case, decided in 1992, did not involve Japanese imports but concerned the rights of European car manufacturers to restrict or terminate the activities of their licensed dealerships. BMW Italia refused to supply spare parts to Automec, a BMW official licensed repairer in Italy. Moreover, BMW Italia refused to allow Automec to use the BMW branding – especially since Automec was importing BMW's from outside Italy for resale in Italy. Automec asked the Commission to order BMW Italia to meet the orders for parts that Automec had forwarded and to authorize it to use certain BMW trademarks. The reason given for those demands was that Automec considered that it met all the requisite conditions for inclusion in the BMW distribution network. Consequently, it asked the Commission to adopt two specific orders in respect of BMW in order to secure compliance with its alleged right to be admitted to BMW's distribution network. The

Commission argued that it had no right to force BMW to comply with Automec's orders and that BMW Italia was free to select its distributors under the terms of the 1985 BE. Automec then challenged the Commission's decision at the CFI.

The CFI ruled that due to the principle of freedom of contract, the Commission was not empowered to issue specific orders requiring BMW to supply the applicant and to allow it to use BMW trademarks. Therefore, the Commission had not infringed Community law by refusing to grant the application to issue such orders on the ground that it had no power to do so. Thus on substantive and procedural grounds, the Commission was exonerated. However, the interesting ruling by the CFI related to the inconsistency of the Commission's arguments related to parallel imports and the 1985 BE. In its decision, the Commission had disregarded a letter sent from BMW Italia to its dealerships. This circular, sent by BMW Italia on 7 July 1988 to all its distributors, aimed to discourage sales to unauthorized dealers and sales 'outside the area' effected with the assistance of 'intermediaries or middlemen'.

The CFI argued that it was contrary to the requirements of Community law as regards both selective and exclusive distribution (SED) and indent 11 of Article 3 of Regulation No 123/85 (the 1985 BE). Moreover, the CFI pointed out that the Commission itself has stated twice namely in its Communication concerning Regulation No 123/85 and in the XVIth Report on Antitrust,[58] that such conduct infringes fundamental rules. Thus although Automec's claims were rejected, the CFI clearly stated that the Commission could not permit the restriction of intra-EU trade by allowing SED.

Eco-System   In this case, Peugeot tried to prevent their Belgian dealers from selling to Eco-System, a company that sought to purchase cars on behalf of French individual customers. The Commission ruled against Peugeot arguing that Peugeot was attempting to prevent consumers from purchasing cross-border. Peugeot lodged an appeal against the Commission's decision at the CFI who in turn rejected Peugeot's appeal. Peugeot then took an appeal to the ECJ. This was the first time in the car distribution issue that the Commission was prepared to tackle anti-competitive behavior of firms. At time of writing, the ECJ had yet to rule on Peugeot's appeal, although on the basis of the past cases reviewed above, it is unlikely to rule in Peugeot's favour.

VW/Audi   A recent case involved a significant prosecution and fine for VW/Audi. VW/Audi instructed their Italian dealerships to refuse to sell to Austrian customers who were seeking to purchase in Italy given the significant price differences between the two countries.[59] They were instructed by VW/Audi to discourage sales by informing customers of the different specifications that existed on models sold in Italy and Austria and to highlight the problems of insurance and guarantee if customers were to re-import the vehicles. In the memo entitled 'Measures to control and prevent re-export', VW/Audi made it clear that it was 'somewhat risky'[60] for the dealers to prevent re-export and it was imperative that the dealers were to deny that they had instructions to this effect should customers ask. In order to ensure that this worked VW and Audi carried out surveillance of the activities of Italian dealerships. VW and Audi cross-checked chassis numbers of VW/Audi vehicles available for sale from German and Austrian intermediaries and traced these vehicles to the supplying Italian dealers and customers. This system made it possible to establish a breakdown of re-imports by customer, dealer and model. In one case, VW/Audi instructed, in a hand written memo, to its dealerships to sell to one intermediary as the re-importing firm had threatened to complain to the Commission.

This was to be done 'on political grounds' in order to avoid the 'withdrawal of the Block Exemption Regulation'.[61] The Commission had discovered that the conduct of VW/Audi went back more than ten years and the fine of 102 million Euros reflected the gravity of the infringement in this case.

Evaluation

From the cases above, the ECJ and CFI appear to be convinced that there are anti-competitive practices of the industry and also in the current and past trade policy arrangements that the EU has agreed to in the car sector. In this sense, they are convinced of the contestability arguments against restrictions on competition. From their judgments, it is equally clear that they view the Commission's monitoring of the BE with suspicion – especially in respect of ensuring parallel importing (*Eco-System* notwithstanding). Implicit in their arguments is that the EU car market is highly segmented. Economic theory would suggest that this would lead to significant price differentials for identical products sold in different segmented sub-markets. This chapter now turns to this issue. The *VW/Audi* ruling by the Commission now suggests a readiness on the part of the Commission to prosecute infringements of the competition rules that frustrate cross-border trade within the SEM – arguably in response to the rigorous enforcement of EU rules by the ECJ/CFI.

SED and Price Differentials

One of the consequences of the BE has been the persistence of price differences for similar brands of car and car parts across the EU. DG IV's XXIInd Report on Antitrust points out that based on its report (May 6 1992) on car price differences in the common market, it found 'very large' price differentials on certain models. It believes that the system of selective distribution 'contribute[s] to sustaining such differentials, in so far as they limit trade between Member States and thereby reduce effective pressure on manufacturers to align prices more closely.'[62] The manufacturers and dealers maintain that other national restrictions (e.g. insurance and guarantees) and the absence of a single currency have caused the differentials and allow them to persist. With the introduction of the Euro on January 1 1999, price transparency will increase considerably and it may be difficult for manufacturers to sustain their price differential arguments. The Commission requires that car manufacturers compile, every six months, on a standard form, comparable price data for one widely sold model in each line. A number of academic studies have sought to explore and account for the perceived price differences between same brands of cars, both import and domestically produced between countries in the EU on the basis of pre-1985 rules and the 1985 BE. The rules of the 1985 BE state that price differentials for a particular make between any pair of EU countries should not exceed 12 percent of the pre-tax price.

One of the main research tasks has been to explain the market structure and firm conduct mechanisms by which these price differentials have occurred. Two studies by Kirman and Schueller (1990 and 1992) focus on price leadership by domestic firms. They show that where domestic firms are higher cost producers then prices will be higher in those markets. Verboven (1995) estimated a structural model of the European car market. His main explanation for price differences was variation in demand elasticity between countries and the presence of trade barriers. Flam and Nordström (1995) studied price differentials for over 40 models and eleven of the EU countries over the period 1989–92. This time period should be hypothesized to be the time when the SEM was coming into force and when, *ceteris paribus*, a unified market should be reducing price differentials through goods arbitrage. The authors find that the maximum price difference between any pair of countries was 50 percent on average and that the 12 percent price margin set as a maximum by the 1985 BE was below the average price variation. Flam and Nordström (1995) also explored the price effects of import restrictions on those countries covered by the 'Elements of Consensus'. The countries are Spain, France, Italy and the United Kingdom. They found that prices for Japanese models were on average 10 to 15 percent higher as a consequence of the agreement and competing European brands were between 5 to 10 percent on competing European models. They show that a combination of the BE, national safety standards and the use of article 115 of the Rome treaty have served to segment EU markets along national lines.

Harbour et al. (1994) point out that the EU Commission does not claim that the BE *causes* price differentials but that it *sustains* historically determined price differentials. The reasons offered by these authors range from persisting tax differentials, registration formalities that differ between member states and technical standards. They contend that price convergence would only increase with a substantial harmonization of the other technical, administrative and fiscal barriers that they cite independent of the BE. This contradicts the conclusions drawn by Flam and Nordström (1995) and Mattoo and Mavroidis (1995) who categorically draw a connection between the BE and price differentials. Interestingly, Flam and Nordström (1995) find higher price differentials on Japanese imports than on domestic brands and at the same time that prices for Japanese imports are higher in those countries that are subject to the EU-Japan deal.

Trade and Antitrust Interactions

This case study highlights that highly internationalized complex production and distribution structures make it harder to separate internal from external policy objectives. In order for the EU Commission to control Japanese imports of cars, it was necessary to restrict competition internally. Similarly, in order to control intra-EU trade within the SEM, it was necessary for the Commission to liberalize Japanese imports away from the member states. This in turn created anti-competitive problems within the EU. The case is not quite so simple in that the nature of complex manufacturing and its associated externalities related to the control of a multi-stage value chain means that there may circumstances in which it is not possible to introduce 'perfect contestability' arguments in the regulation of trade and investment. Both policies in isolation have a number of important effects. The objective of this section is to highlight complementarities and potential conflicts between antitrust and trade policy in the case study above (OECD, 1998a, OECD, 1998b and OECD, 1998c).

The starting point for this analysis is to highlight the EU Commission's explicit acceptance that for the system of bilateral quotas as negotiated under the terms of the 'Elements of Consensus' to work, a significant restriction on the cross-border distribution of cars is essential. This is especially the case since the trade agreement has restricted member state freedoms concerning the use of article 115 and the control of indirect imports. Indeed, in 1994, while the renewal of the 1985 BE was taking place, the EU Commission stated,

> [E]xamining what changes could be made to [the 1985 Block Exemption] [...] taking account of [...] the contribution of the selective and exclusive distribution system to the efficient management of the arrangement between Japan and the EU on trade in automobiles; the efficient management of this arrangement must not be weakened in any way.[63]

The EU Commission came under strong criticism for the renewal of the BE from many quarters. The EFTA Surveillance Authority voiced strong opinions. In November 1994 it expressed its opinion on a draft of the renewed BE that had been adopted in October 1994.

> In [car] markets consumers normally have a choice between products from a number of producers, who are large corporations, *covering substantial parts of the world market*. The products differ in their technical performance, but are to a high degree substitutable. Typically [these] markets [...] are oligopolistic or show oligopolistic tendencies. They are, thus, markets where special attention should be given to attempts to restrict competition and where consumers have a strong interest in retaining the benefits resulting from an effective competition. [...] *The characteristics of this market do not seem to indicate that there would be particular reasons for allowing derivations from the competition line* e.g. through a specific block exemption. [Emphasis added] (EFTA Surveillance Authority, 1994, p. 2).

The implication of EFTA Surveillance Authority criticisms is that the underlying motive for the BE is to aid the organization and administration of trade policy. Mattoo and Mavroidis (1995) agree with this central implication. However, does the slight liberalization in the 1995 BE make the organization of the trade regime any more difficult? The answer to this question lies surely in the willingness of the EU Commission to stick to its word that if price differentials persist, then it may lift the BE. As the EU Commission does not publicly accept that the BE may be a cause of price differentials, it has been unwilling to tackle the persistence of price differentials in excess of the 12 percent level that it set. If the primary objective of the BE is to facilitate the trade policy, then the Commission's preferences are likely to be in favour of rescuing the trade policy at the expense of a unified EU market. On the other hand, by being more explicit in its sanctions in the event of non-compliance with the terms of the 1995 BE, the EU Commission is sending a clear signal to manufacturers and distributors that they mustn't be seen to be blatantly exploiting the BE in their favour. A more hard line approach from DG IV can also be attributed to its decision to raid VW dealerships in Austria and Italy in December 1995 and subsequently pursue prosecutions and impose fines. This policy of the Commission is compatible with the view that although there may be externality arguments in favour of maintaining restraints on distribution, this does not justify restricting intra-EU trade. The pursuit of a BE and VER simultaneously may also be related to the view that encouraging the arrival of Japanese FDI may bring with substantial positive spillovers as analysed in the case above. The arrival of Japanese FDI both from a Japanese MNE perspective and an EU member state perspective may reduce the potential for future protection as Japanese MNEs may serve the EU market from local production. This partially explains why the VER and BE have, to date, worked smoothly.

Mattoo and Mavroidis (1995) have employed a traditional welfare approach in their discussion of the interactions between trade and antitrust. They argue that the combination of a restrictive trade arrangement and a system of SED work together to restrict competition and thereby reduce consumer benefits. Indeed, they refer to 'weakened' antitrust when discussing the BE. Implicitly, they perceive few benefits in SED as the restrictions on intra- and inter-brand competition restrict supply that must raise price and thereby harm consumer welfare. They also implicitly argue that product differentiation and branding which seeks to target specific consumer segments does not significantly impact positively on consumer welfare by supplying the demand for variety. In a related way, Smith and Venables (1992) argue that a VER unambiguously reduces consumer welfare by segmenting markets which allows producers to charge higher prices to consumers who, in a case of trade liberalization, would have a broader range of suppliers and hence increasing variety.

According to Mattoo and Mavroidis (1995), the existence of an EU-Japan VER and the BE owe more to the political economy of the car industry and the highly influential role of the car producers in particular. In this way, the member states have found themselves hamstrung by the commitment to maintain control of trade with Japan. Thus, trade policy, designed to regulate 'bad' external competition has taken preference over the liberalization of 'good' intra-EU competition. It is also important to realize that the EU 'market' has always been segmented i.e. there has never been a SEM as envisaged in the Single European Act (SEA).

An alternative but not necessarily contradictory explanation for the trade and antitrust outcomes in the EU car sector has been that policymakers have employed a different model of competition and efficiency than the traditional welfare approach above. It is arguable that recognition of the market externalities in complex manufacturing have led policymakers to accept a BE. The fact that SED is the common practice in the US and Japan suggests that irrespective of vertical restraints, car retailing is a fundamentally contestable sector as if SED was inefficient, new practices would emerge to replace this method.

Given that the EU member states have committed themselves to a SEM, it has been imperative for the EU Commission to be seen to punishing attempts to prevent cross border sales while pacifying the demands of the EU car industry for protection from Japanese competition. The BE thus has served several purposes. First, as noted above, the Commission concedes that the smooth operation of the EU-Japan *trade* agreement requires the use of *antitrust*. Second, the BE serves to capture the benefits of restrictions on intra- and inter-brand competition at the retail level.

This also can help explain why the ECJ has been strong in its enforcement of EU SEM rules and competition disciplines. It also explains why the Commission has more recently been active in investigating and where necessary prosecuting alleged breaches of the BE and SEM rules.[64] The important challenge for the EU has been to strike the correct balance and to avoid conflicts in trade and antitrust in this sector. Given the nature of complex manufacturing and the political economy of the car industry, these links, as has been demonstrated above are numerous and complicated.

Conclusion

This chapter has attempted to explore the links between trade and antitrust in complex manufacturing. In particular, it has taken the car industry as its focus for analysis. It has made use of interviews with industry and governmental figures in the EU, Japan and the US and detailed appraisal and analysis of industry and government documentation in an attempt to highlight the linkages (both conflicts and complementarities) between trade and antitrust.

The chapter was organized as follows. The first part provided a detailed analysis of the relationship between complex manufacturing conditions. The theoretical analysis was to consider how the nature of production, competition and efficiency occurs in complex manufacturing industries. In particular, it has been argued that complex manufacturing sectors require an economic model that recognizes the existence of market externalities and firm strategy in production and competition. In this sense, a focus on 'markets' and treating the firm as a 'black box' may miss important explanatory variables in these kind of sectors.

The main findings from the case were that first; the agreement has been made to work by the relevant parties in Europe and Japan as it was in all their interests for it to work. Japanese firms realize that after 1999, there are considerable benefits to be gained from European markets. It made little sense, from a political point of view for Japanese firms to have pursued aggressive strategies during the period of the agreement and increase the influence of European interests opposed to presence of Japanese competition in European markets that after 1999 are supposed to be fully liberalized. Second, the impact on European consumers is likely to be affected by the rate at which Japanese producers are able to shift their production from export led to transplant production. On the issue of Japanese exports from the US to the EU, Japanese industry sources were skeptical of Japanese producers' readiness to increase exports from the US to the EU.[65] By restricting Japanese exports only, the agreement allows for the expansion of Japanese FDI in the EU and makes no restrictions on increases of import penetration from third country producers. Third, it may have negative consequences for the competitive process by reducing the number of independent suppliers. Through covert agreements of the type alleged in the UK market preceding the 'Elements of Consensus', market sharing may increase monopoly power of the European producers.

The case study also details the policy development of the BE. It is based around an in-depth analysis of the contributions of the key actors in the policymaking process. It highlights two competing models of competition in car retailing and how the priorities of EU policymakers have been based around the three objectives of controlling Japanese imports, facilitating the most efficient method of car retailing and the completion of the SEM simultaneously. This part was based on interviews and analysis of communications between the actors and internal documentation.

We also drew the implications for and linkages between trade and antitrust. The implications for an *antitrust* analysis are that the usual arguments (as expressed in OECD, 1998a) that antitrust aims to pursue liberalization *per se* may require rethinking. This is because firm strategy that aims to maximize the benefits of an integrated value-chain may need to 'impose' restrictions on competition within the value chain, paradoxically, in order to compete. This is because competition takes a form other than pure price competition. As Porter (1986) suggests, in industries such as complex manufacturing, rather than competing exclusively on cost minimization, firms may compete on their ability to differentiate their product. This may lead to prices that are 'higher' than a traditional economic analysis would regard as maximizing consumer welfare. However, in the case study above, competition in retailing is based on strong branding, significant outlays in advertising and promotion, provision of pre-sales and after-sales service and product differentiation. Given the high sunk costs involved in this form of competition, if producers and their retailers were not able to recoup these costs, it is unlikely that they would provide these services. This reality is somewhat removed from a simple model of price competition. It is closer to Porter (1986) and the need for differentiation as a source of competitive advantage and non-price competition. The implications for antitrust is that policymakers should not slavishly stick to approaches based on perfect competition or contestability.

A similar argument can be used for *trade policy*. In complex manufacturing sectors (and in cars in particular) international trade is not purely determined by country-cost differences (as in the case of natural resource based industries). Several other factors determine the nature of competition and competitive advantage of firms. These include the overall co-ordination of a complex, international value chain and the cost minimization within the value-chain; the ability to innovate and the capacity for branding and marketing. All of these factors lead to an imperfectly competitive or oligopolistic market structure that is dominated by large, multinational producers. As static trade theories are based on a perfectly competitive model, it is unlikely that the predictions of these models will able to offer unambiguous insights into the nature of trade and investment in complex manufacturing. Thus for trade policy, there may be arguments for governments to not pursue trade liberalization *per se*. This is for a number of reasons. First, as trade is determined largely by the strategy of firms, it is not the location of these firms that determines trade but the how the firm's strategy is carried out (Porter 1986).

Second, complex manufacturing sectors generate market externalities or 'spillovers' in production thus as Tyson (1992) and others suggest these spillovers can be captured through trade policies other than pure trade liberalization. Third, as production is determined by MNEs, the ability for nations to attract their production suggests that restrictive trade policies allied to judicious investment attraction policies may allow governments to capture the benefits of production located in their country. Thus in the car industry, the arrival of Japanese assemblers brought with them technical and innovative know-how which has transformed the parts supply chain and the managerial strategy in the countries where they have located. It is also very important to note that there is evidence of traditional negative impacts of a VER in this sector. In particular, interviews with MITI suggest that in order for the EU-Japan agreement to work, the 'forecasts' for Japanese imports require *de minimis*, discussions between Japanese government and the Japanese car producers. It is likely that these discussions will be based on political factors as much as commercial considerations. Potentially, the 'forecasts' may be based on discussions between the firms themselves in which case the anti-competitive effects of inter-firm market sharing may be considerable.

Thus, the *interaction of trade and antitrust* is somewhat more complicated than a story based on mutually reinforcing liberalization of trade and antitrust. From the case study, the following points emerge. First, the EU SEM is unlikely to function as intended if the EU-Japan VER is effectively a set of national restrictions. This is because intra-EU competition disciplines have to be compromised to make the trade agreement work – this is the clear statement of the EU Commission in justifying the renewal of the BE in 1995. Second, this means that current price differentials between member states on the prices of cars may remain – for economists, the hallmark of a lack of competition and a case for antitrust to investigate but caused by trade policy.[66] Third, the necessity for the maintenance of trade barriers has encouraged firm-firm co-ordination (e.g. the SMMT-JAMA). In certain cases, these industry-to-industry agreements to restrict competition have been given tacit blessing by national governments (e.g. SMMT-JAMA and *Asia Motors*). Fourth, the segmentation of the EU market may facilitate collusion of imports between Japanese manufacturers in Japan i.e. which firms get which share of the total quota of the EU market? Fifth, by encouraging FDI through trade restrictions (wittingly or unwittingly), Japanese assemblers' requirements for high quality parts suppliers may in the short term induce parts trade from Japan and in the medium term, may encourage the arrival of Japanese parts suppliers in the EU. In the long term, it will certainly require west European parts suppliers to achieve levels of JIT performance of their Japanese counterparts. Of course this latter point may be viewed as positive for national governments as it encourages structural adjustment in the sector through the arrival of managerial and production 'best practice'.

If trade occurs in a world of finite economic gains i.e. trade is not a positive-sum game (as the literature on imperfect competition and international trade suggests) then it is necessary to tackle the issue of the unilateral v. multilateral interest. In the classic case outlined in chapter 3, there is close to unambiguous support for complimentary trade and antitrust based on liberalization as there are few grounds to support an externality argument. However, where it is possible for nation states to gain economic benefits of production from MNEs, then there is the possibility that nations will launch upon a process of 'beggar thy neighbour' strategic trade policy as nations compete with each other for MNE patronage. As 'System Friction' intensifies with 'Deep Integration', derogations on the application of competition rules in one jurisdiction (designed to capture certain externalities such as R&D) can have negative spillover effects on other nations inevitably leading to conflict.

Postscript: Technological Change and Pressures for Change: The Euro, Internet Sales and New Diagnostic Systems

The current BE expires in 2002 and the EU Commission has launched a new consultation with industry, consumers and 'independent' experts.[67] DG Competition asked a consultancy Autopolis, comprised of former industry managers, to compile a study on the impact of the 1995 BE.[68] While the EU Commission publicly states that it no way have the findings of this report been adopted in DG Competition's re-evaluation, the report notes three important technological changes to car distribution.[69]

First, the introduction of the Euro in the EU has created greater price transparency, allowing consumers to shop across the EU for the best deals. This also dismantles one of ACEA/CECRA's central arguments that the single biggest anti-competitive feature of the car market in the EU is the absence of a single currency. Second, the use of Internet technology has facilitated direct sales to consumers undermining the service-sales dealership relationship. Third, and something that runs counter to the technological forces for liberalization, is the increasing use of in-car diagnostic systems that require higher degrees of repair and servicing expertise and contain components that can only be sold by the car manufacturers.[70] According to Autopolis, the introduction of these systems further enhances the need for SED and while the need for SED is not inherent in car distribution, continued technological advances of this type will encourage SED.[71]

Unsurprisingly ACEA has called for a full and unchanged renewal of the 1995 BE. In response to a questionnaire sent by DG Competition to interested parties, ACEA and CECRA produced a 30–page document reiterating the need for SED.[72]

If the central proposition of this paper is correct: that technocratic issues and transnational solutions hold considerable sway with the EU Commission, it is likely that DG Competition will either refuse to renew the BE or significantly liberalize it as the technological weight of evidence on the need for SED is increasingly against the wishes of ACEA/CECRA. The fact that Autopolis is prepared to suggest that the SED link in distribution is 'unnatural' further weakens the ACEA/CECRA position.

Notes

1   This is similar to Dunning's OLI paradigm but an important aspect for this book is analysing the changes in 'O', 'L' and 'I'.
2   This is evidenced by the UK Labour government to offer a £150 million subsidy to BMW/Rover to maintain production at Longbridge.
3   See Doz (1986) for a discussion of the myriad ways in which governments have attempted to influence the location of multinational production.
4   At this stage, it is worth pointing out that this argument misses a fundamental issue: in whose interest is the capturing of externalities favouring? If all domestic authorities pursued this approach, who would gain? Wouldn't nations be locked in a zero-sum gain with authorities around the world counteracting each other's policies? What should be the balance between the unilateral and the multilateral interest? This argument will be pursued below in chapter 5 but for now, it is worth pointing out that Reich (1991), Tyson (1992), Zysman and Tyson (1983), Thurow (1993) have unambiguous conclusions:

nation-states should attempt to capture these benefits unilaterally as a multilateral framework is unlikely to work and be sustainable. This has engendered opposition among those who defend the multilateral system (Krugman, 1996, Bhagwati and Patrick, 1991).

5   Exogenous to the policy changes, there appear to be a series of important changes in the economics of car distribution itself such as the shift towards electronic ordering, just-in-time servicing and sales and inventory minimization. These changes may, in the final analysis, have a greater effect on the nature of car distribution, intensity of competition and the role of imports.

6   Anderson Consulting has produced several cross-national 'lean manufacturing' surveys. They have found that Japanese based production facilities are still the most 'lean'. However, where Japanese manufactures have set up production facilities as in the UK, these plants have begun to challenge their Japanese counterparts.

7   ...and should the suppliers arrive early, they will be required to pay punitive parking rates for their vehicle as it waits to unload its supply of parts.

8   In fact, German producers hired an additional 46,000 workers in the 1980s.

9   VW closed its plant in the US for example. op cit. 133.

10 While some of the decline in exports may be due to FDI production in the foreign market, another important aspect is that the emergence of East Asian suppliers posed a significant competitive threat to the West European producers and have captured market share from the latter.

11 Ibid. Table 15.2, p. 309.

12 Ibid.

13 For example, differences in insurance and registration rules and the existence of the BE. See Holmes and Smith (1995) and Bourgeois and Demaret (1995).

14 BEUC alleged that the UK government had permitted the SMMT to organize an illicit market sharing agreement with JAMA that amounted to an 11 percent quota. Moreover, BEUC claimed that the EU Commission had not sought to eliminate the agreement in contravention of EU single market rules. This claim was supported by an interview conducted with a member of Toyota's legal department in Japan.

15 See Case T 37/92, Judgment of the Court of First Instance May 18 1994 on the SMMT-JAMA agreement that allegedly restricted the export of Japanese cars to the UK to 11 percent of total car sales.

16 Thus the Chrysler-Daimler merger will allow the new entity to reduce costs of marketing and distribution by pooling costs and consolidating their distribution networks in the US and European markets.

17 Western Europe includes EU + Iceland + Norway + Switzerland (incl. Liechtenstein).

18 A point made by European industry representatives and their Japanese counterparts as well as a senior administrator in MITI.

19 The agreement breaks major ground in establishing a prohibition against so-called 'grey area' measures, and in setting a 'sunset clause' on all safeguard actions. The agreement stipulates that a member shall not seek, take or maintain any voluntary export restraints, orderly marketing arrangements or any other similar measures on the export or the import side. Any such measure in effect at the time of entry into force of the agreement would be brought into conformity with this agreement, or would have to be phased out within four years after the entry into force of the agreement establishing the WTO. An exception could be made for one specific measure for each importing member, subject to mutual agreement with the directly concerned member, where the phase-out date would be 31 December 1999. (Extract of the Uruguay Round Final Agreement). Source: http://www.wto.org/wto/legal/ursum_wp.htm#lAgreement.

20 It is important to remember that although the EU Commission has overall control of the allocation of quotas, not all member states have restricted imports from Japan.

21 This would allow them to price discriminate and to be unconstrained as to their output decision.
22 See Frazer and Holmes (1995) for a discussion of the role of the 'forecasting' in the agreement and FDI.
23 Note that Smith and Venables' industry simulations were for national VERs. Even if the national quotas were replaced by a supposed 'EU-wide' agreement, Mattoo and Mavroidis (1995) point out that in those markets where the EU-Japan agreement was more restrictive, consumers would lose out more than under the national agreements. Where the EU wide agreement was less restrictive, consumers would gain.
24 This could be especially relevant if from January 2000, the EU Commission sticks to its word and does not seek a new EU-Japan agreement.
25 Examples of these alliances are Rover-Honda, Volvo-Renault-Mitsubishi and VW-Toyota.
26 Yoshihiro Yano, Manager, International Trade Section, JAMA made this point. See 4.4 for a more detailed discussion of the points made by JAMA.
27 Riazburo Nezu, MITI and Eugene Tabor, TMMUS.
28 Yoshihiro Yano, JAMA.
29 With the sudden recession in East Asia in 1998, the US administration and the EU Commission have argued over which markets should absorb the excess capacity from these countries. There have been fears expressed that there may be increased pressures for anti-dumping measures as west European and US firms struggle to compete with lower cost supplies from East Asia.
30 ACEA, L'Association de Constructeurs Europeens d'Automobile, is the latest variant of the European car manufacturer's lobby.
31 CECRA is the European Committee for Motor Trades and Repairs.
32 BEUC is the Bureau Européen des Unions de Consommateurs.
33 European Automobile Manufacturers Association (ACEA), *Automotive Dealer Agreement Block Exemption: Request for Renewal*, July 1993, Brussels. ACEA stated that the 1985 block exemption has actually contributed to the achievement of the Single European Market by contributing to the free circulation of goods.
34 Malcolm Harbour, Director, International Car Distribution Programme (ICDP).
35 Ibid. p. 7.
36 European Committee for Motor Trades and Repairs (CECRA) (1993), *Submission for the Renewal of EEC Regulation 123/85 (The Block Exemption Regulation Applying to Motor Distribution Agreements in the European Community)*, CECRA 93 1820/RS/CD. Brussels, 1993. para. 8.3, p. 7.
37 Ibid., p. 8.
38 Letter to Chairman of UK Ford Dealer Associations, February 14 1994.
39 The SMMT and UK Ford Dealers Association.
40 ACEA, *Automobile Distribution in Europe – The European Automobile Industry's Position: Renewal for Another 10 Years*, Brussels, April 1994.
41 UK Ford Dealer Groups.
42 Interestingly, ACEA made it known to UK dealers that they would be prepared to drop the direct sales issue if it would have avoided controversy.
43 Bureau Européen des Unions de Consommateurs, *Regulation No 123/85: Summary of BEUC Position, BEUC/3/94*, Brussels, January 1994. p. 3.
44 Ibid.
45 Ibid. p. 5.
46 Ibid. p. 10.
47 Recent changes in the nature of car retailing may make a significant impact on the question of price differentials. The ability of consumers to purchase cars on the internet has the potential to undermine the entire system of dealerships as it is impossible to allocate territorial exclusivity on the internet. If SED is a cause of price differentials then

if internet purchases in creases, it should be reasonable to expect price differentials to fall. If however the cause of price differentials is related factors other than the SED system, then the internet, by undermining SED, is unlikely to have a manifest impact.

48 Commission of the European Communities Communication to the Council (94/C 379/10)

49 Commission Regulation (EC) No 1475/95, 28.6.95 recital 4.

50 The use of the phrase 'objective reasons' is not defined by the EU Commission suggesting that in the instance of a conflict between a dealer and manufacturer, there could be lengthy and expensive litigation!

51 Complaint from Cesbron of November 18 1985 and complaint from Cesbron, Asia Motor, Monin Automobiles and EAS of November 29 1988.

52 Complaint from Somaco of June 5 1990.

53 Order of 23/05/1990, Asia Motor France / Commission (Rep.1990, p.I-2181).

54 Letter from Peter Farley, Chief Legal Advisor SMMT to Richard Wright, DG III, EU Commission, July 14 1994. Crucially, it was confirmed in a confidential interview with a Japanese industry source that there had indeed been an agreement in force between SMMT and JAMA that restricted imports to 11% as alleged by BEUC.

55 Case T-37/97, p. II-17, para. 59.

56 Case T-37/92, p. II-20, para. 75.

57 Interview with Ursula Pachl, Chief Legal Advisor, BEUC.

58 OJ 1985 C 17, p. 4, section 1(3) and section 30, p. 37 respectively.

59 Case IV/35.733–VW, OJ L 124/60, p. 64, 28.1.98.

60 Ibid. p. 69.

61 Ibid. p. 72.

62 Commission of the European Communities, (1992), p. 168.

63 EC Commission Communication to the Council (94/C 379/10).

64 In a recent speech at EBS London, Karel van Miert made it clear that the SEM must take priority over a BE where the activities of firms, operating under the BE, threatened the rights of EU consumers to make cross-border purchases. In this speech, he also hinted that there may be further investigations in process in addition to the recent VW/Audi decision.

65 Yoshihiro Yano, JAMA.

66 With the introduction of the Euro price transparency will increase. One of the central claims of the car producers was that price differentials were caused in part by the absence of a single currency.

67 Report on the evaluation of Regulation (EC) No 1475/95 on the application of Article 85(3) [now 81(3)] of the Treaty to certain categories of motor vehicle distribution and servicing agreements.

68 'The Natural Link Between Sales and Service', Autopolis, November 2000.

69 This statement is actually rather strange. If the EU Commission asks consultants to write reports, it is clearly seeking the opinions of outside experts in order to inform its own policymaking.

70 In this case, car manufacturers will be reluctant to sell them on the open market to independent garages, preferring to offer them to their exclusive service centers.

71 This is an important claim that SED is not a 'natural' aspect of car distribution as it undermines ACEA/CECRA's central arguments for SED.

72 The document entitled: 'ACEA's Position Paper Regarding the European Commission's Questionnaire on the Application of the Automotive Block Exemption' was backed in a joint ACEA/CECRA press release of October 25, 2000. Of course BEUC produced a paper contrary to ACEA's position earlier in January 2000.

Chapter 5

Trade, Antitrust and Extraterritoriality

Introduction

In the previous two chapters we examined the relationship between trade and competition policy in the context of natural resource and complex manufacturing sectors. In this chapter, we take a slightly different approach by focusing on a specific instance of a transnational merger proposal between General Electric and Honeywell, both US companies involved in avionics. The case has been described recently as an example of 'monopoly leverage'[1] whereby monopolists or quasi monopoly firms in a given sector seek to bundle services together to end-users.[2] The case itself is interesting for three reasons. First, it highlights how differing models of antitrust policy and enforcement can cause 'System Friction' in the international trading system. Second, the relationship between product and service bundling creates dilemmas for antitrust policy – should policymakers seek to protect competitors in order to maintain market contestability or should they focus on the efficiency-related consumer benefits that bundling offers? Third, the case examines an important case of the dangers of extraterritorial application of antitrust policy and the potential harm to the multilateral system.

In July 2001, the EU Commission vetoed the world's largest proposed industrial merger between General Electric (GE) and Honeywell. It failed because of conflicts between the US and European Union (EU) and their differing analyses of merger control. In October 2000, GE and Honeywell announced a merger worth \$42bn to bring the world's largest jet engine manufacturer, GE, together with, Honeywell, the leading company in the world for avionics technology. After having received rapid regulatory approval from the US Department of Justice (US DOJ), GE senior executives expected an equally rapid approval from the EU Commission Competition Authorities (DG Competition). However, DG Competition, headed by EU Competition Commissioner, Mario Monti, requested more time to consider the merger. After several months of investigation, they rejected it on the grounds that it would be anticompetitive.

DG Competition argued that as the merger between two US companies could have an impact on the EU market, GE and Honeywell would need to get permission from the EU for the merger to take place. An ensuing analysis argued that the proposed merger would have an anticompetitive impact on the EU Single Market. As GE CEO Jack Welch stated, 'This shows you are never too old to be surprised'.[3] As a leading CEO of one of the world's biggest companies, Welch had never been confronted with this kind of problem before. Unsurprisingly, the decision by the EU to place severe obstacles in the way of the merger caused political consternation in the US.[4]

While DG Competition contended that their decision was based purely on technical grounds and grounded in a detailed analysis of competition in the industry and the impact the merger would have, this is only part of the story of the emerging conflict. The conflict itself was related to institutional, conceptual and cultural differences between the US DOJ and DG Competition.

It has been argued that with increasing interdependence of markets in the world economy and the increasing scale of global business operations, jurisdictional conflicts over antitrust policy would likely increase in the future.[5] Furthermore, in the absence of international cooperation over antitrust policy, this could lead to the extraterritorial application of domestic laws to regulate transnational business activity. The GE/Honeywell merger case is arguably the result of this. Furthermore, this merger refusal was the first ever by DG Competition to involve two US companies who had already secured authorization from the US DOJ.

Given the importance of this outcome, this chapter seeks to address further the issues related to international antitrust policy in the light of the ruling. The GE/Honeywell merger case is the main empirical focus of our paper. Arguably, while the apparently failed merger has serious strategic implications for the companies involved, this case may force policymakers to consider the increasingly urgent need for cooperation in the area of global mergers and antitrust policy more generally.

The chapter is organized as follows. In the second part, we offer an historical, case overview of the extraterritorial application of antitrust policy. Our third section offers a detailed analysis of the GE/Honeywell case. We argue that the conflict is related to three issues. First, there is a different conceptual importance placed on the key stakeholders in a merger control analysis when we compare US and EU approaches. Second, sharp cultural differences in the weight attached to the role of regulators in the US and EU emerged in the merger investigation of this case. Third, EU regulators are hamstrung by the nature of institutions and procedures that give them little ex-post control of mergers. A result of this is that extraterritorial application of competition laws cannot be ruled out. This has the potential for a 'tit-for-tat' process that could undermine the multilateral trading system based around the emerging WTO Millennium Round proposals. The fourth section argues that there is the potential for an emerging gulf in the antitrust emphasis of the US and EU. A fifth part is devoted to evaluating the public policymaking implications of this case. Lastly, there is also a concluding section, summarizing our findings.

An Historical Anatomy of Extraterritoriality and Antitrust

In the absence of co-operation between states, the resort to extraterritorial application of competition laws cannot be ruled out (Akbar 1999a, Schoenbaum 1996). In particular, where states find that the effect of trade and competition policies in one jurisdiction spill over into their own, the possibility of extraterritorial application increases substantially. Indeed in recent years, the international system has witnessed an increased of extraterritorial application of domestic competition laws by both the US and EU. Of course, both the US and EU are substantial components of the world economy. Any increase in extraterritorial application by these two regions may have a significant impact on the multilateral trading system.

The US and the Sherman Act

As early as 1909, the first major ruling on the extent to which the US Sherman Act had extraterritorial jurisdiction was enunciated in the American Banana Co. v. United Fruit Co. case.[6] The American Banana Company brought an action against the United Fruit Company alleging conspiracy with Costa Rican militia to monopolize production and exportation of bananas from Central America to the United States. In this case, the US court ruled that the Sherman Act had no jurisdiction over activities occurring outside US territory Justice Holmes noted that: 'The general and almost universal rule is that the character of an act as lawful or unlawful must be determined wholly by the law of the country where the act is done'.[7]

Furthermore, the court interpreted US antitrust law 'as intended to be confined in its operation and effects to the territorial limits over which the lawmaker has general and legitimate power'.[8] The clear implication of this ruling is that there are clear limits to extraterritoriality in US antitrust law. This narrow interpretation was to be extremely short-lived. It was widened less than two decades later, in United States v. Sisal Sales Corp.[9] In this case, US companies allegedly conspired with their Mexican counterparts to monopolize the importation of sisal (which is used to make rope). The court ruled that 'here we have a contract, combination and conspiracy entered into by parties within the United States and made effective by acts done therein'.[10] The key aspect of this ruling was that because the anti-competitive acts occurred in the US, foreign firms could be prosecuted. Thus this was extraterritorial to the extent that foreign firms were prosecuted but not to the extent that the alleged infringements of US laws occurred outside of the US.

The most significant step in the extraterritorial direction taken by the US government was when it set an important extraterritorial precedent in the Alcoa[11] judgment as early as in 1945. In Alcoa, foreign defendants were accused of setting up an illegal international aluminium cartel outside the US. In this case, it was recognized that conduct engaged abroad could be found to contravene US antitrust laws if it was intended to affect US imports and did indeed affect them. This is the famous 'effects doctrine'. The Judge Learned Hand in passing judgment stated that: 'any state may impose liabilities, even upon persons not within its allegiance, for conduct outside its borders that has consequences within its borders which the state reprehends…'.[12] Not surprisingly, the Alcoa judgment was met with dismay abroad. The main criticism came from states that held to the view that, under international public law, the principle of respect for national sovereignty is paramount. This is the concept of international comity that presumes equality of all states in international public law. During a debate in the UK parliament over a proposed blocking statute to protect UK interests against US extraterritorial actions, Charles Fletcher-Cooke MP stated: '[o]nce a court system gets an ideology into its mind to such a degree of fanaticism as one can find in the United States it is no surprise, however deplorable it may be, that it becomes a matter of imperialism overseas'.[13] Further action taken by a number of US trading partners was to introduce blocking statutes.

The watershed for collective action came in the uranium cartel case (see below) where Australia, Canada, South Africa, New Zealand and the UK introduced such laws. Canadian authorities summed up their concerns in their *amicus curae* brief in the Uranium Cartel case: 'The Canadian Government submits that there is no legal basis in international law for the extraterritorial application of United States antitrust laws to the activities of non-United States nationals taken outside the US in accordance with the laws and policies of other countries. Such action by United States courts would constitute a direct challenge to Canadian sovereignty'.[14]

Thus, the first response to US extraterritorial actions was retaliatory unilateral action – as many defenders of the multilateral system fear would occur if extraterritoriality increases in incidence. A response of US authorities to this sense of outrage by its trading partners was the introduction of a balancing element to the effects doctrine: 'jurisdictional rule of reason'. This approach has been viewed as an attempt to reconcile the economic and political interests of the state with the reality that state actions at a domestic level have significant impact on the international economy.[15]

This approach was taken in Timberlane Lumber Co. v. Bank of America National Trust and Savings Association.[16] Six factors that US authorities should take into account were enunciated in this judgment. These included the relative significance to the alleged violation of the conduct within the United States, as compared to the conduct abroad and the relative significance and forseeability of the effects of the conduct on the United States as compared to the effects abroad. These conditions could be interpreted as some form of test with a benefit analysis for the US that takes into account the repercussion of such actions for and costs imposed on other states. Not surprisingly, the jurisidictional rule of reason approach was warmly received by international law scholars and was adopted by several Courts of Appeals. However, the results of the 'effects doctrine' and the rule of reason approach have been the same i.e. that US courts have tipped the balance in favour of extraterritorial application of the Sherman Act. This is because the starting point of the analysis from a US legal point of view is that US law has a priori jurisdiction over activities that harm the US government and its citizens. The 1980s witnessed a remarkable shift of opinions on US extraterritorial action. In a period of ten years, the US authorities swung between active extraterritoriality and greater respect for international comity. In 1982, Congress passed the Foreign Trade Antitrust Improvements Act. This act extended the reach of US antitrust law to conduct which did not involve import commerce directly but which had a direct and predictable effect on US commerce i.e. US exports with third countries.

This move was somewhat tempered in 1988, when the US Department of Justice's (DOJ) Antitrust Enforcement Guidelines for International Operations were subsequently altered towards less emphasis on the 'effects doctrine'. This reflected a more co-operative approach towards disputes of an international nature. However, with the election of the Clinton Administration, they were revised in 1992 and took a more hard-line approach more akin to the original doctrine of Alcoa. The 1992 DOJ guidelines referred to above were further amended to encompass greater scope for extraterritoriality. In the most recent revision in April 1995, the new guidelines state: 'Anti-competitive conduct that affects US domestic or foreign commerce may violate US antitrust laws regardless of where such conduct occurs or the nationalities involved'.[17]

Furthermore, the US DOJ will act on the basis of the following actions. First, the extent to which the enforcement activities of another country with respect to the same persons, including remedies resulting from those activities, may be affected and second, the effectiveness of foreign enforcement as compared with US enforcement action. Several cases of US action in this area are worth mentioning during this period. In Hartford Fire Insurance v. California (1993),[18] the US Supreme Court split 5:4 in favour of permitting nineteen US states to launch antitrust proceedings against certain London and UK based insurers in respect of the terms of liability in insurance policies taken out in the US. Justice Souter, writing for the majority, stated that without doubt, Alcoa's 'effects doctrine' applied in this case and that therefore the district court had jurisdiction in this case. Only in a case of true conflict between national laws, could the US Sherman Act be held back from use. Despite the fact that the UK and Canadian governments protested at the decision arguing that the plaintiffs' complaints were not consistent with UK law, the Supreme Court ruled that comity considerations could not be invoked. The US authorities were only concerned if there was a conflict of law between the US and UK law. In this case, there would not have been any such conflict if the defendants had complied with both the US and UK law simultaneously.

The dissenting opinion of Justice Scalia took a somewhat different view to that of Justice Souter. In Scalia's view, two tests were necessary. First, whether a US District Court has genuine jurisdiction and second whether the Sherman Act actually reached the alleged conduct in the case. Scalia argued that any non-frivolous activity might be heard in a District Court and thus passes the first test. More importantly, the second test involved issues over whether a state has the authority to make its law applicable to persons and activities outside its territory. Crucially, Scalia claimed that, in enacting the Sherman Act, US Congress made no presumption that it should be applicable abroad. Thus, there should be a presumption against extraterritoriality. In United States v. S. C. Johnson Inc. and Bayer AG,[19] US authorities alleged that licensing agreements between Bayer and S. C. Johnson for insecticide ingredients reduced competition in the market for household insecticides in the US. The case was settled out of court with a consent decree barring exclusive licensing and preventing S. C. Johnson from acquiring an exclusive licence for insecticide ingredient from the licenser anywhere in the world for use in the US without prior consent of the DOJ.

United States v. Pilkington plc and Pilkington Holdings Inc.[20] involved violations of US antitrust law by the UK firm Pilkington plc, manufacturers of glass. The basis of US jurisdiction according to the judgment was that a subsidiary of Pilkington plc, called Pilkington Holdings Inc. was doing business in the US along with Pilkington plc. The firms were alleged to have contravened US antitrust law by restraining exports of float glass design and construction services through the imposition of territorial patents through licence agreements. Crucially, Pilkington plc were responsible for the anti-competitive practices and that the agreement was reached in the UK. The companies entered into a consent agreement whereby they agreed not to assert rights to the technology against other US licensees with the intention of preventing other firms exploiting float glass technology. These cases demonstrate willingness on the part of the US government to regulate the conduct of non-US firms whenever US trade interests are at stake.

The case law, legislation and US DOJ directives taken together suggest that the US administration is saying to its trading partners: 'you take effective action or leave it up to us'. This would seem to be in line with the new 'results oriented' approach begun by the Bush (senior) presidency and which has been enthusiastically pursued by the Clinton administration.

The EU and Extraterritoriality

The issue of the legal personality of the EU is crucial to a discussion of extraterritoriality. While the EU is a made up of a group of sovereign states, in a number of policy fields, it acts collectively and thus has a legal personality akin to a state in international public law. For the purposes of the analysis that follows, the EU has competence in antitrust and therefore acts like a state.

In 1964, the EU Commission first asserted extraterritorial jurisdiction of its antitrust. In the Grosfillex case, the Commission reasoned that the 'territorial scope of [competition laws] is determined neither by the domicile of the enterprises nor by … where the agreement is concluded or carried out. On the contrary, the sole and decisive criterion is whether an agreement affects competition within the Common Market or is defined to have this effect'.

This statement is very close to the 'effects doctrine' as stated in Alcoa. The Commission subsequently repeated its claims. In the XIth Report on Antitrust in the EU, it asserted '[t]he Commission was one of the first antitrust authorities to have applied the internal effect theory to foreign companies'. It then went even further in the Aniline Dyes Cartel case where the Commission claimed that '[the] decision is applicable to all undertakings that took part in the concerted practices, whether they were are established within or outside the Common Market'.

In the same year, the Dyestuffs case also involved the EU in extraterritorial waters. The EU argued that British and Swiss members of an international cartel in dyestuffs who sold into the Common Market should be prosecuted under EU competition law. Possibly the most important instance of EU extraterritoriality until very recently was the prosecution of a wood pulp cartel organized outside the EU in 1988. In the Wood Pulp case, the EU Commission found that non-EU producers of wood pulp had engaged in concerted actions regarding the prices charged through EU-based subsidiaries to paper makers in the EU. They had set up a horizontal price-fixing agreement whereby they exchanged price information. The Commission imposed heavy fines on the firms involved.

Eighteen Finnish, Canadian and US producers, along with two trade associations, appealed by contending that the Commission lacked jurisdiction in this case. This view was most strongly supported by the United Kingdom. Given the previous case law, the ECJ ruled against the appeal on the same grounds as enunciated in Dyestuffs. The Court stated that: 'Article 85 of the EEC Treaty applies to restrictive practices which may affect trade between member states even if the undertakings and associations which are party to the restrictive practices are established or have their headquarters outside the Community, and even if the restrictive practices in question also affect markets outside the EEC'.

After Wood Pulp, the EU Commission handed down two further extraterritorial decisions. Both cases involved the chemical industry. In PVC, which concerned an agreement by producers supplying bulk thermoplastic PVC in the EU to fix prices and set target quotas, the Commission asserted that: '[I]n so far as the agreements were implemented inside the Community', the EU had jurisdiction. In the second instance, the Commission prosecuted an LdPE (low-density polyethylene) cartel organized along similar lines to the PVC case above. In LdPE, the Commission argued that although Repsol, the Spanish company involved had become an EU based firm, subsequent to Spanish accession to the EU, it would take a retroactive view. It asserted that Repsol's actions before accession affected intra-EU commerce and therefore at that time, EU competition rules applied to it.

One of the central concerns facing EU policymakers has been over the issue of mergers and acquisitions. With the removal of barriers to trade and investment within the EU, focus on how the major firms across industries would respond to the new market opportunities increased. In particular, a merger code was seen as an important complement to maintaining contestability in the Single Market. Given that the EU agreed to keep the Single Market as open as possible to non-EU firms, the issue of takeover activity involving non-EU firms became an increasingly controversial issue. The EU Merger Regulation of 1990 applies to any merger with a 'Community Dimension' defined according to a turnover threshold. If a merger exceeds 250 million Euros, then the EU has the right to intervene. Any such merger proposal must be notified to the Commission in advance of any final agreement. This process could involve divestiture if the EU decides that a merger is to be blocked.

Two interesting cases, both involving the aerospace industry, have involved direct EU intervention in attempted transnational mergers. The first case was the DeHavilland take-over. Alesina of Italy and Aerospatiale of France wished to acquire DeHavilland, a Canadian producer of small-bodied commuter aircraft. Although, in terms of the global market the merger would be relatively small, the EU Commission ruled that the merger would create an overly concentrated market within the EU for this type of aircraft and they subsequently blocked the proposal. The Canadian authorities were not consulted in advance of the EU decision. The Canadian government may have regarded the merger as a sensible restructuring for an ailing firm. Nor were the national authorities in France and Italy consulted.

A recent case occurred over the merger between McDonnell-Douglas and Boeing, two of the world's top three aerospace firms. Airbus, Europe's leading aerospace firm is in direct competition with both Boeing and McDonnell-Douglas in the wide-bodied aircraft market.

It was widely accepted in the US that McDonnell-Douglas was in need of financial restructuring since a large number of its contracts were based on military production that have been reduced following the end of Cold War hostilities. A rescue package by Boeing would on paper seem to be the best solution for McDonnell-Douglas. However, such a merger would have a significant 'Community Dimension', not just in the sense that it would exceed the turnover threshold but also because Airbus would be faced with an even larger competitor. The EU Commission ruled that it would not in principle accept the merger. The Commissioner for Antitrust at the time, Karel van Miert, argued that the merger would create a dominant position for Boeing in the market largely due its long run supply contracts with its part suppliers. Van Miert would only agree to the merger if Boeing could guarantee fair access to parts suppliers for other aerospace companies i.e. Airbus.

Boeing agreed in principle to the EU Commission's demands. Before Boeing's agreement, there was a belief that this strategically vital industry would have ensured that the US government would intervene on Boeing's behalf. Interestingly, the US government declined to intervene arguing that a reasonable settlement between Boeing and the EU Commission was its first priority. Having examined the historical development of extraterritoriality, the chapter now turns to our central case of extraterritoriality: the GE-Honeywell merger.

The GE-Honeywell Merger: Welch's Swansong or Waterloo?

'This is the most exciting day in the 118–year history of GE'. On October 23, 2000, Jack Welch, Chairman and CEO of GE announced plans to implement the largest-ever-industrial merger between GE and Honeywell worth \$42 billion. At the GE press conference he said: 'I'm the one that's putting my neck on the line. If you need a vote of confidence from anybody, I'm the one that's putting 20 years on the line'.[21] Allegedly, the merger agreement was put together in three days. Moreover, Welch announced the merger without consulting with GE's lawyers in Europe at Shearman & Sterling and Clifford Chance.[22] Presciently, Welch identified that although there was a 90 percent overlap between GE and Honeywell in several areas of their activities, they did not produce similar products. He added: 'That's not a speech for the antitrust people. That's a fact'.[23]

It was not the first time that DG Competition had been involved in a merger notification concerning two American firms. In fact, it allowed the merger of Allied Signal and Honeywell to go ahead only after considerable concessions from the parties were offered.[24]

As part of the process of completing the merger, GE and Honeywell's legal staff had to notify relevant competition and merger authorities around the world. Of these, the most important were the US DOJ, their Canadian counterparts and DG Competition of the EU. Both the US DOJ and Canadian authorities agreed to the merger.[25] In the final announcement from the US DOJ, they made no issue of the relationship between GE's position in the large aerospace jet engine sector and Honeywell's pre-eminent place in the avionics business.[26] At a meeting with GE staff and DG Competition on February 26, the latter insisted however on a full-scale in-depth study of the merger. It gave itself until July 14 2001 to arrive at a final ruling. Given that GE is the world's largest producer of jet engines, in its initial research and interviews with industry participants, the EU Commission expressed concern about the nature of the relationship between Honeywell and GE and how that would affect the world market for jet engines. In particular, the DG Competition claimed that GE possessed as much as 62 percent of the large commercial jet engine market compared with only 15 percent and 22 percent for their nearest rivals, Pratt and Whitney and Rolls Royce. GE could use its merger with Honeywell, to secure further market share and undermine the position of its rivals, DG Competition alleged. Their arguments were based on the fact that Honeywell's key service was avionics.

DG Competition suggested that the remedy would be for Honeywell to sell its regional jet engines business, where the newly merged entity would have a 90 percent market share.[27] A second anti-competitive problem with the merger was the role played by Gecas, GE's aircraft finance and leasing arm. DG Competition stated: 'Gecas is therefore used by GE to influence the outcome of airlines' airframe purchasing decisions and act as a promoter of GE-powered airframes to the detriment of GE's engine manufacturing competitors and eventually results, through the use of disproportionate power, in excluding competing engine sales'.[28] DG Competition feared that the newly merged company would seek to use Gecas to leverage the same power over customers for Honeywell's avionics and other equipment. Thus should a customer buy a GE engine, then GE-Honeywell could 'bundle' avionics and other equipment at a lower price then separate purchases of engine and avionics for the buyer.

This, DG Competition argued, was anti-competitive as it would place GE's competitors at a disadvantage and may force them out of business. This bundling argument was the centerpiece of DG Competition's arguments against the merger. It had been used by the US DOJ in their case against Microsoft Corp. and their use of Internet Explorer in the Windows operating system.[29]

The remedy suggested by DG Competition was for GE to divest some its ownership of Gecas while retaining a minority share in the company. In response, GE's offers were manifold amounting to $2.2 billion. First, GE offered to sell Honeywell's regional jet engine business as requested by DG Competition. Second, it would furthermore sell its engines starters business and a sale of its share in a marine gas turbines joint venture.[30] Third, in order to respond to DG Competition's concerns over Gecas, GE offered to set up separate accounts and management of Gecas in addition to an independent board of directors for Gecas.[31] GE responded by pointing out that Gecas only had 10 percent of the market to which DG Competition was referring and therefore did not pose an anti-competitive threat after the merger. Indeed, the views of two of GE's potentially largest customers were skeptical about DG Competition's arguments. Noel Forgeard, CEO of Airbus stated that his company had no objections to the merger as his company had negotiated serious safeguards with GE. By the same token, Harry Stonecipher, Vice-Chairman of Boeing categorically claimed that the merger is '… a short conversation with me because from the get-go, the Boeing Company said it doesn't have any problems with the merger'.[32] Mauricio Boatel, Chairman of Brazilian aircraft manufacturer Embraer described the deal in March as 'fantastic'.[33] By contrast, Lufthansa representatives asked to give evidence to DG Competition's merger hearing requested GE and Honeywell representatives to leave the room before they would give evidence.[34]

The remedy suggested by DG Competition would have arguably undermined the rationale for the merger in the first place. GE insisted that the divestitures were an attempt to eliminate Honeywell's aerospace business thus nullifying the merger. In reply, DG Competition argued that GE was selling only those parts of Honeywell that would not be viable without the rest of the business.[35]

Following a meeting on June 13 between Jack Welch and senior DG Competition officials, the following day, GE and Honeywell submitted a final package of measures they were prepared to make.[36] Crucially, they were not prepared to meet the terms on Gecas as demanded by DG Competition. Welch commented: 'Jeff Immelt and I wanted to complete the transaction but we have always said there is a point at which we wouldn't do the deal. The Commission's [DG Competition] extraordinary demands are far beyond that point. In this case, the European regulator's demands exceeded anything I or our European advisers imagined, and differed sharply from antitrust counterparts in the US and Canada'.[37] GE did not formally withdraw its merger bid and instead asked Honeywell to decide. Honeywell refused to withdraw the bid initially. As late as the last week in June, Honeywell wrote to GE offering to reduce the merger price but GE refused. At the end of June, the Honeywell CEO, Michael Bonsignore resigned to be replaced, ironically, by former GE Executive Larry Bossidy. Finally, in a 155–page ruling, DG Competition refused on July 3 against the merger. The key obstacle was the issue of 'bundling' on which GE was unprepared to waver.

Jack Welch, in an interview, stated: 'It hasn't been antitrust in the US for 75 years and it hasn't really been antitrust anywhere'.[38] It appeared that in Mario Monti and his team at DG Competition, Jack Welch, 'had finally met his match'.[39]

The strategic implications for Honeywell, and to a lesser degree for GE, are quite far reaching. First Honeywell's new leadership could consider suing GE for failure to pursue the merger effectively by taking all reasonable steps.[40] Second, the more pressing question of whether it seeks to revive its merger with United Technologies, which it rejected in the light of GE's original offer, will need to be addressed. This merger itself could remain in doubt because of fears that DG Competition may need to consider that merger too. It could remain independent and seek to reduce its cost base by selling off parts of the company. Whichever route it chooses, Honeywell in investing significant resources into the merger process will need to time to regroup. Within days of becoming CEO, Bossidy has set proposals to restructure Honeywell in motion. The new structure will reduce Honeywell from its current eight divisions to four.[41]

GE's situation is clearly less troublesome. In some senses, the failed merger reflects more on Jack Welch's leadership of the process rather than GE itself.[42] Indeed, Jack Welch is unlikely remain as CEO until the end of 2001 as originally planned. GE's share earnings will be affected by the failed merger. The company's owners will have to sacrifice estimated additional earnings of eleven, fourteen and seventeen cents a share in the coming three years.[43] In addition, the relatively imbalanced nature of the company's earnings, with over fifty percent coming from GE Capital will not be counterbalanced by this industrial merger. Interestingly, Welch's successor at GE, Jeffrey Immelt had gone on record for the French newspaper Le Monde that the merger proposal had 'virtually zero' chance of regulatory approval.

The Emerging Gulf Between US and EU Attitudes to Antitrust Policy

In 1991, the EU Commission, on behalf of the EU member states, and the US DOJ signed an agreement on co-operation in antitrust enforcement.[44] It was revised in 1998. The agreement calls for notification and co-operation in non-confidential information sharing when both the US and EU authorities have a common interest. While DG Competition stated when they opened the investigation into the GE/ Honeywell merger that they were collaborating with the US DOJ on matters of 'common competition concerns that might require a joint remedial action', the outcomes of the two investigations were dramatically different.[45] The aim of this section is to analyse the causes and consequences of this difference between the respective American and European regulators.

It is not the first time that DG Competition had blocked mergers. Table 5.1 below outlines mergers not authorized by the EU from 1998 to the present day. It has also forced significant concessions before allowing mergers such as the Novartis and AstraZeneca merger.[46] However, the GE/Honeywell case is the first time US companies, having received authorization from the US DOJ, have been refused by DG Competition.[47]

Table 5.1 Mergers Blocked by EU, 1998–2001

Date	Companies
May 1998	Deutsche Telekom and Beta Research
May 1998	Bertelsmann/Kirch/Premiere
September 1999	Airtours/First Choice
March 2000	Volvo/Scania
June 2000	MCI WorldCom/Sprint
Jan 2001	SCA Moinlycke/Metsa Tissue
May 2001	Bertelsmann/EMI

Source: DG Competition, EU Commission

DG Competition's activist approach is in stark contrast to the US DOJ. This is arguably for both philosophical and procedural reasons. While both authorities adopt a rule of reason approach to most antitrust policy statutes, on philosophical grounds, US DOJ views on effective contestability of markets has swung from being skeptical of the ability of markets to maintain contestability without effective regulation towards a laissez-faire attitude.[48] The Microsoft ruling reflected a concern about the absence of competition in the market. The GE ruling suggested that the US DOJ were less concerned about contestability. The EU by contrast, has largely favored a more activist approach. This arguably is due to the nature of European integration and the relative 'youth' of the EU Antitrust policy authorities. Moreover, Europeans have always been less convinced of laissez-faire approaches to understanding market contestability.

Procedural and institutional issues are also very important. First, the degree of ex-post control of mergers that the US DOJ has is considerably greater than that of DG Competition. This includes the possibility of allowing private cases to be accepted offering treble damages for successful suits in the US.[49] This lack of control means that DG Competition is likely to be more wary of future anti-competitive actions of newly merged companies than the US DOJ. It certainly engenders a more thorough working through of all of the facts of the case before it delivers a decision. As Commissioner Monti stated at a EU Press Conference to announce the decision to block the merger: 'We have a one-shot possibility to approve or block a merger'.[50]

Second, while it is possible for companies to appeal a decision by DG Competition at the European Court of Justice (ECJ), the slow-moving nature of the EU institutions means that it is unlikely that they would receive an answer quickly enough to make the merger worthwhile. For example, Airtours' proposed takeover of First Choice Holidays was blocked by DG Competition. After two years, Airtours finally won an appeal against the decision to block the merger. The problem of course, is that it came far too late for Airtours who was forced to change its strategy in the light of the first rejection.[51] By contrast, the relative speed with which the judicial process in the US operates allows companies to seek appeal if they are not satisfied with a US DOJ ruling.[52]

In terms of resources compared with the workload facing DG Competition, it is short staffed.[53] When the EU's Merger Taskforce was set up in 1990, it was staffed with 47 experts dealing with approximately sixty cases per year. While having doubled staffing resources, the Taskforce is required to consider over 345 cases per year currently.[54] This means that decisions take longer and policymakers that are working on them tend to be more thorough because they know that changes to the decision following appeal could take a long time to implement given the backlog of cases already facing the Merger Taskforce of DG Competition.

A problem, succinctly pointed out by Welch himself, is that there is a lack of independent assessment of DG Competition decisions: in effect, it is jury and judge.[55] This means that the team carrying out the analysis handles the final judgment. If the analysts form strong opinions early on in the case, this may mean that may be less than objective when they deliver the final judgment. US DOJ officials cannot block a merger without gaining permission from an independent judge.

Three other factors could be considered in explaining the different approaches taken by European and US authorities, First, is the plausible issue of cultural differences between US and European regulators. More specifically, DG Competition regulators focus heavily on due process and issues of legal fairness whereas, arguably, the US DOJ has a results-oriented approach and economic theory is predominant over legal issues. Furthermore, the corporate culture of GE, based around the strong results-based orientation of Jack Welch may have misunderstood the institutional culture of DG Competition.[56] This is certainly not the first case of a significant cultural understanding gap between societies. Recent US-EU disputes over agricultural and audiovisual products highlight a significant cultural difference between US and European societies that could plausibly be reflected in the actions of policymakers from these societies.

Second, there could be a hidden industrial policy agenda being pursued by DG Competition. This is because the GE-Honeywell merger may weaken Rolls Royce's position in the world market for jet engines and may make Airbus dependent on a US supplier for its engines and avionics. This could undermine its competitive position with Boeing, who throughout the merger case strongly supported GE.[57] Several US politicians at senior levels have claimed this. US Treasury Secretary, claimed: '[w] hat the EU is doing is a far reach from looking at questions that are directly of interest to the European Union'.[58] Senior Republican Senator, Phil Gramm claimed: 'my concern is that we don't have bad policies imposed by us as

Europeans trying to protect themselves from competition'.[59] This view was echoed by Democrat Senator Ernest Hollings when he claimed that the EU was 'using its merger review process as a tool to promote and protect European industry at the expense of US competitors'.[60]

However, at least two factors mitigate this claim. Historically, DG Competition has largely resisted attempts by member states and by DG Industry (the industrial policy department of the EU Commission) to pursue activist industrial policy. In fact, DG Competition has been swift to condemn use of unjustified State Aid and has strongly proposed and encouraged privatization of state-owned industries in the EU. Moreover, in this specific case, the breakdown of opposition to the GE/Honeywell merger did not fall along European versus American lines. For example, Pratt and Whitney also strongly opposed the merger as did Rockwell International, both North American companies. As cited in section 3 of this paper, the CEO of Airbus went on record as supporting the merger proposal.[61]

Third, the US DOJ has been argued by GE and Honeywell to be favoring consumer interests by permitting GE/Honeywell to offer a more comprehensive, lower priced service to them through bundling engines with avionics. By comparison, DG Competition was more concerned with competitor interests by claiming that GE/Honeywell, through its merger, would have the potential to force rivals out of the market through the mechanisms outlined in section 2. Put another way, US DOJ analysis over time has become less concerned with the number of firms in a given industry and more with the conduct of the firms while EU rules emphasize that an EU Single Market needs to have a plurality of players for it to function.[62] US Federal Reserve Chairman Alan Greenspan recently told US Congress when asked about the merger: 'We don't try to protect the competitors. Our focus is solely on the consumer. That's not true in Europe'.[63] US Assistant Attorney General, Charles James stated that while US antitrust policy held that competition rather than competitors was paramount the EU approach 'reflects a significant point of divergence'.[64]

In some senses, the EU approach is also favoring consumer interests. This is because should GE/Honeywell be able to reduce the number of competitors in the industry, given the high fixed costs of entry and exit in aerospace, it would have reduced choice for consumers. Therefore, DG Competition was taking a dynamic view of competition in the sector in the pursuit of the furtherance of competition. The US DOJ, by contrast, was assuming that entry and exit costs did not present a sufficiently high barrier to allow GE/Honeywell to force out competitors. Thus, the issue to focus on would be the lower costs that the merger would provide in the short term. Logically, these lower costs would be passed on to customers in lower prices for engines and avionics. Moreover, Gecas did not have a dominant position in the global aerospace jet engine sector and therefore leveraging possibilities were small for GE. It is interesting to quote DG Competition's statement on the reasons for blocking the merger.

> The combination of the two companies' activities would have resulted in the creation of dominant positions in the markets for the supply of avionics, non-avionics and corporate jet engines, as well as to the strengthening of GE's dominant positions in jet engines for commercial and large regional jets. The dominance would have been created or strengthened as a result of horizontal overlaps in some markets as well as through the

extension of GE's financial power and vertical integration to Honeywell's activities and of the combination of their respective complementary products. Such integration would enable the merged entity to leverage the respective market power of the two companies into the products of one another. This would have the effect of foreclosing competitors thereby eliminating competition in these markets, ultimately affecting adversely product quality, service and consumer prices.[65]

If we strip away the language of antitrust, some of the very claims to anticompetitive conduct were at the heart of the strategic objectives of the merger. Thus, in some respects, the difference in opinion between the US DOJ and DG Competition is reflected in the difference between market power arguments for internalization activities (through merger) of MNEs and those that emphasized the efficiency type arguments of internalization.[66] DG Competition arguments resemble the market power motives whereas the US DOJ view emphasizes the internal efficiency arguments for the merger. This is summed up aptly by Assistant Attorney General James: '[the EU] apparently concluded that a more diversified and thus more competitive GE could somehow disadvantage other market participants'.[67]

It is not possible to evaluate the validity of arguments on either side within the scope of this paper except to recognize these important differences. However, we argue that these differences: institutional, cultural and analytical (philosophical) will become increasingly salient as multinational enterprises (MNEs) seek to defend market positions through extending their existing reach through merger and acquisition. In the past twelve months, DG Competition, in addition to ruling on the GE/Honeywell case, has opened an investigation into several other cases. These include the merger of Brazilian Iron Ore groups and their impact on the EU steel sector prosecuted IMS Health, a US health-information firm for an abuse of a dominant position in Germany, and allowed one European acquisition to proceed and granted a German joint venture authorization.[68] This problem is particularly acute for US MNEs, whereas European MNEs are used to DG Competition's approach given the large number of intra-EU mergers that have taken place in recent years. The next section attempts to consider the implications for international public policymaking and for MNE strategy in the light of this case.

Policymaking Issues

It is necessary to consider the public policy fallout from the failed merger. We argue that policymakers should, and are probably are, becoming more aware that GE/Honeywell is not, and will not remain, an isolated incident. This suggests that deeper cooperation between antitrust policy authorities is necessary. The current investigation into Microsoft's bundling of Media Player into its XP operating system also could raise the possibility of corporate restructuring of a US company by EU authorities. Moreover, the draft proposed remedies being suggested by DG Competition exceed those of the US DOJ and could increase conflict in Transatlantic trade.

In this context, a recent survey examined the question of the relative efficacy and competence of the US DOJ and DG Competition in antitrust cases.[69] The survey argued that based on eight criteria,[70] the US DOJ was ahead of DG Competition. In particular, the US DOJ's strongest area was merger control.[71] For public policymaking, the outcome of the GE/Honeywell case is potentially far-reaching indeed. While it is arguable that the EU has a right to vet mergers that effect the EU Single Market, where that it the relevant market, the GE/Honeywell merger's relevant market is the global aerospace industry i.e. all major regulatory authorities are affected by the merger. While it is not an immutable fact that global mergers will continue, the probability of similar mergers in globally consolidating sectors such as the automotive and chemical industries is likely to strain jurisdictional practices based on the notion of (extra)territoriality.

Indeed, it has been argued that there is a 'governance gap' emerging between the intensification of global competition and the inertia of state-bound antitrust policymaking.[72] Several senior managers of MNEs have expressed the hope that in the light of this case, policymakers will work together to develop new mechanisms that consider transnational policy solutions. Fran Rooney, CEO of Baltimore Technologies, argues: 'the big issue […] is the lack of coordination and different interpretations between regulators. The uncertainty that is emerging now makes it difficult for corporations to fulfill the strategies they have'.[73] Phillipe Camus, Co-CEO of European Aeronautic Defense & Space Co. argues similarly that it is 'a question of appreciation of the situation by two regulatory bodies [each using its own approach] that create a divergence'.[74] Alejandro Rivas-Micoud, CEO of Spanish Telecommunications Company Alo Communicaciones SA is more forthright in his suggestions: 'This [case] highlights the need for the World Trade Organization or some other international organization to deal with antitrust'.[75]

While senior managers may have expressed concern about this situation, it is vital to understand the politics of ICP and in particular the challenge facing state sovereignty from the transfer of antitrust policy to the WTO or OECD. Part of the reason why the Multilateral Agreement on Investment (MIA)[76] proposed by the OECD was rejected was its far-reaching impact on national sovereignty. OECD Member States felt that this would be too great an infringement on their policy autonomy. In a similar way, the failure of the Seattle meeting of the WTO to move further on antitrust policy reflects this concern. We argue however that the difference in the GE/Honeywell case is that it is so high profile in terms of its size and the companies involved that it may force policymakers across the Atlantic at least to consider other ways of resolving this dilemma. The remainder of this section is devoted to considering in what areas greater cooperation could develop within the EU-US relationship. A reading of public statements from the case portrays DG Competition seeking to underplay the differences between them and their US DOJ colleagues. To quote DG Competition in its press release:

> The European Commission and the US Department of Justice have worked in close cooperation during this investigation. It is unfortunate that, in the end, we reached different conclusions, but each authority has to perform its own assessment and the risk of dissenting views, although regrettable can never be totally excluded. This does not mean that one authority is doing a technical analysis and the other pursuing a political goal, as some might pretend, but simply that we might interpret facts differently and forecast the effects of an operation in different ways. The GE/Honeywell case is a rare case where the transatlantic competition authorities have disagreed. I am determined to strengthen our bilateral cooperation in the future to try and reduce this risk further.[77]

Thus, on the surface at least, there is a commitment to enhance co-operation from the EU side. Commissioner Monti's comments on co-operation were echoed by the US DOJ.[78] Above all, co-operation develops from greater mutual understanding. Both the US DOJ and DG Competition have undertaken several regular meetings to build a strong relationship.[79] Indeed, the EU-US antitrust policy relationship is probably the strongest bilateral antitrust relationship in the world. The 1998 agreement on cooperation in the areas of antitrust policy is a good basis for a deepening of the relationship.[80] We argue that co-operation could be enhanced in the following areas.

First, where antitrust policy questions such as transnational merger are likely to lead to two separate investigations, EU and US authorities should agree to hold a joint investigation. This implies changing confidentiality rules but it would allow for joint consideration of a case and reduce the costs and uncertainty to MNEs. A joint investigation would require a meeting of minds on the competition issues in the case. Presumably, both authorities should develop common conceptualizations of competition models and their applicability to specific cases. Co-operation and joint investigation would be likely to force minds on the theoretical and conceptual issues.

Second, broadening the scope of the geographical boundaries of the 'relevant market' in merger cases could also help. Under the current EU Merger Directive,[81] DG Competition is obliged to investigate a merger that has turnover of over $225 million within the EU irrespective of nationality of the firms concerned. This creates a jurisdictional and extraterritorial problem if the merger concerns non-EU companies and other authorities have agreed the merger. If the EU and US could agree common scale of a merger for the purposes of investigation, then this would reduce duplication of effort and clarify the jurisdictional question.

Third, on a practical level, personnel exchange between the US DOJ and DG Competition could enhance further cooperation by breaking down institutional barriers to potential misunderstanding and further build trust between authorities. We believe that these three suggestions will reduce uncertainty for business and begin a process of creating effective international institutions to deal with antitrust policy.

Of course, we are aware that the fundamental issue remains the political veto that could be used to prevent further institutional progress. Democratic systems, by their very nature, tend to reform more slowly than business practices evolve. However, incremental reform can reap significant benefits. One of the best examples of this is the creation of the EU itself. Part of the success of the integration process in Europe has been its emphasis on technocratic policymaking, which has led to comprehensive policy shifts from a national to a supranational level. If a compelling but limited process of technocratic reform could take place between the US and EU authorities, this could improve the current, highly politically charged situation.

Conclusion

When Mario Monti and his Merger Taskforce decided to veto the GE-Honeywell merger, a significant new precedent had been set. For the first time in business history, the EU had thwarted two US corporations in their business strategy even after the US government had agreed to the merger. While historically, the US DOJ had been seen to be the most rigorous enforcers of antitrust, it appeared that the EU Commission was prepared to wield its regulatory power.[82]

This decision has once again brought into sharp focus the 'governance gap' between the strategies of MNEs and the ability of national and regional authorities to regulate the activities of these firms. We have argued that the main reason why DG Competition did not agree with the US DOJ ruling is due to institutional, conceptual and cultural differences. First, DG Competition does not have the same degree of ex-post merger control as the US DOJ therefore making it more cautious in authorizing mergers. This is compounded by resource constraints facing the Merger Taskforce. Second, it is clear that the American and European authorities had different perceptions and 'models' of competition underlying their analysis. The US DOJ looked more at direct cost efficiency gains to consumers whereas DG Competition focused on contestability and the monopoly power that GE-Honeywell could exert on its rivals. Third, in the negotiations between GE and DG Competition, strong cultural differences emerged in the results-oriented approach of Jack Welch and the process-oriented nature of EU decision-making. This is related to a broader difference between US and European attitudes to regulation where regulation is regarded as a 'non-market' issue in the US by many strategists.

We believe that this case highlights the urgent need for progress on the development of de minimis, bilateral institutions for antitrust policy between the US and EU. These institutions should be created incrementally and focus on areas of common concern such as merger notification. The possibility of joint investigation of cases between the US DOJ and DG Competition, once confidentiality issues are dealt with, could help this process. It is unlikely that in the short term, major multilateral agreements could be forged given the political sensitivity of such issues. Having said this, the problems that the current US President is having in gaining authority from Congress to begin the WTO Millennium Round doesn't augur well for the future. Nor does the decision of the Bush Administration to impose trade tariffs on imported steel and the subsequent European response to target industries in Republican states in retaliation.

Notes

1   A comment made by William Kolasky, Head of the DOJ's international antitrust division, cited in 'EU Plans Tough Line on Microsoft', *Financial Times*, May 10 2002.
2   A similar case, referred in footnote 177 is Microsoft's attempts to clear antitrust obstacles for its Windows XP operating system.
3   'The Day The Neutron Got Nuked By Brussels', *The Economist*, June 16 2001.
4   Phil Gramm, US Republican Senator stated on CNBC, the business news television channel part owned by GE. 'It's a very real question what power the EU should have in dealing with two companies that are American companies.' Senators Mike DeWine and Herb Kohl, the top Republican and Democrat on the antitrust subcommittee, said they would make 'further inquiries' into the EU's role. CNBC, June 16 and *Financial Times*, June 17.
5   Yusaf Akbar. 1999. 'The Extraterritorial Dimension of US and EU Competition Law: A Threat to the Multilateral System?' *Australian Journal of International Affairs*, 53 (1): 11 3–126. Yusaf Akbar. 2000. 'The Internationalization of Antitrust: Implications for International Business.' *Thunderbird International Business Review*, (1), Jan.-Feb: 1–25.

6   213 U.S. 347 (1909).
7   Ibid.
8   Ibid.
9   274 U.S. 268 (1927).
10 Ibid.
11 148 F.2d 416 (2d Cir. 1945).
12 Ibid.
13 Quote taken from Kapranos-Huntley (1981).
14 In re Uranium Antitrust Litig., 480 F. Supp. 1138 (N.D. Ill. 1979).
15 An interesting, if somewhat legalistic interpretation of the jurisdictional rule of reason approach is that of Donald Turner. He states that 'a strict territorial test, while it may minimize conflicts, is sufficiently responsive to legitimate national economic interests.' Turner (1985).
16 549 F.2d 597 (9th Cir. 1976).
17 US DOJ Antitrust Enforcement Guidelines for International Operations April 1995 §3.1.
18 113 S. Ct. 2891 (1993).
19 CA No. 94–50249 (N.D. Ill 1994).
20 Civ. No. 94–345 TUC (WDB) (D. Ariz. 1994).
21 'Welch stakes his reputation at GE on Honeywell deal', *Financial Times* October 24 2000.
22 'As Honeywell Deal Goes Awry for GE, Fallout May Be Global', *Wall Street Journal*, June 15 2001.
23 Ibid.
24 Commission Decision of 1.12.1999 C (1999) 4057 Final, Case No Comp/M 1601.
25 The US DOJ did however put pressure on GE to make minor changes to the proposal. The US government were concerned that GE should sell off parts of its two helicopter engine companies as the merger may limit competition in the helicopter engine market – whose principle clients are military. 'US worried over competition in helicopter engine market if Honeywell merger goes ahead', *Financial Times*, March 30 2001.
26 'Justice Department Requires Divestitures in Merger Between General Electric and Honeywell', US DOJ Press Release, May 2 2001.
27 'General Electric Offers More Concessions', *Financial Times*, June 10 2001.
28 'GE to face Brussels call for Gecas separation', *Financial Times*, June 6 2001.
29 Not all analysts agreed with the use of this theory. GE hired Yale Management School Professor Barry Nalebuff, a notable scholar on 'bundling theory', who argued that while this theory may work in mass consumer goods markets, the aerospace jet engine sector was made up of sophisticated buyers and that these buyers would not necessarily rely upon a sole supplier.
30 Op cit. endnote 8.
31 'GE And Honeywell Submit Final Undertakings to European Commission', GE Press Release, June 14 2001.
32 'GE's Standoff Didn't Catch All Boardrooms by Surprise', *Wall Street Journal*, June 18 2001.
33 'How Monty turned a deal into a flight of fancy', *Financial Times*, July 6 2001.
34 'GE plans robust defense at merger hearing', *Financial Times*, May 29 2001.
35 'As Honeywell Deal Goes Awry for GE, Fallout May Be Global', *Wall Street Journal*, June 15 2001.
36 According to media sources, the meeting was attended by Welch, Mario Monti, Enrique Gonzalez-Diaz, head of DG Competition's team on this case, Henrick Schaub, Director-General of DG Competition and Gotz Drautz, head of the Merger Taskforce.
37 'GE sends final proposals to the EU', *Business Wire*, June 14 2001.
38 'How Monty turned a deal into a flight of fancy', *Financial Times*, July 6 2001.

39 'When Neutron Jack was nuked by Brussels', *The Economist*, June 18 2001.
40 'GE and Honeywell Consider a Future Apart', *Financial Times*, July 2 2001.
41 'Honeywell Chief Bossidy Revamps Management', *Financial Times*, July 13 2001.
42 This is especially the case given the nature of Jack Welch's management style.
43 Op cit. 19.
44 'Agreement between the Government of the United States of America & the European Communities on the Application of Positive Comity Principles in the Enforcement of Their Competition Laws. June 4 1998.
45 'Commission opens full investigation into the General Electric/Honeywell merger', EU Commission Press Release, March 1 2001.
46 Case M1806, AstraZeneca and Novartis. Notification with conditions and obligations, July 26 2000.
47 The other case of a US merger being thwarted by the EU was the EMI/Time Warner merger.
48 This is loosely correlated with the Presidency with Republicans favoring laissez-faire and Democrats favoring more activism.
49 'Neutron Jack and the one that got away', *The Economist*, June 21 2001.
50 'EU Officially Blocks GE-Honeywell Deal', *Wall Street Journal*, July 5 2001.
51 'GE's Standoff Didn't Catch All Boardrooms by Surprise', *Wall Street Journal*, June 18 2001.
52 An example of this is the relative speed with which Microsoft has been able to challenge the US DOJ and subsequent circuit court ruling against them.
53 Interview with Mario Monti on CNN in November 2000.
54 'Europe's Fearless Diplomat', The Economist, July 5 2001.
55 'We just couldn't believe what happened. It's a tough deal having the prosecutor be the judge'. Welch, quoted in 'Welch will step down earlier as GE revenues fall', *Financial Times*, July 12 2001.
56 This is summed up nicely by a quote from a *Wall Street Journal* article: 'From GE's perspective, dealing with members of the taskforce seemed like a through-the-looking-glass tumble into an unfamiliar world where process-oriented technocrats, answerable to no-one, made law and changed their rules as they saw fit. To the Europeans, Mr. Welch and GE embodied the stereotype of a scheming and arrogant American multinational, throwing its considerable weight around and unwilling to consider any objections that might stand in the way of its getting even bigger.' Taken from *Wall Street Journal* article cited in footnote 16.
57 *The Economist* claims that Boeing accused Airbus of trying to scupper the deal through lobbying the DG Competition. 'When Neutron Jack was nuked by Brussels', *The Economist*, June 18 2001.
58 'Monti's block makes waves across Atlantic', *Financial Times*, July 4 2001.
59 'EU Rejection of GE Honeywell Deal May Spark Trade Fight', Dow Jones Newswires, July 3 2001.
60 'US Antitrust Chief Chides EU for Rejecting Merger Proposal', *Wall Street Journal*, July 5 2001.
61 This is a highly plausible outcome given the increasingly transnational nature of markets such as aerospace, where firms do not regard their principle market as being a domestic one. See Helen Milner, *Resisting Protectionism* (New York: Columbia University Press, 1988) and David B.Yoffie (ed.), *Beyond Free Trade: Firms and Governments in Global Competition* (Boston: Harvard Business School Press, 1993) for an excellent analysis of this phenomenon.
62 'EU Antitrust policy on Trial', FT Marketwatch, June 19 2001.
63 Op cit. 39.
64 Op cit. 42.

65 'The Commission prohibits GE's acquisition of Honeywell', EU Commission Press Release, IP/01/939, Brussels, July 3 2001.
66 Market power arguments are forwarded in Stephen Hymer. 1968. 'La Grande Firme Multinationale', *Revue Economique*, 19: 949–973, whereas the internalization motive is developed in Peter J. Buckley and Mark Casson, *The Future of the Multinational Enterprise*, London: Macmillan. This is a considerable debate outside the scope of this paper. Interested readers should see John Cantwell, 'A Survey of Theories of International Production', chapter 2 in Christos Pitelis and Roger Sugden (eds.) *The Nature of the Transnational Firm* (London: Routledge, 1991) and Lorraine Eden and Evan H. Potter (eds.), *Multinationals in the Global Political Economy* (London: Macmillan, 1993) for a discussion of these issues.
67 'Justice Department Chief Questions EU on GE-Honeywell', Dow Jones Newswires, July 3 2001.
68 'Europe's fearless diplomat', *The Economist*, July 5 2001.
69 *Global Competition Review*, a London-based journal of antitrust law and policy.
70 These are Merger-handling, Cartel handling, Economic expertise, Independence, Transparency, Informal guidance, Confidentiality, Leadership.
71 The survey was based on practitioners' viewpoints. See www.global-competition.com.
72 Akbar and Mueller (1997).
73 'GE's Standoff Didn't Catch All Boardrooms by Surprise', *Wall Street Journal*, June 18 2001.
74 Ibid.
75 Ibid.
76 The MIA was a treaty designed to significantly liberalize investment rules in the OECD, granting greater freedom and flexibility to MNEs.
77 Op cit. 45.
78 Op cit. 47.
79 These meetings are at both high and middle levels. They seek to develop institutional substantive understanding of antitrust policy issues. They are based with the framework of EU-US relations.
80 Of note, was a claim by the *Financial Times* that a new problem between the US and EU authorities is that there was greater shared views on competition theories between the Clinton DOJ and the EU than between the EU and the new Bush administration. 'How Monti turned deal into a flight of fancy', *Financial Times*, July 6 2001.
81 Council Regulation (EEC) No 4064/89 of December 21 1989 on the control of concentrations between undertakings.
82 Views of Edward Bannermann, Head of Economics and Business Unit, Centre for European Reform.

Chapter 6

Conclusions

Introduction

This book has analysed the relationship between trade and competition policy. The starting point of the book was to explore in what ways the changing nature of economic interdependence has altered explanations for trade and investment. This interdependence is sometimes termed economic globalization. It is a new phenomenon because of the pre-eminence of FDI over trade flows and the increased scrutiny of domestic policy regimes and how they affect international trade and investment. Liberalization and de-regulation has proceeded both on the level of trade and in capital markets. The consequence of de-regulation and liberalization has been the growing interdependence of economies. The success of the GATT/WTO negotiations, in which industrial goods tariffs have been lowered progressively has been coupled with attempts to liberalize emerging services trade through the General Agreement on Trade in Services (GATS) and agreements on the protection of intellectual property (TRIPs). Importantly in the context of globalization, there are agreements on the liberalization of rules on foreign direct investment that are necessary for the provision of services internationally (TRIMs).

The rapid growth of global capital markets has been one of the distinct features of the latest phase of liberalization. As commonly cited in the globalization literature, the Thatcherite and Reaganite de-regulation of capital markets coupled with technological change has rendered 'floor trading' obsolete.[1] This has necessarily allowed financial institutions to carry out portfolio capital transactions instantaneously and has severely weakened the ability of states to control monetary policy. The most visible cases of the increased influence of the global capital markets have been in the recent 'Asian Crisis'.

The essential consequence of this process is the concept developed by Ostry (1990, 1997) called 'System Friction' (see chapter 1). Differing industry conditions generate conflicts between different national policy regimes e.g. trade and antitrust and is itself a function of the increasing scrutiny of different models of national economic governance. As Lawrence et al. (1996) suggests, this is due to 'Deep Integration' which has occurred at a regional level through deliberate policy decisions e.g. the EU and the creation of a single market and single currency. However, the interesting aspect for Lawrence and others is that the current process of 'Deep Integration' that is occurring at a global level is somewhat haphazard and led by corporate decisions as much as by governments.[2] Importantly, the international economy has witnessed the emergence of new forms of international corporate governance that have outstripped the capacity of industrialized states to regulate their activity. As Akbar and Mueller (1997) suggest, the international system is witnessing a governance gap, as firms are able to develop and implement new strategies faster than states can respond with sufficient regulation. This is the problem facing states in their attempts to control economic activity.

Traditionally, economists have relied upon models of country comparative advantage to explain the causes of international trade. The theories of David Ricardo, Hecksher-Ohlin argued that *countries* should specialize in the production of goods for which the relative cost of production was lowest. Production cost is determined by relative factor endowments and in the case of Ricardo, relative labour costs internationally. Two important assumptions were central to the models: a perfectly competitive model or one in which barriers to entry are negligible and the non-mobility of factors internationally. Thus where countries specialized in production of goods for which they had a comparative advantage and countries removed all barriers to trade, there would be global welfare gains due to the maximization of allocative efficiency brought about by falling prices for internationally traded goods.

While clearly the current international economy is not completely free from trade barriers, there are industries that display the characteristics of the standard or static trade models above. As a generalization, these would be industries where access to country-specific resources is the overriding source of competitive advantage for firms. In this book, natural resource industries are this case.

However, the static trade theories struggle to explain the reality that many industries do not approximate the standard competitive model. This is related to the presence of market imperfections and externalities (Dunning 1998). These imperfections imply a role for firm strategy as imperfect competition implies strategic interdependence. Firm strategies play an important, if not decisive, role in determining trade and investment. The work of Porter (1986), Yoffie (1993), Zysman and Tyson (1983) among others offers new perspectives on this issue. In particular, it is the decisions of *how* and *where* firms produce which play a significant role in explanation the explaining the flows of trade and investment.

From the perspective of government policymakers this implies that comparative advantage can be *created* rather than being dependent upon 'natural' sources related to country factor endowments. Importantly as firms develop competitive assets, with judicious interventions from governments, firms may decide to develop those assets in particular countries. Thus in an imperfectly competitive world, two implications for government policy arise. First, governments can attract the 'asset-building' and employment creating potential of MNEs. Countries may 'compete' with each other for the benefits of MNE production and investment. Second, new industries do not develop purely due to competitive pressures with the most 'inefficient' firms being forced to exit. In fact, national industries require time to develop in order to learn from production; to build up sustainable market share; to exploit economies of scale. Governments, by providing incentives such as R&D subsidy; offering temporary protection, can aid the development of such 'strategic' sectors (Doz, 1986, Yoffie, 1993, Tyson, 1992).

Underlying these analyses is that the concept of economic efficiency is also somewhat broader than the standard use by economic theory of allocative or static efficiency. In other words, analyses of changes in efficiency must take into account not just price effects as used in comparative static analysis but also dynamic efficiency changes caused by economies of scale, learning economies and transaction cost externalities. Partly in response to the realization that international markets are imperfectly competitive, the economics literature has developed models of imperfect competition and trade as an attempt to tackle this issue (e.g. Grossman, 1992, Helpman and Krugman, 1985, and Krugman and Smith, 1996). The problem faced by economists with trade and imperfect competition was that there was a multiplicity of models to capture the nature of imperfect competition. It was therefore necessary to accept that each case of imperfect competition and trade may be unique (see Krugman and Smith, 1996).

In a standard competitive model, trade and antitrust should be regarded as mutually reinforcing tools of liberalization. However, the role for trade and antitrust in an imperfectly competitive context is somewhat different. First, governments can exempt sectors from standard rules on antitrust. This can take a number of forms, depending on the objectives. For example, where policymakers perceive that co-operation between firms can enhance R&D, they can allow the existence of R&D consortia.

Second, in terms of trade policy, governments can offer temporary trade production such as VERs in order for industries to adjust to changing global competitive structures. The presumption here is that structural adjustment for firms in imperfectly competitive markets requires time. For example, firms may need to respond to changing technological processes or managerial systems in order to compete. Thus, governments can offer them protection in order to develop competitive responses.

Third, governments can use restrictive trade policies in order to attract the sources of global competitiveness through the arrival of foreign firms and FDI. As Belderbos (1998) has shown, market access through local presence in technology industries has emerged due to the presence of trade barriers such as anti-dumping.

Fourth, governments could also support export drives through export subsidy. This is a corollary of points two and three above. Again, where economies of scale internal to the firm are important, there is a need for firms to recoup their fixed and sunk costs. By supporting a firm's export drive, governments can facilitate cost reduction by enabling firms to capture foreign market share. This is especially important where a domestic market is not large enough to permit the firms to reach minimum efficient scale (MES). This issue is also important in the context of small countries where there is insufficient market size to support the existence of firms that require large market share to recoup costs.

Two important *normative* implications emerge from this analysis. First, trade policy is not a positive sum gain: countries can gain at the expense of each other. Second, government intervention is not unambiguously harmful to welfare.

Yoffie (1993) offered an excellent framework within which these concepts can be explored (see chapter 1). In particular, Yoffie (1993) developed a framework in which he attempted to differentiate industries by the nature of competition that emerged in each sector. The means by which he differentiated industries were by (a) the degree of global market concentration and (b) the level of government competition. Thus, where markets were segmented and where government intervention was low, trade could be explained by the traditional concepts of comparative advantage. However, where global market concentration was a feature of competition, then the role of the MNE and its strategy became a crucial explanatory factor in international trade.

Where government regulation of an industry was such that national markets were subject to differing regulatory standards *inter*-nationally, then the role of government was crucial in explaining trade and investment. Lastly, where a combination of global market concentration and government intervention combined, it was necessary to consider how industrial policy and the promotion of corporate strategy interacted – thus the extent to which MITI industrial policy facilitated the development of Japanese MNEs (Doz 1986). This in turn could explain trade and investment.

This book used a broad classification by 'industry conditions'. It classified four 'kinds' of industry: scarce natural resource based industries, complex manufacturing sectors, R&D intensive industries and internationally traded services. By setting up this classifications, the book sought to demonstrate how different market structures create different linkages (and conflicts) between trade and antitrust.

Relative to complex manufacturing, scarce natural resource sectors are likely to be depicted by traditional cost-country advantages with firms (even MNEs) choosing to produce based on access to natural resources. MNE strategy is of course relevant in this sector but it is often dedicated to accessing those essential resources. While R&D is a feature of complex manufacturing, relative to R&D intensive industries, the key source of competitive advantage (and therefore the pattern of trade and investment) is determined by the ability of MNEs to minimize costs and risks in the management of complex international value chains (Porter 1986). As the name of the third classification suggests, the source of trade and investment in R&D intensive sectors is going to be determined by the extent to which the return on R&D can maximized by the MNEs undertaking that investment.

Internationally traded services may require the management of complex value chains and the need for product and process research. Relative to the other three sectors, it is the pervasive regulation and standard-setting of national governments which is a key factor in this 'kind' of industry which determines the location of production and patterns of trade.

This book thus suggested that when an analysis of the complex manufacturing or R&D intensive sectors is carried out, it is necessary to 'recalculate' the welfare function and to define efficiency other than in the static sense. As dynamic efficiency is by necessity a complex concept, rather than trying to develop an explicit 'calculation' or definition, the definition of this form of efficiency is implicit in the case studies in this book.

Implications for Trade and Antitrust

Given these different industry classifications, the dissertation then sought to develop relationships between trade and antitrust. Methodologically, it adopted a case-study approach. Justifications for this approach were given in chapter 2.

The existing literature on trade and competition linkages in R&D intensive and internationally-traded services is rich (see chapter 2 above for references). This dissertation sought to develop cases in the two relatively under-researched (in terms of trade and antitrust) categories: scarce natural resources and complex manufacturing (chapters 3 and 4).

As expected, the relationship between trade and antitrust cannot be meaningfully generalized – it is necessary to make comparisons by industry 'type'. This is an important implication for policy making. In particular, it suggests that policies (and their associated modes of analysis) in natural resource industries may be inappropriate if applied to the other industry types such as R&D intensive sectors. Thus, as Thurow (1993), Tyson and others suggest, a slavish adoption of liberalization policies in R&D intensive sectors may fail to allow firms to capture the market externalities inherent in these sectors.

This leads to a normative discussion of unilateral v. multilateral interest. Inevitably, if one nation decides to 'pick winners', it will involve a process of 'national preference'. Thus industrial policy aimed at stimulating an R&D intensive sector may maximize national dynamic efficiency, it may be achieved at the cost to other nations (Bhagwati and Patrick, 1991, Krugman, 1996). This itself is amplified by 'System Friction': MITI industrial policy may have had direct effects on the success of US MNEs in their competition with Japanese MNEs. This in turn may encourage a round of retaliatory action by US legislators and the overall outcome is that both nations lose out. This leads to the inevitable question: is competition between states desirable? What implications does this process have for the multilateral system?

For domestic trade and antitrust, the key question is the correct relationship between the two. Thus, should trade and antitrust be complimentarily pro-liberalization in a sector which is R&D intensive when it is evident from industry conditions that (a) market share and the ability to recoup costs from R&D are inseparable, (b) R&D consortia can significantly enhance the success of R&D activity and (c) there are important 'external spillovers' to other sectors from the presence of locally-based R&D activity i.e. a national system of innovation? Why might restrictive trade policies foster domestic collusion where the main source of competition is import competition blockaded by the trade policies?

Findings and Conclusions from the Case Studies

Natural Resource Industries

In *natural resource based industries*, the driving force for trade and investment is access to scarce resources. Those firms who can minimize costs on this basis will survive. Conversely, if there are firms who suffer from significant cost disadvantages; there are strong motives for these firms to erect barriers to entry to new more cost efficient firms. Furthermore in sectors where natural resource industries are imperfectly competitive (by virtue of the existence of economies of scale internal to the firm), then the propensity for swings in demand to significantly impact on capacity maintenance may further enhance motives for collusive activities. As discussed below, the natural resource based sectors lead to classic cases of regulatory capture and collusion.

There were two industries explored in chapter 3: tanner crab and soda ash. In the former case, poorly enforced antitrust in Japan permitted Japanese seafood companies to impose import barriers against the most competitive source of tanner crabmeat. In tanner crab, Japanese trading firms may have used an import cartel to minimize imports of tanner crabmeat. This was in order to (a) ensure that higher-cost Japanese fishing fleets could supply some of the Japanese market and (b) create a wedge between Alaskan fishing companies and the Japanese market in order to purchase at low price and sell at a higher price in Japan. In accepting Japanese firms' guilty pleas, the US court that tried the case alleged that it was poor enforcement of the Japanese AML that permitted the import cartel. Implicitly, the court's argument related to "System Friction" – i.e. conflicting systems of national governance. Thus in this instance, weak antitrust frustrated free trade.

The main case study for chapter 3 is provided in the detailed analysis of the soda ash industry. Soda ash production requires significant economies of scale in order to minimize these costs. In addition, as it is an intermediate product, it is dependent on the demand for final products that use it.

Economies of scale ensure that the soda ash sector can only really support a few large firms. Internationally, US firms benefit from significant cost advantages over their west European and Japanese rivals in that US producers process naturally occurring sources of soda ash whereas EU and Japanese suppliers have to produce soda ash through an energy-intensive process of electrolysis. Thus even if transport costs are taken into account, it is likely that US producers would be the dominant suppliers of soda ash to the world market in a case of free trade. Taken together, this case has the ingredients for a classic case of regulatory capture, collusion and protectionism. Indeed, this case demonstrates each of these posing some straight dilemmas for trade and antitrust. The principal findings from this case were:

(a) In a sector where competitive advantage is determined by access to natural resources, trade barriers such as anti-dumping serve to frustrate lower-cost supplies of the good. Where the industry is made up of a small number of large firms, the reduction in competitive supply facilitates domestic collusion. Thus in the soda ash case, not only did anti-dumping shelter high-cost producers from competition, it allowed Solvay and Brunner Mond to orchestrate an intra-EU cartel. The fact that all sources of viable import competition had been effectively eliminated by anti-dumping measures against US and ECE producers lends further credence to this argument. By successfully getting these measures imposed, the necessary barriers to entry to facilitate the cartel were in place. When anti-dumping duties were briefly lifted, the entry of US soda ash imports shook up the cartel by forcing intra-EU shipments of soda ash.

(b) The exemption of ANSAC, an export cartel based in the US, may have further enhanced the competitiveness of US exporters. Under the terms of the EU anti-dumping measures and antitrust measures, the ANSAC cartel was required to cease operations in the EU market.

(c) There was a lack of co-ordination between the EU Commission offices in charge of antitrust (DG IV) and trade policy (DG I) respectively. DG IV's analysis of the competitive conditions in the EU soda ash industry made it clear that US imports of soda ash represented a significant threat to Solvay and that these imports did not need to be dumped to be a threat. Opposed to this view was DG I's analysis that claimed to have shown that US firms had indeed dumped soda ash in the EU market. They also underplayed the intra-EU cartel.

(d) When the cartel was broken up and coincidentally anti-dumping duties were lifted, 'mutually reinforcing' liberalization of trade restrictions and enforcement of antitrust led to a more competitive and more efficient market. This supports the view of Patrick Messerlin: '[I]t makes little sense to have two types of rules, one for domestic competition and one for external competition' (Messerlin, 1990, p. 48). Free trade in the absence of enforced antitrust is unlikely to ensure contestability. Nor is a rigorously enforced antitrust likely to maintain contestability given the interdependent nature of trade and investment in the contemporary international economy especially if the source of competitive advantage resides in importing firms who have access to natural resources which higher-cost domestic producers do not possess. In the more interdependent economy as depicted in chapter 1, the links between traditional policy boundaries have become blurred and thus as Ostry (1997) and Jacquemin and Sapir (1991) suggest, a restrictive trade policy effectively acts as a barrier to entry into an oligopolistic domestic market. In the starkest terms, anti-dumping facilitates domestic collusion.

Complex Manufacturing Sectors

In *complex manufacturing sectors*, the relationship between trade and antitrust is somewhat different and considerably more nuanced. This is due to at least two factors. First, due to the imperfectly competitive nature of markets and the externalities that flow from this, the role of MNEs as coordinator of complex international value chains becomes central to understanding the causes of international trade and the location of international production. Second, because of the imperfectly competitive nature of this sector, the role of government intervention goes beyond classic cases of 'at-the-border' trade protection into "System Friction" cases of domestic subsidy, poor enforcement of antitrust etc. Of course, complex manufacturing sectors are not immune from cases of regulatory capture and protectionism. This is a reality of international business. However, the arguments for protection from domestically located producers may go beyond arguments of static comparative cost disadvantages. There may be justifiable arguments that dynamic efficiencies can be gained if competition can be minimized for a given period of time.

Thus, the role of government becomes important to the extent that it is regulators who will determine the degree to which domestically located firms can benefit from a temporary minimization of competition (Doz 1986). This implies that trade and antitrust may be related in both contradictory and complementary ways.

In the car industry, there is historical evidence of strong forces attempting to capture the trade and antitrust process in the classic case (as in soda ash). The west European assemblers have historically sought to resist trade liberalization from more competitive Japanese sources. This is evidenced by national restrictions on Japanese imports that preceded the EU-wide agreement with Japan. At the same time, the attempts by EU assemblers to extend the 1985 BE can be interpreted as a case of rent-seeking behaviour: by maintaining the BE, price differentials across the EU may have been maintained and intensified to the benefit of the assemblers and their associated distributors. In using a static conceptualization of economic efficiency, economists would argue that this situation harms consumer welfare and undermines the concept of the SEM (Mattoo and Mavroidis 1995). This is in line with Milner's type IV industries that are depicted by a high degree of multinationality but rely heavily upon local markets for profitability (a hallmark of international market segmentation). This is also supported by data from Jones (1999) in table 4.2 that showed the high degree of dependence of European car producers on domestic markets.[3]

An alternative (but complementary) explanation is that the economics of car manufacturing is considerably more complex than the 'simple' models that predominate in trade theory. This book has analysed the retailing and distribution part of the value chain. One argument is that as car distribution and retailing does not involve simple models of trade, without it, there would be inadequate provision of sales related services. At the same time, temporary protection (in the form of VERs) serves two purposes from an EU industry and policy making perspective. First, it offers 'breathing space' for west European manufacturers in their attempts to achieve similar levels of competitiveness as their Japanese rivals. Second, as there is a link between trade restrictions and the arrival of FDI as evidenced in other sectors similar in their 'complexity' to cars (Belderbos 1998), EU policy makers can encourage the sources of competitive advantage in Japanese management and production systems into the EU. This both encourages emulation on the part of west European suppliers and it reduces the political influence of those rent-seeking forces who would find it harder to get protection against Japanese-owned but locally-based production.

The main findings from the primary research for this case study are as follows:

(a) The EU SEM is unlikely to function as intended i.e. the free movement of goods if the EU-Japan VER is effectively a set of national restrictions. This agreement requires that rules on competition are compromised – this is the clear statement of the EU Commission in justifying the renewal of the BE in 1995.[4]
(b) The necessity for the maintenance of trade barriers has encouraged firm-firm co-ordination (e.g. the SMMT-JAMA agreement). In certain cases, these industry-to-industry agreements to restrict competition have been given tacit blessing by national governments (e.g. SMMT-JAMA and *Asia Motors*).
(c) The segmentation of the EU market may facilitate collusion of imports between Japanese manufacturers in Japan i.e. which firms get which share of the total quota of the EU market?

Thus the central message of the car industry case study is that a standard model of competition used to set trade and antitrust is likely to miss the important complexities of the sector and thus ignore the inherent complex and rich interactions between trade and antitrust itself.

Extraterritoriality and Antitrust Policy

In chapter 5 we examined a case of 'monopoly leverage' involving a proposed merger between GE and Honeywell of the US, both firms involved in avionics. By merging the two firms hoped to become the world's largest supplier of avionics equipment and services. While passing DOJ antitrust scrutiny, the merger was scuppered by the decision of DG Competition to veto the merger on the grounds that the bundling of avionic services and products would lead to unfair competition by the newly merged entity.

The case highlighted three key issues. First, it highlighted how differing models of antitrust policy and enforcement can cause "System Friction" in the international trading system. Second, the relationship product and service bundling creates dilemmas for antitrust policy – should policymakers seek to protect competitors in order to maintain market contestability or should they focus on the efficiency-related consumer benefits that bundling offers? Third, the case examined an important case of the dangers of extraterritorial application of antitrust policy and the potential harm to the multilateral system. Moreover, it suggests, as is currently being experienced, that these kinds of cases are unlikely to disappear in the future and may mark a trend in the years ahead.

Broader Policy Implications for Trade and Antitrust

In a study that is based on specific case studies and deals with specific instances, a researcher should always be wary of broadening the conclusions of the case studies to a more general application unless the findings of the case studies can justify such a broadening. We have just summarized the findings of the natural resource and complex manufacturing cases. The aim of this section is to see where these specific findings may be of use to inform a more general debate. Before undertaking this task, it is important to note that in recent years, several academic studies (Nicholaides, 1996, Scherer, 1995, Waverman et al., 1997, Hope and Maeleng, 1998), international organizations (OECD, 1998a, 1998b and 1998c) and think-tanks (e.g. International Antitrust Code Working Group) have sought to analyse the links between trade and antitrust. This has been with a view to discussing the prospects for the internationalization of antitrust (ICP).

Most of this work has been based on general theoretical and conceptual propositions. Virtually none of the work has used detailed case studies to illustrate actual examples of the trade and competition linkages that may mitigate in favour of an ICP. Thus from the detailed cases in this book, the following findings could be of use for more general policy guidance to aid those scholars and policymakers who are engaged in a more general policy debate.

(a) In both the soda ash and car industry cases, there is a problem of *institutional disagreement and constraints within the EU* itself. In *soda ash*, DG IV and DG I arrived at diametrically opposing analyses of the nature of competition in world soda ash trade. Although both departments were investigating the same industry, there was no attempt to combine activities and perspectives on the events in this sector. In the *car industry*, the ECJ and CFI were required to prioritize the functioning of a liberalized SEM in car trade as for the ECJ and CFI, this is one the basic principles that it is required to enforce. By contrast, the EU Commission was in a more difficult position. On the one hand, the Commission had sought agreement with the Japanese government on restricting import trade. This required them to restrict intra-EU trade, through relaxing the rules on competition through the BE, in order to make EU-Japan agreement work. In this context, the EU Commission was responding in part to pressures of regulatory capture. Furthermore, the EU Commission also recognized the arguments that in a complex manufacturing sector, it may be necessary to recast the antitrust regime for car distribution.

The differences in the Commission and ECJ/CFI approach can be explained as follows. First, as the ECJ and CFI are non-majoritarian bodies, they are not so prone to regulatory capture as other EU institutions such as the EU Commission. Second, the EU Commission has used a different model of competition to formulate trade and antitrust in the car sector than the ECJ. This was the main thrust of the argument under 'Trade and Antitrust Interactions' in chapter 4.

Soda ash suggests that if DG IV and DG I could co-operate more regularly, then the problems of trade and antitrust conflicts may be solved. If DG IV and DG I were to formally notify each other of their ongoing investigations into the activities and events in particular sectors, they may be able to find situations in which trade policy measures (DG I's remit) may impact adversely on the monitoring and maintenance of competitive conditions in the EU single market (DG IV's task). However, the procedural framework of the EU institutions prevents DG IV from sharing information with other departments as it must behave in a completely independent manner when dealing with competition cases. This makes it impossible for the kind of consultation required in anti-dumping cases. A more radical solution would be to make anti-dumping rules subject to competition code disciplines, thereby implying that the burden of proof would shift from accused foreign firms towards complainant firms. In other words, complainant firms would have to prove that there were anti-competitive intentions underlying the lower prices of imported goods.[5]

In the car industry, it is also not clear how the differences in approach of the Commission and the ECJ could be mediated. Again, the ECJ is not a policymaker in the same sense as the EU Commission. Its role in the EU is as an enforcer of the policies introduced by the other institutions. This further implies that it can only enforce the principles of the EU Treaty and thus cannot create derogations and exemptions as the EU Commission can. Moreover, it is unable to co-operate and share information with other institutions as that would compromise its role as an impartial judge.

This implies that the general policy stance of the EU institutions taken together have to reflect the very important complexity of imperfectly competitive markets while at the same time recognizing that the SEM should not be overly compromised. Indeed, this appears to be the trend given the case law analysed in the latter part of chapter 4, especially the *Eco-system* and *VW/Audi* rulings where the principle of the SEM was held as key priority but the

Commission did not withdraw the BE as a consequence of Peugeot's or VW's actions.

(b) The findings in the soda ash strongly point to a *link between domestic cartelization and anti-dumping.* Subjecting anti-dumping rules to competition case disciplines may shift the emphasis of the measure away from a tool of protectionism towards a genuine policy designed to eliminate anti-competitive, predatory pricing. As DG IV suggests, the US exporters benefited from substantial cost advantages which they were seeking to exploit in a relatively high cost EU market. The anti-dumping measures merely protected and fostered collusive activities among EU firms. The competition-restricting impact of trade policy compounded the collusive nature of the intra-EU market thereby reducing the contestability of the EU market. Taken with the work of Messerlin (1990), this offers further evidence in support of reforming or even abolishing anti-dumping measures. In terms of reform, one possible solution would be to subject anti-dumping investigations to the same burden of proof as competition cases. Most mainstream economists are unconvinced by the price-discrimination/injury link that anti-dumping cases claim.

(c) In a related fashion to the issue of anti-dumping in (b), in global oligopolistic markets such as the car industry (a Type IV sector in Milner's typology), policymakers should be aware of the anti-competitive impact of VERs not just in the traditional sense of a trade barrier but in two additional, but important ways. First, the antitrust-weakening effects of the VER and the need to create exemptions in antitrust rules. Second, the need to allocate market share in VER-type measures can foster government-industry co-ordination and may have also required firm-firm co-ordination in order to hand out shares of the total quota. Past experience of the UK-Japan bilateral accord demonstrates the need for firm-firm coordination. This further reinforces the central message of the complex manufacturing case that in these kinds of sectors, the relationship between trade and antitrust is likely to be more characterized by conflict than in natural resource industries.

(d) Where there are important externalities in global production and where the existence of MNE activity and strategy are central to understanding trade and investment outcomes i.e. in complex manufacturing, liberalization *per se* in competition and trade policy may not be the optimal policy. Policymakers need a much richer understanding of the relationships between trade and antitrust. In particular, where there are genuine arguments for a relaxation of competition rules e.g. the BE, antitrust policymakers must also be aware of the 'spillover' effects of such policies e.g. the non-existence of a SEM. Similarly, where a trade policy such as a VER is introduced, policymakers must be aware of the competition effects of these policies in sectors where firm strategy is an important determinant in international trade and investment.

As 'System Friction' intensifies with 'Deep Integration', derogations on the application of competition rules in one jurisdiction (designed to capture certain externalities such as R&D) can have negative spillover effects on other nations inevitably leading to conflict (Akbar, 1999). Furthermore, this creates uncertainty in the regulatory environment for MNEs (Akbar, 2000). Moreover, if trade occurs in a world of finite economic gains i.e. trade is not a positive-sum game (as the literature on imperfect competition and international trade suggests) then it is necessary to tackle the thorny issue of the unilateral v. multilateral interest. Where it is possible for nation states to gain economic benefits of production from MNEs, then there is the possibility that nations will launch upon a process of 'beggar thy neighbour' strategic trade policy as nations compete with each other for MNE patronage.

The first best solution to tackling the problems of 'System Friction' would be to seek agreement among states on ways in which differences in policies can be harmonized. This has been the preoccupation of a significant portion of the literature on the internationalization of antitrust policy (e.g. Scherer, 1996, Waverman et al., 1997, Hope and Maeleng, 1998). Grandiose schemes and draft agreements have been drawn up in this literature yet there has been little movement at a multilateral level towards such a process.[6] Short of undertaking a new analysis of the political economy of international policy making, it is necessary to emphasize that the existing literature in creating these schemes have ignored the political impossibility that shifting to a global governance regime would entail (see Akbar and Mueller, 1997).

While there has been limited bilateral agreement between states and jurisdictions,[7] it is still largely the case that internationalization of antitrust policy is a long way off. The limited agreement between states has tended to be based on voluntary codes rather than new mandatory agreements. Thus there is a lack of consensus among the major parties in the field of antitrust. What is left is a system of national trade and competition policies that are increasingly brought into conflict through the extraterritorial application of domestic competition laws. It is interesting to explore the extraterritorial phenomenon as the incidence of extraterritoriality is related to the increasing degree of interdependence in the world economy.

Evaluation

This book has argued that as industry conditions become more complex, the relationship between trade and antitrust becomes more interrelated and nuanced. In particular, when market structures are imperfectly competitive, straightforward relationships between trade and antitrust policy appear to break down. As Ostry and others have argued, 'System Friction' increases as the activities of firms becomes increasingly transnational as it brings into focus differences in national models of trade and competition regulation. As can be seen in chapter 5, one of the aspects of the use of extraterritoriality in recent years by the EU and US has been in industries that are widely regarded to be imperfectly competitive and to some extent highly internationalized or globalized.[8] Pharmaceuticals and aerospace are industries where R&D is an important determinant of trade and investment. In the latter case, global MES is vital for cost reduction due to the huge sunk costs and learning economies inherent in aerospace. As it is increasingly the case that industries are imperfectly competitive as a rule rather than by exception, if transnationalization of economic activity intensifies, then without attempts to develop co-operation on the setting of trade and antitrust, Ostry's 'System Friction' is likely to increase.

The current reality is that international policy management in these fields is somewhat *ad hoc* and frequently unilateral as demonstrated with the analysis of extraterritoriality. From a multilateral perspective, this is likely to enhance rather diminish conflict. This necessarily leads to a discussion of current and potential directions for policy reform.

Policy Reform: Current Directions

The reality is that there has been little progress towards internationalization of antitrust. Moreover, having offered limited policy suggestions on the basis of the case study work in chapters 3, 4 and 5, it may be instructive to conclude with a brief discussion of current directions in international policymaking at the heart of trade and antitrust nexus. There is no attempt to offer a detailed analysis of the current situation.[9] The GATT/WTO system has proven itself to be remarkably durable (Hoekman and Kostecki, 1998 Low, 1995) and has maintained a process of multilateral bargaining and negotiation. It has significantly reduced industrial tariffs and has begun to tackle the issue of agricultural trade in a multilateral framework.

For the purposes of this book, it has also developed new policy regimes that may inform policy reform in trade and antitrust. Two agreements in particular are of interest: the General Agreement on Trade in Services (GATS) and in Trade Related Intellectual Property Rights (TRIPS). Both GATS and TRIPs are a response to the reality that traditional trade liberalization measures 'at the border' fail to capture the importance of these issues. GATS is based on the principle of market-access as the provision of services is crucially related to local presence (see chapter 2). TRIPs recognized the issue of 'created' assets related to trade i.e. not based on the notion of national comparative advantage and national factor endowments. The basic principle of GATS is non-discrimination. It prohibits six types of market-access restrictions. Signatories cannot restrict the number of service suppliers allowed into their country; the value of transactions or assets; the total quantity of service output; the number of people employed by service provider; the type of legal entity providing the services; nor the participation of foreign capital in terms of absolute value of capital. Signatories to the agreement were allowed to register exemptions by mid-1994 and not surprisingly over sixty members registered. The most common sectors were audio-visual, financial services and transportation. While the GATS may be replete with exemptions, the importance of the agreement lies in the acceptance of the principle that as 'Deep Integration' proceeds, states will need to consider approximation of domestic policies: thus could antitrust be considered in this framework?

On paper at least, TRIPs is a far-reaching agreement which, if fully implemented, implies significant restrictions on the signatories to interfere with the rights of owners of IPRs. In particular, the agreement:

(a) Establishes minimum substantive standards on the protection of IPRs.
(b) Prescribes procedures and remedies which should be available in signatory nations should IPRs be infringed.

(c) Allows the Dispute Settlement Mechanism (DSM) of the WTO to be used for TRIPs related conflicts.
(d) Extends GATT/WTO principles to TRIPs.

Again the agreement offers a significant challenge to domestic policy regimes – implicit in the TRIPs is that a set of common codes on IPR protection should be introduced. Critics of the TRIPs would argue that although on paper, the agreement appears far-reaching, the actual implementation of the TRIPs accord would require significant resources that currently many signatories to the agreement do not possess. Moreover, one of the main culprits of IPR violation is not a member of the WTO i.e. China. As the broadest international forum, the WTO has the advantage of representing a broad plurality of views. In this context, the GATS and TRIPs agreement is a remarkable piece of international rulemaking. The fact that the WTO is so broad may also militate against the potential for radical new policymaking given the inherent difficulties of negotiating with a large and diverse group of states.

However, in the specific context of trade and antitrust, the OECD has been the most active for the longest time. It produced guidelines on the regulation of international restrictive business practices (1986), it has produced numerous policy and discussion documents (e.g. OECD (1998a, 1998b and 1998c)) and it recently held a high level meeting in Paris in June 1999 to discuss the links between trade and antitrust. Of course, the MAI was an attempt by the OECD to develop a more consistent set of guidelines on the treatment of FDI implicitly accepting the increasing importance of FDI in firm strategy.

However, the MAI floundered on the reluctance of OECD member states to accept the sovereignty pooling implications that standard rules for FDI treatment across the OECD would imply. A similar implication for internationalization of antitrust is unavoidable.

Only once states have first explored the linkages between trade and antitrust and second reconciled the inevitable clash between the pursuit of national economic and political objectives and the multilateral interest can a series of rules emerge. Having said that, the current trend appears to be towards developing limited 'mini-lateral' co-operation between states rather than grander multilateral accords.[10] This is probably because it is easier to forge a limited consensus between parties that more or less share similar views on the limited issues covered by the negotiations. While being very important, this latter issue is beyond the scope of this book as it encompasses broader issues of legal procedure and political economy. This could be the subject for further fruitful research.

Notes

1   Once the US and UK governments started the de-regulation process, arguably other states had to follow suit in order to avoid their financial centres losing their competitive position in the global financial markets.
2   This is certainly the implication of Milner (1988).
3   But also to extend Milner's analysis, the data demonstrates an increasing degree of export dependence as the traditional domestic markets are eroded by import or locally-based

foreign competition. This can also help explain the merger wave currently occurring in the sector as MNEs reposition themselves in a new global competition.

4   The ongoing investigation of the Office of Fair Trading into car retailing in the UK is a demonstration of the concern of regulators and policymakers have when dealing with SED systems. Volvo UK's admission that it imposed rules on its dealerships to maintain artificially high prices for its cars is also further evidence of the potential for anti-competitive conduct that SED can foster.

5   See Holmes and Kempton (1997) for a discussion of the issues on anti-dumping reform.

6   *The Economist* magazine (November 26 1999) reported that the US government regards the enthusiasm of the EU to discuss trade and antitrust at the forthcoming WTO summit in Canada as an attempt to avoid talking about agricultural reform.

7   Examples of such agreements include the US-EU, US-Canada agreements and the US-Japan joint seminars on international anti-trust co-operation.

8   This does not deny that extraterritoriality has been invoked in more 'traditional' issues such as over Cuba where the Helms-Burton Act sought to prosecute non-US nationals in US courts for maintaining business interests in Cuba which may have been 'stolen' by the Castro regime from US citizens (i.e. Cubans who fled the revolution and went to live in the US).

9   See Hoekman and Kostecki 1998 and Trebilcock and Howse 1998 on the current state of regulation of world trade and investment.

10 Examples include the EU-US agreement on antitrust co-operation; a similar accord between Canada and the EU; US agreements with Australia and New Zealand; and increasing discussions and seminars between EU and Japan and the US and Japan.

Bibliography

Adelman, C., Jenkins, D. and Kemmis, S (1977), 'Rethinking Case Study: notes from the second Cambridge conference', *Cambridge Journal of Education*, 6.

Alford, R.P. (1992), 'The Extraterritorial Application of Antitrust Laws: The United States and European Community Approaches', *Virginia Journal of International Law*, Vol. 33, No.1, pp. 1-50.

Akbar, Y. (1997), 'EC-Japan Relations: Future Directions for EC Policy', *Proceedings from the 13th Annual Student Conference*, Council on Western Europe, Columbia University, New York.

———— (1999), 'The Extraterritorial Dimension of US and EU Competition Law: A Threat to the Multilateral System?', *Australian Journal of International Affairs*, Vol. 53, No. 1, April 1999, pp. 113-26.

———— (2000), 'The Internationalisation of Antitrust: Implications for International Business,' *Thunderbird International Business Review*, January-February 2000.

———— and Mueller, B. (1997), 'Global Antitrust: Issues and Perspectives'. *Global Governance* Vol. 3 No.1 January 1997, pp. 59-81.

Baldwin, R.E. (1990), 'The U.S.-Japan Semiconductor Arrangement', *Centre for Economic Policy Research Discussion papers*, 387

Barack, B. (1981), *The Application of Competition Rules (Antitrust Law) of the European Economic Community to Enterprises and Arrangements External to the Common Market*, Luxembourg: Commission of the European Communities.

Bar, F. and Borrus, M. (1997), 'Why Competition is Necessary in Telecommunications and How to Achieve It: The Experience of the Advanced Economies'. *BRIE Working Paper* 102, September 1997.

———— and Murase E. (1997), 'The Potential for Transatlantic Cooperation in Telecommunications Service Trade in Asia', *BRIE Working Paper* 107, November 1997.

Belderbos, R. (1996), 'The Effects of EU Anti-dumping: Lessons from the Japanese Electronics Cases', SPRU, University of Sussex, typescript.

Bhagwati, J.N. (ed.) (1983), *Essays in International Economics*, Princeton UP.

———— and Patrick, H.T. (eds) (1991), *Aggressive Unilateralism: America's 301 Trade Policy and the World Trading System*, Harvester Wheatsheaf New York.

Borrus, M., Millstein, J. and Zysman, J. (1983), chapter 4 in Zysman, L. and Tyson, L. (1983).

Bourgeois, J. and Demaret, P. (1995), 'The Working of EC Policies on Competition, Industry and Trade: A Legal Analysis', in Buiges, P. Jacquemin, A. and Sapir, A. (eds) (1995), *The Coherence of European Policies Towards Trade, Competition and Industry*, London: Edward Elgar.

Brander, J., and Spencer, B. (1983), 'International R&D Rivalry and Industrial Strategy', *Review of Economic Studies*, No. 50, pp. 707-22.

Brander, J., and Spencer, B. (1985), 'Export Subsidies and Market Share Rivalry', *Journal of International Economics*, No. 18, pp. 83-100.

Brown, J. (1994), *Selective Distribution Legislation 123/85 – Commentary on the BEUC Position, International Car Distribution Programme (ICDP) Research Paper No. 4/94*, Solihull: ICDP.

Casson, M. (1997), *Information and Organization: a New Perspective on the Theory of the Firm*, Oxford: Clarendon Press.

Chenais, F. 'Globalisation, World Oligopoly and Some of their Implications', chapter 2, pp. 12-21 in Humbert, M. (ed.), (1993), *The Impact of Globalisation on Europe's Firms and Industries*, London: Pinter.

Commission of the European Communities (1981), *XIth Report on Antitrust*, Luxembourg: Commission of the European Communities.

Commission of the European Communities (1992), *XXIIth Report on Antitrust*, Luxembourg: Commission of the European Communities.

Dicken, P. (1998), *Global Shift: Transforming the World Economy*, 3rd ed, London: Paul Chapman.

Doz, L. (1986), 'Government Policies and Global Industries', chapter 7, pp. 225-66, in Porter, M. (1986), *Competition in Global Industries*, Boston: Harvard Business School Press.

Dunning J. (1998), *Alliance Capitalism and Global Business*, London: Routledge.

Economist Intelligence Unit (1994), 'The New Car Market in Europe – 1992/93 Edition', *EIU Special Report No. R308*, London: The Economist Newspaper.

EFTA Surveillance Authority, *View of the EFTA Surveillance Authority on the Draft Commission Regulation (EC) on the Application of Article 85(3) of the Treaty to Certain Categories of Motor Vehicle Distribution and Servicing Agreements*, Doc. No. 94-16245-I; Dec. No. 153/94/COL. Brussels, November 9 1994.

Financial Times, January 31 1998. 'Competition: Van Miert seeks global rules accord'.

Financial Times, December 21 1990. 'Brussels ready to take on the biggest: Lucy Kellaway assesses the significance of cartel-busting against ICI and Solvay'.

Fingleton, J. (ed.) (1996), *Antitrust and the Transformation of Central Europe*, London: CEPR.

Flam, H. and Nordström, H. (1995), 'Why do Pre-tax Car Prices Differ So Much Across European Countries?', *Centre for Economic Policy Research (CEPR) Discussion Paper Series*, No. 1181, London: CEPR.

Frazer, T. and Holmes P. (1997), 'Self Restraint: Cars, Complaints and the Commission', *European Public Law*, Vol.1 No. 1 pp. 85-95.

Freeman, C. (ed.) (1990), *The Economics of Innovation*, Aldershot: Edward Elgar.

GATT (1993), *Trade Policy Review*, Geneva: GATT.

Graham, E.M. (1995), 'Antitrust and the New Trade Agenda', in OECD (1995), *New Dimensions of Market Access in a Globalising World Economy*, Paris, pp. 105-188.

Grossman, G. (ed.) (1992), *Imperfect Competition and International Trade*, Cambridge: MIT Press.

Groves, P.J. (1995), 'Whatevershebringswesing: DGIV rebukes the Car Industry', *European Competition Law Review*, Vol. 16, Issue 2, March 1995, pp. 98-103.

Guardian, The, December 5th 1995. 'Dawn Raids as VW denies Austrian Buyers were shunned'.

Harbour M., Brown, J. and Wade, P. (1994), 'Competition in European Car Distribution', *ICDP Research Paper 2/94,* Solihull: ICDP.

Helpman, E. and Krugman, P.R. (1985), *Market Structure and Foreign Trade: Increasing Returns, Imperfect Competition and the International Economy,* Cambridge: MIT Press.

Hirst, P. and Thompson, G. (1996), *Globalization in Question,* London: Polity Press.

Hobday, M. (1995), *Innovation in East Asia: the Challenge to Japan,* Aldershot: Edward Elgar.

Hoekman, B. and Mavroidis, P. (1994), 'Competition, Antitrust and the GATT', *CEPR Discussion Paper* No. 876, Centre for Economic Policy Research, London.

———— and Kostecki, M. (1998) *The Political Economy of the World Trading System: from GATT to WTO* (2nd edition), London: Oxford UP.

Holmes, P. and Smith, A. (1995), 'Trade, Competition and Industrial Policy for Cars: Conflicts of Aims and Instruments', in Buiges, P., Jacquemin, A. and Sapir, A. (eds) (1995), *The Coherence of European Policies Towards Trade, Competition and Industry,* London: Edward Elgar.

Hope, E. and Maeleng, P. (eds) (1998), *Competition and Trade Policies: Coherence or Conflict?* London: Routledge.

———— and Kempton, J. (1997), 'Study on the Economic and Industrial Aspects of Anti-Dumping Policy.' *SEI Working Papers in Contemporary European Studies,* 22.

Japan Automobile Manufacturers Association Inc. (JAMA), *Japan Automobile Manufacturers Association Comments concerning Selective Distribution of Motor Vehicles in the European Community.* Brussels, January 25 1994.

Jacquemin, A. and Sapir, A. (1991), 'Europe Post-1992: Internal and External Liberalisation', *American Economic Review Papers and Proceedings,* May 1991, pp. 166-170.

Johnson, C. (1982), *MITI and the Japanese Miracle: The Growth of Industrial Policy 1925-1975,* Palo Alto: Stanford University Press.

Jones, D.T. (1999), 'The Car Industry' in Dyker, D. (1999), *The European Economy,* 2nd edition, London: Longman.

Jovanovic, M. (1997), *European Economic Integration: Limits and Prospects,* London: Routledge.

Kahn-Freund, O. (1955), 'English Contracts and American Anti-Trust Law: The Nylon Patent Case', 18 *Modern Law Review* 65.

Kapranos Huntley, A. (1981), 'The Protection of Trading Interests Act 1980: Some Jurisdictional Aspects of Enforcement of Antitrust Laws', 30 *International and Competition Law Quarterly* 213, 224 (1981).

Kirman, A.P. and Schueller, N. (1990), 'Price Leadership and Discrimination in the European Car Market', *The Journal of Industrial Economics,* 39, pp. 69-91.

———— (1992), 'Market Structure, Producer Costs and Location: an Alternative View of Pricing in the European Car Market' in Dagenais, M. G. and Muet, P.A. (eds), *International Trade Modelling,* London: Chapman and Hall.

Kronstein, H.D. (1972), *The Law of International Cartels,* Cornell University Press: Cornell NY.

Krugman, P. R. (1996), *Pop Internationalism*, MIT Press, Cambridge, MA.

——— and Smith A. (eds) (1996), *Empirical Studies of Strategic Trade Policy*, National Bureau for Economic Research, Chicago: Chicago University Press.

Lawrence, R. Z. (1993), 'Japan's Different Trade Regime: An Analysis with Particular Reference to Keiretsu', *Journal of Economic Perspectives*, Vol. 7 No. 3, pp. 3-19.

———, Bressand, A. and Ito, T. (1996), *A Vision for the World Economy: Openness, Diversity and Cohesion*, Washington DC: Brookings Institution.

Leamer, E.E. (1984), *Sources of International Comparative Advantage*, Cambridge: MIT Press.

Locke, S. and Bovis, C. (1994), 'The Supply of New Cars and the EU Block Exemption', *Consumer Policy Review*, Vol.4, No.1, pp. 38-46.

Low, P. (1995), *Trading Free: the GATT and U.S. Trade Policy*, New York: Twentieth Century Fund Press.

Marques-Mendes, G. (1991), *Antitrust in a World of Interrelated Economies*, Brussels: Presse Universitaire de Bruxelles.

Martin, S. (1997), 'Public Policies Towards Co-operation in Research and Development: The European Union, Japan and the United States', in Waverman, L., Comanor, W. S. and Goto, A. (eds) (1997), *Antitrust in the Global Economy: Modalities for Cooperation*, London: Routledge.

Matsushita, M. (1991), 'The Role of Competition Law and Policy in Reducing Trade Barriers in Japan', *The World Economy* Vol. 13, No.3, pp. 181-197.

——— (1993), *International Trade and Competition Law in Japan*, Oxford: Oxford University Press.

Mattoo, A. and Mavroidis P. C. (1995), 'The EC-Japan Consensus on Cars: Trade and Antitrust Trade-Offs', *The World Economy*, May 1995, pp. 345-365.

McGee, J. and Thomas, H. (1988), 'Explaining Complex Industries' in Hood, N. and Vahlne J., (1988*), Strategies in Global Competition*, London: Croom-Helm.

Messerlin, P. (1990), 'Anti-Dumping Regulation or Pro-Cartel Law: The EC Chemical Cases', *PRE Working Paper Series*, 397, World Bank.
[NB: a version of this paper was later published in *The World Economy*. The data and references in the book refer to the working paper and not the published article.]

Milner, H. (1988), *Resisting Protectionism*, New York: Columbia University Press.

Monopolies and Mergers Commission (1992), *New Motor Cars*, Cm 1808, London: HMSO.

Nicolaides, P. (1996), 'For a World Competition Authority: The Role of Antitrust in Economic Integration and the Role of Regional Blocs in Internationalizing Antitrust', *Journal of World Trade*, Vol. 30, No. 4, (August), pp. 131-145.

Ohmae, K. (1993), 'The Rise of the Region State' *Foreign Affairs* 72 (Spring), pp. 78-87.

Organization of Economic Co-operation and Development (OECD) (1987), *The Costs of Restricting Imports: The Automobile Industry*, OECD: Paris.

——— (1995), *New Dimensions of Market Access in a Globalising World Economy*, Paris.

——— (1998a), *Consistencies and Inconsistencies between Trade and Competition Policies*, Paris: OECD COM/TD/DAFFE/CLP (98) 25/FINAL.

———— (1998b) *Complementarities between Trade and Competition Policies*, Paris: COM/TD/DAFFE/CLP (98) 98/FINAL.

————(1998c) *Competition Elements in International Trade Agreements: A Post-Uruguay Round Overview of WTO Agreements*, Paris: COM/TD/DAFFE/CLP (98) 26/FINAL.

Ostry, S. (1990), *Government and Corporations in a Shrinking World: Trade and Innovation Policies in the United States, Europe and Japan*, Council on Foreign Relations: New York.

———— (1991), 'Exploring the Policy Options for the 1990s', in OECD, (1991), *Technology in a Changing World*, pp. 13 – 35, OECD: Paris.

———— (1994), 'New Dimensions of Market Access: Overview from a Trade Policy Perspective.' Typescript, OECD Roundtable on the New Dimensions of Market Access in a Globalizing World Economy, June 30 – July 1, Paris.

———— (1997), 'Globalization, Domestic Policies and the Need for Harmonization', in Waverman, L., Comanor, W.S. and Goto, A. (eds) (1997), *Antitrust in the Global Economy: Modalities for Cooperation*, London: Routledge.

Pauly, L. and Reich, S. (1998), 'National Structures and Multinational Corporate Behaviour: Enduring Differences in the Age of Globalization'. *International Organization*, Spring pp. 1-30.

Petropoulos, S. (1994), 'Parallel Imports, Free Riders and the Distribution of Motor Vehicles in the EEC: The *ECO System/Peugeot* Case', *Consumer Law Journal*, Vol.1 No. 1, pp. 9-16.

Porter, M. (1986), *Competition in Global Industries*, Boston: Harvard Business School Press.

Pugel, T. (1986), *Fragile Interdependence*, London: Macmillan.

Reich, R. (1991), *The Work of Nations: Preparing Ourselves for 21st-century Capitalism*, London: Simon and Schuster.

Roth, P.M. (1992), 'Reasonable Extraterritoriality: Correcting the "Balance of Interests"', Vol. 41, April 1992, *International and Comparative Law Quarterly*, pp. 245-286.

Sako, M. (1992), *Prices, Quality and Trust: Inter-firm Relations in Britain and Japan*, Cambridge: Cambridge University Press.

Scherer F. (1995), *Competition Policies for a Integrated World Economy*, Washington DC: Brookings Institution.

Schoenbaum, T. J. (1996), 'The Theory of Contestable Markets in International Trade: A Rationale for "Justifiable" Unilateralism to combat Restrictive Business Practices?', *Journal of World Trade*, Vol. 30, No. 3, June, pp. 161-190.

Smith, A. and Venables, A. (1992), 'Completing the Internal Market in the European Community: some industry simulations', *European Economic Review*, 32, pp. 1501-1525.

Smith A. 'Strategic Trade Policy in the European Car Market', pp. 67-81 in Krugman, P.R. and Smith A. (eds) (1996), *Empirical Studies of Strategic Trade Policy*, National Bureau for Economic Research, Chicago: Chicago University Press.

Society of Motor Manufacturers and Traders Limited (SMMT), 'Selective Distribution (Block Exemption)', *Parliamentary Briefing*, February 1994.

Stocking, G.W. and Watkins, M.W. (1946), *Cartels in Action: Case Studies in International Business Diplomacy*, New York: Twentieth Century Fund.

Stocking, G.W. and Watkins, M.W. (1948), *Cartels or Competition: The Economics of International Controls by Business and Government, with the report and recommendations of the Committee on Cartels and Monopoly*, New York: Twentieth Century Fund.

Stopford, J. and Strange, S., with Henley, J. (1991), *Rival States, Rival Firms: Competition for World Market Shares*, Cambridge: Cambridge University Press.

Strange, S. (1996), *The Retreat of the State: The Diffusion of Power in the World Economy*, London: Cambridge University Press.

Sutton, J. (1991), *Sunk Costs and Market Structure*, Cambridge Mass.: MIT Press.

Suzumura, K. and Goto, A., 'Collaborative R&D and Antitrust: Economic Analysis in the Light of Japanese Experience', chapter 8 in Waverman, L., Comanor, W. S. and Goto, A. (eds) (1997), *Antitrust in the Global Economy: Modalities for Cooperation*, London: Routledge.

Telser, L. (1960), 'Why Should Manufacturers Want Fair Trade?', *Journal of Law and Economics*, vol. 3, pp. 86-105.

Thurow, L. (1993), *Head to Head: the Coming Economic Battle Among Japan, Europe and America*, London: Nicholas Brealey.

Trebilcock, M. and Howse, R. (1998), *The Regulation of International Trade*, London: Routledge.

Trenor, J.A. (1995), 'Jurisdiction and the Extraterritorial Application of Antitrust Laws after Hartford Fire', The *University of Chicago Law Review*, 62, 1995, pp. 1583-1617.

Trompenaars, F. and Hampden-Turner, C. (1991), *The Seven Cultures of Capitalism*, London: Piatkus Press.

Turner, D.F. (1985), 'Application of Competition Laws to Foreign Conduct: Appropriate Resolution of Jurisdictional Issues', in Hawk, B. (ed.), *Fordham Corporate Law Institute* 231, 233, 1985.

Turner, L. and Hodges, M. (1992), *Global Shakeout*, London: Century Business.

Tyson, L. (1992), 'They Are Not Us: Why American Ownership Still Matters', *The American Prospect* no. 4 (winter 1991), pp. 37-49.

Verboven, F. (1995), 'International Price Discrimination in European Car Market', Centre for Economic Research, Tilburg University, typescript.

Vigier, P. (1992), 'La Politique Communautaire de l'Automobile', *Revue du Marché Unique Européen* 3, pp. 73-126.

Vogel, S. (1996), 'International Games with National Rules: Competition for Comparative Regulatory Advantage in Telecommunications and Financial Services', *BRIE Working Paper* 99, June 1996.

Waverman, L., Comanor, W.S. and Goto, A. (eds) (1997), *Antitrust in the Global Economy: Modalities for Cooperation*, London: Routledge.

Wilks, S. (1995), *The Revival of Japanese Antitrust and its Implications for EU Japan Relations*, London: Royal Institute for International Affairs.

Williamson, O.E. (1983), *Markets and Hierarchies: Analysis and Antitrust Implications*, New York: Free Press.

Womack, J., Roos, D. and Jones, D. T. (1990), *The Machine that Changed the World*, Cambridge MA: MIT Press.

Woolcock, S. (1993), *Market Access Issues in EC-US Relations: Trading Partners or Trading Blows*, RIIA. London: Pinter.

Yoffie, D.B. (ed.) (1993), *Beyond Free Trade: Firms and Governments in Global Competition*, Boston: Harvard Business School Press.

———— (1997), *Competing in the Age of Digital Convergence*, Boston: Harvard Business School Press.

Zysman, J. and Tyson, L.D. (eds) (1983), *American Industry in International Competition: Government Policies and Corporate Strategies*, Ithaca, N.Y: Cornell U.P.

Index

For Product Safety Concerns and Information please contact our EU representative GPSR@taylorandfrancis.com Taylor & Francis Verlag GmbH, Kaufingerstraße 24, 80331 München, Germany

T - #0123 - 160425 - C0 - 219/153/10 - PB - 9781138715370 - Gloss Lamination